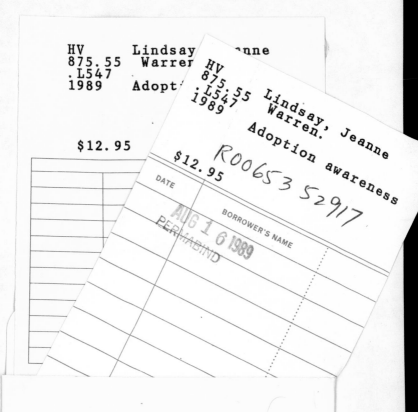

By Catherine Monserrat and Linda Barr:

*Teenage Pregnancy: A New Beginning*

*Working with Childbearing Adolescents*


By Jeanne Lindsay:


*Pregnant Too Soon: Adoption Is an Option*

*Parents, Pregnant Teens and the Adoption Option: Help for Families*

*Open Adoption: A Caring Option*

*Teens Parenting: The Challenge of Babies and Toddlers*

*Do I Have a Daddy? A Story About a Single-Parent Child*

*Teenage Marriage: Coping with Reality*

*Teens Look at Marriage: Rainbows, Roles and Reality*

# ADOPTION AWARENESS:

## A Guide for Teachers, Counselors, Nurses and Caring Others

**Jeanne Warren Lindsay, M.A., C.H.E.**
and
**Catherine Paschal Monserrat, Ph.D.**

Morning
Glory
Press

Buena Park, California

Copyright © 1989 by  Jeanne W. Lindsay and Catherine P. Monserrat

## All Rights Reserved

**Library of Congress Cataloging-in-Publication Data**
Lindsay, Jeanne Warren
    Adoption Awareness.

    Bibliography: p. 237-267
    Includes index.
    1. Adoption--United States. 2. Birthparents--Counseling of--
United States. 3. Teenage mothers--Counseling of--United States. I.
Monserrat, Catherine Paschal. II. Title.
HV875.55.L547  1989    362.7'34'0973       88-34540
ISBN 0-930934-33-4
ISBN 0-930934-32-6 (pbk.)

MORNING GLORY PRESS, INC.
6595 San Haroldo Way        Buena Park, CA 90620
Telephone (714) 828-1998
Printed and bound in the United States of America

To the birthparents
with whom adoption begins

# Contents

# Preface

Nearly 500,000 teenagers give birth each year in the United States, and the majority are single. Many of these young women did not intend to parent so early in their lives, yet less than five percent release their babies for adoption. Most of the others apparently never consider adoption as an alternative.

Sometimes older women become pregnant at the "wrong" time in their lives. They may wish to consider the adoption alternative, yet they seldom are offered support in doing so.

Many people are strongly opposed to adoption. They can't imagine a mother letting someone else rear her child. Some people think adoption must be a selfish choice, something a mother does only if she doesn't care about her baby. On the contrary, adoption is an extremely difficult choice, a decision birthparents make because they want more for their child than they can offer at the time.

Other people think of adoption as a solution to the teenage pregnancy "epidemic." They say, "There are wonderful couples wanting to adopt children. Teenagers shouldn't keep those babies. They can't be good parents. They ought to place them for adoption."

We feel strongly that either extreme is wrong. The decision to place one's child for adoption is perhaps the most difficult decision a parent can ever make, one that requires a great deal of love and caring. The parent considering the adoption alternative needs lots of support from all of us.

Adopted adolescents also need to know that adoption is a loving choice. Whatever we can do to normalize adoption will benefit all those involved in the adoption triangle.

Adoption, however, is not an alternative that's right for every parent under eighteen, or even all under fourteen. It's a decision which must be made by the parents themselves, a decision that absolutely must not be forced on them because of their age.

Our concern is two-fold. We would like women with unplanned pregnancies to make conscious decisions either to parent or to make adoption plans for their babies. We want them to receive the support they need for the decisions they make.

This book is written for all those professionals who may work with pregnant women and their partners, whether it be occasionally or frequently. It is designed to help teachers discuss adoption with pregnant students — and with non-pregnant teenagers. It is for staff in health clinics and in other problem pregnancy services who want to discuss the adoption alternative with their patients. It is for hospital staff who are a crucial part of the birthparent's decision-making after she gives birth.

*Adoption Awareness* is also for attorneys, clergy, doctors, counselors, and others who may work directly with pregnant women who are considering an adoption plan. It is for adoption counselors who might like to generate more support for adoption in their communities as well as among their clients.

We've included a variety of forms and other materials in the Appendix which may give concrete help in developing support services for birthparents.

Forty years ago about eighty percent of pregnant, unmarried Caucasian teenagers released their babies for adoption. At that time, many felt they had no choice. There were almost no social services supporting single mothers and their children. Today that adoption statistic has changed radically to less than five percent, but support services for single mothers and their babies still are far from adequate. This is a serious problem. The fact that adoption planning receives little support is also a serious problem.

We hope *Adoption Awareness* will accomplish what our title implies, awareness of the adoption alternative in a positive fashion as a choice one has when one is pregnant.

# Foreword

This book aptly speaks to a pressing unmet need to educate all those whose lives are touched by adoption and to a better understanding of that institution. Adoption as we know it today is grossly oversimplified, overemphasized, and misunderstood.

As the authors point out, too often our actions and reactions to adoption are based on misconceptions and personal biases. All too often we view adoption as simply bringing together a teenager faced with an unplanned pregnancy with an infertile couple who can provide a home for that child.

The fact that the decisions made by these vulnerable teenagers may be the most important ones they make in their lives is totally overlooked. The fact that birthmothers and birthfathers need the very best counseling available to help them with these decisions is all too easily passed over. The fact that they will have to live with these decisions for the rest of their lives and mourn the child they have relinquished somehow escapes us.

We have badly failed to help all those in need of pregnancy counseling, not only to explore all the alternatives available to them, but to help them clearly understand the implications for themselves and those whose lives will be affected by the decisions they are about to make.

*Adoption Awareness* speaks clearly to these issues. It truly provides a much-needed guide for teachers, counselors, nurses, clergy, and caring others to be better prepared when confronted with these problems.

My first preference in providing such help would be professional counselors trained in pregnancy counseling, knowledgeable about pregnancy alternatives, knowledgeable about adoption as a lifelong process, and familiar with community resources. Since we cannot depend on such counselors to be available when we need them, those in our communities who are often the first to be confronted with these problems must make themselves as knowledgeable as they can so that they can provide useful and meaningful guidance.

In their exploration of alternatives, the authors do not lose sight of the fact that we need to acknowledge that the first and best place for a child is with his own family, in his own community, in his own country. We must recognize that adoption is not appropriate unless all efforts have been made to salvage his family for the child. Adoption should not be employed unless it is clear that the child's own family is not likely to be able to provide the care that the child needs and is rightfully entitled to receive.

This would suggest that family welfare is the best child welfare. This means that the community is obliged to provide the birthfamily with those resources and services that would enable that family to maintain the child at home. If substitute care is needed, the first efforts should be made to find such a home in the child's own racial, national, ethnic, and religious community. Only if it is clear that such resources are not available should efforts be made to find an adoptive home outside the child's community. In my view, the primary purpose of adoption is to provide a permanent family for children who cannot be cared for by their birthparents. Therefore the child's welfare, the child's needs, the child's interests are the basic determinants of good adoption practice. Homes should be selected for children rather than children selected for homes.

*Adoption Awareness* speaks to these issues, as a brief look at the chapter headings indicates. Chapter Two, "Why Don't Teens Consider Adoption?" deals with the importance of the decisions teens face, societal changes that affect these decisions, fantasies of teen parenthood and finally, what teens can expect from their peers when exploring alternatives.

Chapter Three, "Agencies Emphasize Counseling," contains a most important suggestion that one may need to look at several agencies before one finds one that meets the needs of the particular client. Independent adoptions, which are used by well over a majority of birthparents, are discussed in Chapter Four. The pitfalls, and there are many, are talked about as well as the reasons why so many birthparents turn to independent adoption.

Chapter Five deals with open versus closed adoption, a very timely and crucial issue in today's adoption plans. Open adoption, which usually leads to the parents and the selected adoptive parents meeting and then deciding the degree of openness with which they are comfortable, is slowly becoming the prevailing practice in current adoptions. It has much to offer the birthparents as well as the adoptive parents who are able to see one another as real people.

An exploration of both options in my opinion will lead most birthparents to choose open adoption. This permits the birthparents to meet and select the people to whom they will entrust their child. Most important, I believe, is that it gives the adoptive child direct information about the birthparents. Open adoption provides honest and more complete answers to the adopted child's inevitable questions about who the birthparents were and why they chose adoption. An understanding of open and closed adoptions will present the alternatives counselor with invaluable insight in dealing with this most important aspect of adoption planning.

The importance of the family, too often left out, is dealt with in Chapter Six, "Family Support Is Crucial." Decisions about alternatives, such as parenting the child or adoption planning, are often made by the family. Leaving them out can indeed be disastrous to any exploration of alternatives.

The father, the forgotten person in adoption planning, is reviewed and discussed in Chapter Seven. Having written extensively on this subject, I am particularly pleased to see an entire chapter entitled "Birthfathers Need Help Too." I would differ with attorneys who say that birthfathers are indifferent or they are not concerned with their offspring or with the women they impregnate. This is not only a disservice to birthfathers, but to the child who is the result of such a union, for the child can only be left with a negative image of his birthfather which he then incorporates as a part of his own self-identity.

A quote from this chapter summarizes my feelings and states the case for birthfathers. "The wise and caring approach is to assume, with each birthfather we encounter, that there is a Larry inside, a young man who does care about his family and who needs help." Larry refers to one of the rich and poignant case illustrations contained throughout the book.

Other chapters in *Adoption Awareness* discuss such important topics as the grieving process, support through alternatives groups, and the long-term needs inherent in alternatives counseling. There will surely be times for most, if not all, birthparents "to remember, rethink, rework, or regrieve" the decisions they have made about their children. Hopefully those adoption services or other helping services will be there when that need arises.

The chapters that deal with the role of teachers, hospital staff, and clergy are an invaluable contribution to the literature on alternatives counseling, and especially in helping these professions to gain a greater awareness of adoption as a possible alternative. The insights that these chapters offer are invaluable to teachers, hospital staff, and clergy. They are often the very first to confront the problem or to be called upon to provide advice and counseling. What can they do when confronted with these problems? They can make themselves as knowledgeable as they possibly can about the issues talked about in this book so that the help and guidance they are offering is indeed the very best they have to give.

Reading this book and the invaluable learning it provides cannot help but contribute to that end.

Reuben Pannor
Co-author: *The Unmarried Father: New Approaches for Helping Unmarried Young Parents*
*The Adoption Triangle: The Effects of the Sealed Record on Adoptees, Birth Parents, and Adoptive Parents*

# Acknowledgments

This book was a long time in the making. It reflects a journey for each of us as we've learned about adoption. There have been many stops along the way with many who have shared our work and provided us with guidance.

This work has also been a journey for us together both as colleagues and friends. We want to acknowledge each other for the growth and commitment that this has fostered.

Our primary acknowledgment belongs to the birthparents with whom we have worked over the years. Some of them are quoted here, many are not. Their real names by agreement have not been used. We hope that we have represented their stories accurately and respectfully. Our lives have been enriched by having known each one of them. Their caring, their concern, and their love for their children is touching. We admire them and we respect them.

Our goal with this book was to provide guidance for professionals who may occasionally or frequently offer help to those dealing with untimely or crisis pregnancy. To meet this goal we decided not only to depend on our own resources, but also to interview others who work in this field.

We have talked with countless teachers, nurses, counselors, social workers, attorneys, clergypersons, and other helping people during the seventeen years we have been working with pregnant and parenting teenagers. Many of these people offered specific help for this book. As they are quoted throughout, they are identified by title, agency and location.

Reuben Pannor and Sharon Kaplan have had a great impact on adoption practice through their efforts at normalizing more open adoption. Reuben wrote the Foreword for *Adoption Awareness,* and Sharon critiqued the manuscript and offered helpful suggestions. We appreciate them.

Counselors and social workers especially helpful include Helen Magee, Claire Priester, John Holzhuter, Marge Driscoll, Fran Thoreen, Randy Perin, Joan Anderson, Kathleen Silber, Margaret Svetlauskas, Laurie Cooley, and Humberto Jimenez.

Nurses, social workers and counselors in hospitals or other medical facilities who contributed to *Adoption Awareness* include K. C. Sharrard, Sherri Finik, Karen Sakata, Barbara Gant, Pam Peevy-Kiser, Mary Ghiglione, and Radonna Tims.

We have discussed adoption with many teachers. We especially thank Bev Short, Julie Vetica, Marge Eliason, and Nancy Minor for their contributions to this book. Julie Vetica and Pat Alviso helped edit the manuscript.

Attorneys sharing their adoption expertise with us were Linda Nunez, Deborah Crouse Cobb, Dan Farr and Glenna Weith.

Clergypeople we interviewed cover a wide range of faiths — Lois Gatchell, Fred Trevino, Linda Pickens-Jones, Jeff and Karyn Johnson, Michael Gold, Norman Cluck, Don Mohlstrom, Elwood Wissmann, Dennis Adlof and John P. McAndrew. Their titles and religious affiliations are included with their quotes.

Sandra Musser, Mary Ann Liebert, Jim and Judy Glynn, Christine Verduzco and Morris Chestnut also provided input to the book. David Crawford helped with photos. We're grateful.

Bev Short, Fran Thoreen, Mary Ghiglione, Linda Howrey and Laurie Cooley contributed wonderful material for the Appendix. Permission is granted for copying these items as needed providing author and source are listed on the copies.

Carole Blum again provided excellent help in editing, proofreading, and generally keeping the office fires burning. Tim Rinker designed the cover, and Steve Lindsay assisted in the general design of the book. Erin Lindsay helped with last-minute editing and livened up the process with funny comments.

We each want to express our deep appreciation to our best friends and husbands, Bernardo Monserrat and Bob Lindsay. We value their input and are especially grateful for their support and companionship during the writing of this book.

# Introduction

The drop in the adoption rate among pregnant, single women, especially pregnant teenagers, is amazing. During the fifties, the vast majority of pregnant teenagers, as high as eighty percent, released their babies to adoptive couples. Today less than five percent do so.

Why such a tremendous change?

Forty years ago our culture was quite different. The concept of the nuclear family was strong. As a society, we thought a single woman could not support a family. Many mothers did, of course, but they were not the norm. Teenagers at that time, especially our daughters, were expected to be obedient and dependent. Pregnancy outside of marriage was deeply shameful. When it happened, the pregnancy was kept secret if at all possible. After all, the child born to that single mother would be illegitimate, a terrible label to give a baby.

In the sixties our culture started changing. Youth became more independent, and "Do your own thing" was the guiding principle for many. The sexual revolution stormed through our society and changed forever the lives of many people. The concept of illegitimacy faded. We finally realized that a baby is not "illegitimate," whatever the marital status of his/her parents.

The rise of the women's movement continued through the seventies and single parenthood was more respectable. Abortion became legal and "problem" pregnancies were more likely to be terminated than to be continued with adoption in mind.

By the early eighties, the adoption rate among pregnant and single teenagers dropped to four percent. Adoption was not something most pregnant women, whatever their age, considered at all.

Today most pregnant teenagers either terminate their pregnancies or parent their children themselves. Amazingly, we have even heard a few young women comment that abortion is "better for the baby than adoption." This comment reveals a great deal about some people's negative attitudes toward adoption.

Throughout these changes in our society, the practice of adoption did not change significantly. Adoption continued to be shrouded in secrecy in most parts of the country. The birthparents continued to be the forgotten corner of the adoption triangle. We think this accounts partially for the drop from an eighty percent adoption rate among single and pregnant teenagers to only four percent.

Even now, most materials written about adoption apply to adoptive parents and adoptees without much concern for the birthparents. *Yet it is with the birthparents that infant adoption begins.*

In the last few years, however, adoption has been changing. More and more, agencies are encouraging letter and picture contact between birth- and adoptive parents. The birthparents often are involved to some extent in choosing the adoptive parents for their child. Some licensed adoption agencies in various areas of the country are fostering more open adoption in which the birthparents may meet the adoptive parents and may continue contact after the adoption is finalized.

Private or independent adoption accounts for the vast majority of infant adoptions, as high as seventy-five percent in some states. Many independent adoptions are arranged through attorneys, sometimes with involvement of doctors or friends of the birthparents and/or adoptive parents.

Recently, independent adoption services have been established which emphasize the importance of counseling both for birthparents and adoptive parents. In some of these adoption services the birthparents are considered the primary clients, and their needs are given first consideration.

We think the changes occurring in adoption practice in the last few years are making it more possible for birthparents to consider the adoption alternative. As more and more people realize that adoption does indeed start with the birthparents, support for this alternative may grow.

The decision to keep or place one's baby for adoption is a sacred one. We treat it, or at least we should treat it, with some reverence.

## Alternatives and Older Birthmothers

People tend to think of birthmothers as teenagers, yet according to some adoption counselors, at least half the women who release their babies for adoption are past their teen years. Several women mentioned to us their frustration at the dearth of reading materials and other resources for "older" women considering an adoption plan.

*Adoption Awareness* is meant to apply to pregnant women and their partners, whatever their ages, who need support in considering their alternatives. Several chapters, specifically "Why Don't Teens Consider Adoption?" and "Teachers Discuss Alternatives" are written primarily for professionals working with teens. Many of the quotes in the other chapters come from teenagers. The philosophical base for this book, however, is that birthparents of all ages care about their babies and want to make the best possible plan for those babies and for themselves. Those who release their babies for adoption will grieve intensely whether they are fifteen or thirty-five. They all need to be as informed as possible on the different choices available within adoption. The trend toward openness in adoption will interest many birth-parents regardless of their age. Birthfathers, whatever their age, need support along with the birthmothers. Traumatic hospital experiences have been related by very young birthmothers and by birthmothers in their thirties.

Good pregnancy alternatives counseling starts with respect for the woman involved, whatever her age. The concepts covered in *Adoption Awareness* are useful not only for those working with pregnant teenagers, but also for those who counsel older women facing untimely pregnancies.

## Our Interest in Adoption

Both of us became interested and involved in presenting the
adoption alternative to pregnant teenagers through our work
with special schools for pregnant minors. I (Catherine) was a
teacher and counselor at New Futures School, Albuquerque,
New Mexico, for fifteen years. I was there as the program grew
from a tiny one-room class to a large comprehensive program
for pregnant and parenting teenagers. When it was a small
program, the staff found it easy to talk with each girl individually and make sure she was aware that she had choices. As the
program grew, this became increasingly difficult.

Over the years the adoption rates in our program reflected the
national trend. Few of the teens we saw were interested in
adoption. The adoption option began quietly to fade out of the
picture. The staff was faced with the challenge of serving the
growing population of teen moms.

One day I walked down the hall of the school and realized
there were mothers and babies everywhere. Ours was a program
equipped to help teenagers become good parents. This was not
bad. We were dealing with young women who were intending to
be mothers.

However, I was concerned that perhaps the physical environment did not emanate a feeling of choice. It spoke primarily to
motherhood. I didn't know much about adoption at that time, so
I began to educate myself. I visited adoption agencies, spoke
with people involved in the adoption field, and tried to figure out
what might be done to turn some of that around.

Our director and other staff members joined me in working to
enhance our services for those who might be considering
adoption. I began to conduct weekly alternatives discussion
groups for the students who were interested in pursuing their
choices in more depth. I also began to provide counseling for
those who made adoption plans and for their families.

We held staff trainings on adoption and began to offer an
annual Adoption Awareness Week for all of our students.

Most recently I designed and conducted a research study of
birthmothers for my doctoral dissertation. The research con-
sisted of in-depth interviews with sixteen birthmothers who had

placed their children within the past three years. Many of the quotes contained in this book came from these interviews.

I (Jeanne) started the Teen Mother Program in Cerritos, California, in 1972. This is an alternative program offered as a choice to pregnant and parenting teenagers in the ABC Unified School District, a small district in Los Angeles County. I, too, have always been concerned that, because most of our students parent their children, the adoption alternative does not receive the support it deserves.

Each year two or three students in our Teen Mother Program made and carried out adoption plans. With each student, we tried to be as supportive as possible. However, we found little help in written materials. Books on adoption invariably dealt with adoptive parents and/or adoptees with little or no mention of birthparents.

I, too, started learning as much as possible about adoption. I began interviewing former students who had carried out adoption plans. *Pregnant Too Soon: Adoption Is an Option* (1980, 1988: Morning Glory Press) was the result, a book written directly to pregnant teenagers who might consider the adoption alternative.

As I heard more and more about openness in adoption, I became intrigued with this new, yet age-old concept of child placement. After interviewing many professionals as well as birth- and adoptive parents involved in this type of adoption, I wrote *Open Adoption: A Caring Option* (1987: MGP).

If the birthparents are teenagers, their parents are likely to be involved in the decision-making process and in the grief which follows losing a child or a grandchild through adoption. Once again, I found nothing written for this part of the adoption scene. Again I interviewed extensively, then wrote *Parents, Pregnant Teens and the Adoption Option: Help for Families* (1989: MGP).

Both of us have felt for a long time that we needed a book which would offer guidance to professionals dealing with individuals who might be considering the adoption alternative. We have spent several years researching this topic, and we have discussed with literally hundreds of professionals how best to

offer the adoption alternative to adolescent and older women
facing untimely pregnancy.

The implications for the young woman, her child, her child's
father, her family, and society as a whole are monumental.
Young people need a tremendous amount of assistance in
sorting through their alternatives and their feelings about adoption and about parenting. Their families and partners are often in
need of such help. Yet, assistance with this decision is not as
readily available as one might think. Advice-givers are plentiful,
but skilled, supportive helping persons are often unavailable.

## Some Counselors Don't Discuss Adoption

Some, perhaps many, pregnancy counselors seldom mention
adoption as a viable alternative. Edmund Mech (1984) studied
the orientations of 132 pregnancy counselors toward adoption.
In terms of attitude, these counselors were far more positive
toward adoption than toward parenting as a choice for pregnant
teenagers. However, in actual practice, adoption was discussed
with clients by only sixty percent of these counselors. Further-
more, the counselor proficiency about the topic was consistently
low. These researchers found that the counselors were influenced by the lack of utilization of adoption as an alternative and,
therefore, considered it a risky topic to address.

As one reflects upon these findings, it is not difficult to form
an image of what it must be like to be an adolescent or an older
woman considering adoption in a milieu where peers, helping
professionals and community are, at best, reticent to discuss it,
and, at worst, extremely negative toward the idea. In fact,
research seems to indicate that the lack of perceived and actual
support may be critical factors in the subsequent adjustment to
the loss of a child through adoption.

The self-fulfilling prophecy is a useful concept to consider in
a discussion of the reasons so few teenagers consider adoption
as a possible alternative. Most pregnant-too-soon teenagers
parent their children themselves. Many exhibit absolutely no
interest in the adoption choice. Are we therefore to assume no
teenager is willing to discuss adoption as one of her options? If
we don't discuss it, we imply it's not a possible alternative. The

obvious follow-up is that those who hear nothing about adoption will not consider this alternative.

It is far better to continue to present adoption as a loving, unselfish, and extremely difficult choice available to any woman — and to her partner — facing untimely pregnancy. It's not a choice they *should* make. Neither is parenting a choice they *should* make. They should look at their options and come to the best possible decision for them. And they should receive support from helping professionals for their decision.

Teachers, nurses, counselors, social workers, clergy and attorneys are most likely to be in a position to offer this support. How to do so may sometimes be a problem. *Adoption Awareness* provides guidance for helping persons wishing to encourage the consideration of the adoption alternative in crisis pregnancy.

# Carrying a heavy load this semester?

**Call the Adoption Information Center**
**1-800-522-6882**

In Milwaukee, call: 453-0403.

Creating a climate for alternatives may involve displaying
adoption posters along with parenting materials.

# CHAPTER 1

# Creating
# The Climate

*Of course I'm keeping my baby. I wouldn't give him away. I'm not that selfish. I'll love him and I'll take care of him. (Luanne, 15)*

*I wanted to finish college, maybe go on to graduate school. Why did I let this pregnancy happen? I'd like to consider adoption, but when I mentioned it to the nurse at the clinic, she was startled. And my roommate was horrified. (Tommy, 20)*

*Pregnant again — and we can hardly feed the kids we have. I don't believe in abortion. I wonder about adoption. . . (Jayne, 32)*

*I thought we were getting married, and now he's gone. I want this baby to have two parents, but I don't think I could handle adoption. (Sara, 17)*

Pregnancy is wonderful — at the right time. There are times, though, when it can be devastating. The woman who is pregnant at the wrong time has four legal options. If she doesn't consider abortion a possible choice and marriage is out of the question, her options are halved. Many women don't consider adoption a viable option either. So, for them, there are no options. If she's pregnant, she'll be parenting in a few months.

Becoming a parent after pregnancy is a rational, often happy course of events for many people. For others, the timing is drastically off. Adoption might be a workable option after all.

## Is Adoption for Pregnant Teens?

People who work with pregnant teenagers, however, have a standard concern: the young women aren't interested in learning about adoption. Teachers and counselors are tired of bringing up a topic that no one seems to want to discuss. At the same time, they feel it's important that young women at least become aware of adoption as a viable alternative.

"It's easier to ride the horse in the direction it's going." Life will be smoother if one goes with the flow. The wisdom in these statements is obvious, but an exception may be in the area of teenage pregnancy and decision-making.

As helping persons, we are responsible for keeping our services and our presentations of the options balanced. If we assume that most young people with whom we work plan to be mothers, we risk investing all our energy in preparing them to be parents and supporting them in that decision. We are too likely to ignore the needs of those who may not be ready or willing to parent a child.

Profound decisions are constantly being made concerning parenting. Choosing to continue one's pregnancy is a decision. Choosing to rear the baby oneself is a big decision, regardless of whether this decision is made consciously or not. It's a decision which affects the lives of many people for a long time.

## Older Women and Adoption Planning

Older women considering adoption report facing negative reactions from professionals as well as friends. Marion, who shares her story in Chapter Five, was thirty-two when she released her baby for adoption. She found practically no support because most people direct their energies toward teenagers.

"I think it's harder for people to understand why an older woman would choose adoption. Society in general thinks if you're old enough to support yourself, you should be able to support this baby," commented Karen Sakata, clinical social worker at Kaiser Permanente, Downey, California.

"It's embarrassing for an older woman to consider adoption," commented Sherri Finik, program director of Adoption Affiliates, Tulsa, Oklahoma. "Society is very judgmental. We have two strongly conflicting values. Everybody should applaud a woman who is willing to continue her pregnancy and provide another family with a child. On the other side is the American virtue of loving your child and doing whatever you can to keep your family together. Many believe that nobody old enough to work and support a child should be 'selfish' enough to place that child with another family.

"I think this needs to be a more possible option. If you're twenty-five and you already have three children, and you're struggling, if you're trying to raise those three children well and you know that having one more is not going to enhance their lives or yours, you need to realize you can make a positive choice through adoption. Choosing adoption does *not* mean you don't love this child," Finik explained.

## Encourage Conscious Decision

Making a conscious decision is usually better than simply accepting one's fate, especially when something as important as parenting a child is involved. A young couple faced with the choice of whether or not to parent now needs to examine their options thoroughly. They need to stand in them and see how these options fit. Only then can they make a conscious choice, a decision with which they can live most peacefully.

If the young woman is alone as she faces these choices, it may be even more important that she make a conscious decision. Adolescents have a lot of shoulds pressed on them concerning their decisions. We owe them our support and guidance as they consider the possibilities available to them.

When a teenager hears an adult's strong message about what she ought to do, she's likely to respond with rebellion and do the opposite. To take a strong stand with a teenager only defeats our purpose. Our focus need not be on what she *should* do. Our focus is upon her awareness that she has choices and helping her explore those choices. Simply riding the horse in the direction it's going is not adequate.

## Create a Supportive Atmosphere

Whether you're working with teenagers in a school program, supporting women through childbirth, or working with women with problem pregnancies in some other setting, it's important to support both the adoption and the parenting alternatives rather than assuming that all women who continue their pregnancies will rear their babies themselves.

Making the extra effort to bring *adoption awareness* into your program is important. This can be done in several ways, some requiring very little effort, others requiring more.

Most of us who work with pregnant women have wonderful pictures of mothers and babies, fathers and babies, and other parenting topics on our walls. We have parenting books and brochures on the shelves. We think it's important to help pregnant women and their partners become *good* parents. We talk about the bonding experience.

Much of our society is geared to families, mothers and fathers and their children. Marion, unhappily pregnant, commented on this phenomenon: "All this time these wonderful couple-oriented things were like another knife in my side — couples at Lamaze, couples on TV, in magazine ads. Everything is mom and dad."

We're not suggesting that we stop supporting parenthood and families. Obviously we'll continue to do that.

What do we do then, and how do we do it?

Our job, our mission is to create a supportive atmosphere for alternatives. This is one of the most significant things we can do to make a contribution in the realm of decision-making.

You can do this by starting where you are, in your own setting. Try walking into it with brand new eyes and looking around. Notice what is on the walls. What types of pamphlets are laying on the tables? What books are available for check-out? Ask yourself, "What is the message this environment gives to the people with whom I work?"

The physical environment is very important. While people are sitting in an area waiting for an appointment or for a class session to begin, they're absorbing a tremendous amount of nonverbal data. They're looking around, they're picking up leaflets and pamphlets, and they're reading posters on the walls. They are, in short, receiving some very definite messages. What is the message your environment is offering people? Specifically, what is being conveyed about the options available to a young woman and her partner?

Once you start scrutinizing the atmosphere, begin to ask yourself the next important question. What can you do, in this setting, to create an atmosphere that supports the exploration of choices? The answers will vary with each setting. It may be helpful to brainstorm ideas with a colleague or a friend. Keep in mind that your focus is heightened awareness of the alternatives and not a strong message about what you want someone to do.

## Providing Adoption Materials

Display posters that convey the themes of support, alternatives, and adoption. Put them in prominent places along with the customary pregnancy and mothering posters.

Some pro-adoption posters are so strongly in favor of adoption that they might be misinterpreted as being anti-birthparents. A poster proclaiming "Adoption builds families," for example, is not suitable for classrooms or offices dealing with problem pregnancies because adoption *doesn't* build birthfamilies. If you can't find what you want, make your own. When you make your own posters, you control such factors.

Get pamphlets and brochures about adoption and have them laying out in clear view with the other brochures. The local adoption agencies and independent adoption services may have something you can use, or they will be able to tell you where to get appropriate materials. Make sure that the pamphlets are descriptive but not pushy. Also, if you have a choice, choose those that are colorful and easily read.

Add books about adoption to your bookshelves. You probably have books about pregnancy, childbirth, and parenting, with only a sprinkling on adoption. You may want to have available for your clients several copies of Lindsay's *Pregnant Too Soon: Adoption Is an Option, Open Adoption: A Caring Option,* and *Parents, Pregnant Teens and the Adoption Option* (Morning Glory Press). If you choose only one title, *Pregnant Too Soon* is probably the most appropriate.

Other good titles are *Dear Birthmother: Thank You for Our Baby* by Kathleen Silber and Phylis Speedlin (Corona), and *To Keera with Love* by Kayla Becker (Sheed and Ward). Others are described in the bibliography (pages 269-283). The style of adoption planning varies from state to state and among communities. It's important to read these books yourself first so you'll know which titles are most appropriate for your various clients.

## Staff Must Support Alternatives

Being human, we all have our biases, attitudes, prejudices, and feelings. This makes us all unique. However, some of our biases are based on misinformation, fear, or unresolved feelings. Staff members in your program will, most likely, have a whole range of feelings, opinions, and interpretations of the adoption alternative. It is important to work with these individuals as much as possible. The staff *is* the atmosphere.

Each of us has a value system we've carefully constructed over the course of our lives. When we work with young people, this value system may come strongly into play, especially if we're convinced those young people will have difficulty parenting.

All of us make judgments about what others should do. When we have a very young girl sitting in the office with us, one who has no money, no support system, and few resources, we're likely to have feelings and biases about her choices.

Advice-giving, however, is not our role. Telling someone else what to do with her life is not our job. We'll be out of her life in the future, but she'll have to look in the mirror every day and live with the decisions she makes.

## Sharing Our Values

The choices we make are made because we deeply value families. Even the child of a dysfunctional family values those primary relationships, according to Rev. Lois Gatchell, Episcopal Deacon and founder of the Margaret Hudson Program for pregnant and parenting teens in Tulsa, Oklahoma.

"With long careful counseling, a young person's values may become more informed and may change over time. If a client learns how families can function positively to provide a nurturing environment, she may adopt such a family as her personal goal. She may reject the other influences that undermine that goal. Thus her value of the 'ideal family' has been changed and this begins to influence her decisions," Rev. Gatchell explained.

A counselor knows that values cannot be coerced. They must be freely chosen among alternatives and will be based on internalized learning.

"Knowing this, the counselor refrains from judgment," Rev. Gatchell continued. "Instead, she sees the professional role as that of gentle leader providing all the sound information the client can absorb and reinforcing it as necessary. In this process, as trust and friendship develop, the professional becomes a role model."

As professionals, we must consider the feelings we have about adoption. Do some of us consider it abandonment? Or do we think it's "so sad" to see a fifteen-year-old keep her baby? What are our biases?

Have you ever had an unwanted pregnancy? Perhaps you need to consider your feelings toward that pregnancy and how these feelings may affect the way you look at the whole issue.

If you have ever adopted or attempted to adopt a child or have had a close friend who did so, this experience may have created strong pro-adoption feelings. If your client is a young birthmother, the adoptive parents waiting out there are *not* your primary concern.

People in helping professions usually have high standards for work performance. We expect ourselves to be objective, non-judgmental, and unconditionally caring. We expect it every time, with every client.

This is a tall order, particularly when we're dealing with very young pregnant women. Regardless of how objective we try to remain, we're still human beings. We have formulated our belief systems over the years, and they are the lenses through which we view the world.

We may feel ashamed of ourselves when we're feeling judgmental or opinionated. To compensate, we deny it, or at least we do our best to cover it up. By doing so, we're attempting to suppress a very real part of ourselves. The result is that we become uncomfortable and unnatural when we work with people. The cover-up does not work, and our suppressed feelings begin to run us.

## Importance of Acknowledging Beliefs

Being consciously aware of our values and beliefs can be an asset. Once we acknowledge these values and beliefs, they belong to us. They are something we *have,* rather than something we *are.*

Having beliefs is freeing. The beliefs can be observed, changed, looked upon, evaluated, and verbalized. You won't need to defend your beliefs and values because your selfhood is no longer dependent upon their preservation. Even more significant is your freer position as a helping person. You have beliefs, and your client also has his or hers. You are free to listen and feel and respond without having to defend your position. She may have different beliefs than you do, but that doesn't mean either of you is wrong.

This is particularly important in alternatives counseling. Perhaps we believe that no one under fifteen can be a good mother, a commonly held opinion among people in our field. When a thirteen-year-old comes to us for help with her decision, we already "know" she shouldn't parent. If we deny that we are biased, we're more likely to be judgmental, opinionated, and possibly very rigid as we work with her.

Whenever she talks about being a mother, it will be extremely difficult for us really to listen to her. We will have the tendency to push her into other lines of thought. In short, we'll not truly be with her, and we'll not be exploring options. We will be too busy defending our own beliefs.

---

*Some young women under 15*
*have become competent parents.*

---

What if we've already admitted to ourselves that we feel this way? What if we have shared this idea with a colleague and worked on our discomfort? Once we have acknowledged and explored our beliefs, we are much freer.

First, we're in a position to notice that our belief has not always held true. We'll be able to notice that some young women under fifteen have become competent parents. Suddenly it is no longer a universal truth that determines our behavior. Instead, our belief is reduced to a concern we have about *some* young mothers.

We still may have this concern, but now we can listen to the young mother fantasize about her motherhood. We can explore adoption with her without pushing. Why? Because we don't need her to make either choice. We can now make ourselves available to assist her in her decision-making.

Another widely held bias is the idea that young fathers don't care about their babies. We may come to that conclusion based on watching the misery a  mother endures when the father of her baby splits as soon as he learns she's pregnant, or he denies that the baby is his.

Apparently that young father doesn't care about his child and, we think, should have no part in the adoption decision. We may extrapolate from that situation to all young fathers. Presto, another bias is born.

This bias, too, can be faced. We can allow ourselves to realize that some young fathers care about their children and need help and support just as their partners do. We may continue to feel a bias against a young father's adverse involvement in the decision-making process, but we can step ahead of that bias to provide the help and the support that our client needs because we know he's not "all young fathers." He's simply a young man who needs assistance.

## Provide Staff Training

Staff training provides the opportunity for staff members to explore their attitudes and feelings about adoption as an alternative. There are a number of ways to approach staff training. It is ideal to set aside time when the staff members can be together to explore the topic.

If at all possible, bring in a panel of birthparents who can discuss their feelings, their experiences, and their reasons for making an adoption plan. It may also be helpful to invite an adoptive couple and an adult adoptee to share their experiences with the staff.

If such people are not available, another approach is to use a film or video that deals with adoption as a choice. We have listed several in the Appendix. Following the presentation, encourage staff members to share their thoughts and emotional reactions. Encourage those who disagree or have ambivalent feelings to share during this time.

Cultural and familial patterns may be important areas for discussion. Very likely, at least one staff member will have a personal adoption story to share.

As time permits, feature other activities that facilitate sharing among staff members. One method is to divide participants into smaller groups to discuss specific case situations. Encourage them to respond individually to the case content. Then, as a team, they can develop suggested approaches for their own professional responses.

## Words Make a Difference

Often it's not so much what we say but how we say it. Terminology carries with it a tremendous amount of feeling. This is particularly true of words and phrases used in describing the adoption process.

Many adoptive parents cringe when someone inquires about their child's "real" parents. Certainly they feel they are the parents committed to the day-to-day, year-to-year upbringing of a child and are "real" parents in every sense of the word.

Young women considering adoption are also victims of careless use of terminology. Take, for example, the comment, "She's giving her baby up for adoption." The phrase "to give up" often is used in our society to mean "to quit, to cease to try." Obviously, when it is connected with a baby, it carries the connotation of giving up on the infant or of being unwilling to try to raise him. "Making an adoption plan" is a better description.

A similar example carries an even more negative connotation. Sometimes people say, "I don't see how she can give her baby away." The phrase "giving away" is usually connected with objects. To use such a phrase to describe a mother's choice for her child makes it sound like a degrading and selfish act.

For awhile we tried the word "surrender," but this sounds like losing a war.

The terms "release" and "relinquish" are two of the more popular ones. In many areas, "relinquish" signifies the placement of one's child with an adoption agency while "release" refers to independent or private adoption. "Release," however, is commonly used to signify the placement of one's child with an adoptive family whether or not the placement goes through a licensed agency or directly from birthparents to adoptive parents with the help of an attorney and/or other adoption facilitator. Both of these terms are somewhat neutral and have a more professional sound. However, "making an adoption plan," "arranging for an adoption," or "placing the child in an adoptive home" are better ways to describe the adoption alternative. These phrases imply the birthparents' involvement in planning for the child's future.

"Deciding to parent the child" is a better description of this decision than is "keeping the baby." "Keeping" suggests ownership of a possession. A baby is not a possession.

Whatever terms you choose, it's most important to be sensitive to the connotations they may carry for the young people with whom you work. Using neutral language may help your client make a good decision for herself and her child.

## Dealing with Peer Pressure

Peer pressure is a common problem cited by people who work in our field. Since the majority of pregnant adolescents intend to keep and raise their children, there is a tendency for them to exert pressure on those considering adoption.

Nancy, sixteen, had an extremely mature way of interpreting the unkind comments she heard at school:

> *The other girls were nice to me until I told them I was releasing my baby for adoption. Then they weren't nice at all. They acted like they hated me. I think they were jealous because after my baby was born, I had to go through the pain of losing someone I dearly love, but they're never going to stop struggling unless they find a man to take care of them.*
>
> *They thought I was copping out, but actually I think they were the ones that copped out when their babies were born. It's much easier to hold a cute little baby and say, "I'll keep him" than to say, "I'm going to release." But in the long run, it's harder to keep. Those girls who said those things weren't real happy.*

You can help your client deal with peer pressure by bolstering her self esteem. Help her understand the value of her love and her caring concern for her baby's future whether she chooses the adoption or the parenting option.

Perhaps you can help her find a different peer group. Can you locate some volunteers, young birthmothers, who would be willing to get together with either a pregnant teen or an older woman and talk about their realities? These birthmothers could share their unselfishness in making the adoption decision. They could demonstrate that their lives are going on, that the grieving does become less strong as the months pass.

If you don't have other birthmothers willing to share their experiences, utilize books, articles, poems and films to help your clients understand the realities of adoption.

At the time she became pregnant, Lana was not enrolled in school. When she was five and a half months pregnant, she enrolled in an alternative program which served both pregnant and non-pregnant students. She remained in that program until after the birth of her child.

Lana remembers the negative comments, but she was able to withstand them because of her own self esteem and her strong conviction that an adoption plan was best for her child. Now she likes to talk with pregnant teenagers about her adoption decision:

> *A lot of people told me to keep my baby, but they don't put me down now. My life is going well and they can see I made a good decision.*
>
> *So many people think, "That's your baby, keep it." My thinking is so much different from a lot of people I know. I've seen people who ruined their lives because they got pregnant. One girl got pregnant at fourteen, kept her child, and is now fighting her mother for the privilege of raising her own child. To me, it's not worth it. I'd rather have someone else have that joy and privilege rather than fight my family to let me raise my own child because they think I'm too young to do it.*
>
> *Most of the people I know kept their babies because they couldn't do it, they couldn't carry a child for nine months and then place it with someone else. It makes me mad. How are they going to support this child? What is their thinking about this child they say they love so dearly? Why do they do this?*
>
> *I feel happy about my decision. I feel happy too when people in that situation want to talk to me. I can say I've been there. For a lot of people, it's easier to have a peer, someone their own age say, "I know how you're feeling." Sammy's happy, he's getting all the things I couldn't give him. He's living the life I wanted him to live.*
>
> *I tell other people considering adoption, "Look at what these people who can't have kids can do. Look at all the love they can lavish on a child." That feels good to me.*

When peer pressure for parenting and against adoption exists, a guest speaker like Lana may help students accept each other's decisions. Hearing a birthmother talk about her reasons for choosing adoption for her child and her comfort in knowing her child is loved and well-cared for can put a different and much needed perspective on the subject.

## Student Agreements Are Helpful

Teen parent programs can utilize student agreements to stress respect for each person's decision. A student agreement outlines clearly that a policy of the program is the support of a wide variety of life choices. The agreement is read to each student upon enrollment. Signing it indicates that the individual understands the expectations set forth in the policy.

The practitioner doing the initial intake explains what the policy means in practice. She may say, "In our program we have many young women who are in a variety of situations. Some are single, some are married. Some are planning to keep their babies, and some are making adoption plans. It's very important that we understand that everyone's situation is different and that we be understanding and supportive. How do you feel about this? Can you agree to do so?"

The value of an agreement of this type is two-fold. First, it sets the tone for the program. Second, the signed agreement is kept in each student's file and can be referred to in the future if the need arises.

Few students feel that the opportunity to hassle another is worth expulsion from the program. The choice is clear, to cooperate or to leave. Over the years we never found it necessary to ask a student to leave due to harassment of another student based on differing decisions.

The form of such an agreement or program policy will vary from one setting to another. Whenever such a policy is set up as a guideline for behavior, however, it is of value in establishing a supportive tone for the program. If we are committed to supporting the exploration of alternatives, we must also be responsible for protecting those young women who are involved in such an exploration.

## Different Decision, Still Friends

Incidents are bound to occur. Yet, the effective handling of peer pressure can bring about positive results for the people involved. I (Catherine) had such an experience while working in a teen parent program:

> *One day Gloria came into my office highly distressed and near tears. Another student had made remarks to her on two occasions about Gloria's decision to release her baby for adoption. The student making the allegations, Becky, was the mother of a toddler. She had said things to Gloria like, "I don't see why you had to give your baby away! Why didn't you just give him to me?" Gloria responded on the first occasion by explaining that she chose adoption because she wanted her baby to be raised by a couple in a healthy and secure environment. On the second occasion, she was hurt and frustrated, and simply walked away.*
>
> *Gloria and I talked at length about her feelings before we made any decisions about appropriate action. She stressed that she did not want to hurt Becky or to get her in trouble, but that her remarks were painful and embarrassing. Finally, we agreed that Becky's counselor could call her in to discuss the issue. Ultimately, Gloria, Becky and their two counselors met together.*
>
> *Both Gloria and Becky were obviously nervous when the meeting began. I asked Gloria to tell Becky how she felt when Becky made her remarks. Becky, far less verbal, sat in silence looking at the floor. Finally, she burst into tears and exclaimed that it had been very hard for her to raise a toddler in her situation, and that she was exhausted and lonely. Gloria, with sincere concern in her voice, responded, "I'm so sorry. Would you like to have lunch with me today?"*

This is an example of a potentially volatile situation that can arise over the issue of decision-making. Although it takes extra time and energy on the part of the staff person, such conflicts can usually be resolved. Certainly not everyone is as quick to forgive as was Gloria, and not everyone will be so ready to let go of her position as was Becky. Yet, most conflicts can be brought to resolution through guided communication. Of course, when all else fails, there is always the back-up measure of the agreement forbidding such behavior.

Creating a climate for the exploration of the adoption as well as the parenting alternative in pregnancy counseling requires, first of all, helping professionals who are aware of our biases. We know our role is to help each client look at her life and her goals, and to consider the needs of her partner and their child. Only then can we talk with her about decision-making regarding alternatives.

Emelda talked briefly about her adoption decision. She feels strongly that other women should have a chance to look at their alternatives, then make their own decision:

> *The best thing was that I got to spend four days with my baby. The worst thing is he had to go.*
>
> *This was a difficult decision, one I didn't want to make. People should understand that I wasn't doing this because I didn't want my baby. I did it because I wanted it to benefit both of us. I wish there was something I could say to make people understand why girls some- times make this decision. I think it has to do with the way your family feels about it and the kind of options you think you have. People need to know they have options. They need to be able to talk this all over and maybe they can figure out what's best for them. They shouldn't feel they have to make any decision that's not best for themselves and their baby.*

# CHAPTER 2

# Why Don't Teens Consider Adoption?

*I'm only 17 and not financially ready, but I'll love my baby. I'm trying to graduate so I can support it. (Jan)*

*I don't want to give away something that is mine and that I care for. (Mary Jane, 16)*

*I feel if you can carry a baby for nine months, then you should have a bond or will to keep it. (Sally, 14)*

*I wanted a baby and I love him. I don't want anyone else to have him. (Gloria, 15)*

You may have heard most of these comments. You probably have also heard some of the following questions:

"Why do so few teenagers choose to release their babies for adoption?"

"Why do so many keep and raise their children? Don't the girls know how *hard* parenting is? Aren't you telling them?"

"There are so many stable couples out there dying to have a child! Don't these girls know adoption would be better for their babies?"

The first question is actually the basis for the others, and there are several answers. The first and most often ignored reason teenagers decide to parent their children is that teenagers are human beings.

Teenage women are human beings who bond with their babies during pregnancy just as older women do. They *want* to parent their babies. Neither of us has ever yet worked with a young woman who made an adoption plan because she did not want her child.

The dreams and fantasies pregnant teenagers have about the children they carry belong to them. It is their birthright as human beings. Nature has designed human beings to bond with their offspring, and to want to nurture them after birth. The reasons for this are obvious. Without consistent nurturing following birth, the human infant would not survive.

The natural, healthy progression of a pregnancy involves the mother identifying with her maternal role, giving birth, and bonding with the infant. This, of course, is the ideal preamble to healthy maternal-child interaction and ongoing nurturance.

Those of us who work with mothers and children know that there are a number of physiological, psychological, and socio-logical factors that can alter or inhibit this process. Nonetheless, the alternative of bearing a child and then releasing it for adop-tion is usually a threatening one. It is inconsistent with the established biological patterns of childbearing.

## Societal Changes Affect Decisions

There are also social reasons that help to explain why so few teenagers today elect to make an adoption plan for their chil-dren. We have been working with pregnant teenagers for nearly twenty years, and we have seen profound societal changes. Twenty years ago, never-married motherhood was not accept-able in our society. Most pregnant teenagers at that time were reluctant to face the kind of societal pressure they would receive if they chose to parent as a single person.

Today the picture is extremely different. Half of the children in our country will at one time live with a single parent. Societal pressure against single parenthood has lessened significantly. The stigma associated with unwed motherhood among teenagers has diminished. This is simply no longer a major motivating factor in the decision of whether or not to parent one's child oneself.

Today's children are growing up quite accustomed to the concept of single parenthood. Thus, rearing a child alone doesn't carry the same connotation today.

When we talk to young women who are planning to parent alone, they frequently express this philosophy. They feel their mothers (or fathers, aunts, cousins, friends) have been able to go it alone and, therefore, they see no reason for not following the same life style.

## Looking Ahead Is Difficult

Another important reason so few teenagers make adoption plans is that they're teenagers. When we were teenagers, we did all kinds of crazy stuff. For example, we would get on the freeway and floorboard the gas pedal to see if we could go fast enough for the windshield wipers to pop open. It *never* occurred to us that we might have an accident and die. We were living for the moment.

Many teenagers have difficulty projecting into the future and hypothesizing potential outcomes. This relative inability to think ahead, coupled with peer pressure and inexperience, makes the decision-making process a difficult one indeed. As teenagers, many are simply unable to project into the future sufficiently to contemplate potential consequences.

To talk to someone about planning her life when she has barely had experience with her weekly allowance is extremely hard. And, when she can think ahead, she tends to be like all of us. She sees her beautiful and loved baby in her future, and she longs for that child.

Recently Erin and her mother came in to see me (Catherine). They were accompanied by the school nurse and counselor from Erin's midschool. Erin had learned she was pregnant a few days earlier. She and her mother wanted information and they wanted help in considering alternatives:

> *Erin was barely thirteen. She was attentive and cooperative throughout the visit, but she obviously did not comprehend the significance of the discussion. Erin's mother and the nurse became tearful several times as we talked. Erin looked at them with concern, but could not understand why they were so upset. She responded to most questions by thinking a moment, then replying, "I don't know," or "I haven't thought about that."*
>
> *Erin's mother was seriously considering an abortion for her daughter. Erin didn't appear to have much feeling about the matter one way or another. At one point I said, "You know, the decision of whether or not to have an abortion is a hard one. Often the decision is based on what the person believes about it. Some people believe it is killing. Other people believe there is not a living person until later on. Do you have some ideas about that?"*
>
> *Erin puzzled long and hard in trying to answer my question. Finally she said, "I don't think I believe anything about it." This, I'm sure, was an honest answer.*

The session continued in this vein. At times Erin made an extraordinary effort to draw herself into the conversation. She seemed eager and indifferent at the same time. How could this be? What was transpiring?

## Concrete Stage of Thinking

The young person of twelve, thirteen, even fourteen is generally still in a concrete stage of thought. Although she may begin to project somewhat into the future, she still functions mostly in the present. Her thoughts center around what is happening to her now. It's not only difficult, but often impossible for someone in this cognitive stage to look at her options in pregnancy. She

finds it a monumental task to imagine what it would mean
to have a baby.

It is equally difficult for her to project what it would mean to
release her child for adoption, or to think about the life and
death issues surrounding abortion. She has probably never
thought about it. Her values are not yet set. No one was ever less
prepared for such a difficult decision than Erin at thirteen. She
faced a decision that would affect her the rest of her life, one
that would profoundly affect the future of her child. Her choice
would significantly impact her parents, the baby's father, and
possibly his family.

## Cognitive Immaturity Requires Concrete Approach

When cognitive immaturity and lack of experience play such
an important role, the young person needs a great deal of assistance. Although it is ultimately her decision, it is important that
her family be counseled with her. The approach will have to be
concrete, directed at the feelings and ideas she is able to grasp
rather than at fantasizing about the future.

As you work with a pregnant teenager, ask her about the key
people in her life. What are they like? How are they reacting to
her pregnancy? What do they think she should do about this
decision?

You may want to assign lots of homework researching cost of
delivery, independent housing, continuing education and other
needs. Suggest that she interview her key people. You can help
her work out the questions. Explain that she needs to interview
these people to find out just what help she'll be getting.

Sara had extensive counseling concerning her pregnancy
alternatives. She decided to make an adoption plan, but after her
baby was born, wondered if she could handle releasing Billy to
his adoptive parents. Sara explained how her mother helped her
face reality through some very concrete thinking:

> *At first I didn't want to hold my baby after he was
> born because I felt I wouldn't want to give him back.
> The nurse finally took me to my room and brought Billy
> in. I did okay until they left me alone with him.*

*I thought, "They can't take my baby away, they can't. Nobody's going to take my baby away." Then somebody came in and I calmed down and everything was okay again. I made the right decision, he's going to be happy.*

*I got out of the hospital on Thanksgiving Day and I told them, "I'm not going to give my child up on Thanksgiving. I don't care if you have to pay for this baby to stay in the hospital for two extra days, I'm not giving him up today." So they kept Billy in the hospital for another day and I went home.*

---

## "He's yours now.
## Take good care of him."

---

*That night I went hysterical. My mother was with me, and I kept saying, "They can't take him away from me, they can't. It's my baby and they can't do this."*

*My mom and I sat down in her bedroom and talked. It's real stupid what made me decide again, a real subtle type of humor. Mom said, "If you brought that baby home tomorrow, what would you do with him? You don't have bottles, you don't have a crib, you don't have diapers, you don't have anything. What would you do, use your hand?" And at that time it was funny. We cracked up. We sat there and laughed because she had made that comment. I know it sounds stupid, but after that point I was actually fine.*

*I hadn't met the adoptive parents yet, and I decided I needed to do that. My mom and I talked a lot about bonds, the bond that's created between the mom and the child she carries. I decided it was important to hand Billy to his new parents, that that would help break that bond between us, and it did.*

*Of course there was a lot of crying, and I was very upset when I handed Billy to these people. I said, "He's yours now. Take good care of him." And it was okay. It hurt, but I knew it was okay, the way it should be.*

> *It was a decision that was made, and it was some-*
> *thing that needed to be done. I knew Billy would*
> *be happy. I feel comfortable with the decision I made*
> *and the life Billy is leading.*

## Adolescence Is a Time of Transition

The teenage years are a training ground, a transition time when the young person is moving out of the safety and security of childhood toward the autonomy of adult maturity. Adolescence in our nation today is usually accompanied by school and perhaps job experiences. It is a somewhat nebulous time when she is neither child nor adult. It is during this time that the young person attempts to carve out an identity for herself.

All of this sounds, in theory, very simple and straightforward. Why, then, is adolescence such a stormy period for many young people? Why do we see teens taking serious risks with their lives and the lives of others?

Let's take a typical example. Recently we were driving down a main street. While stopped at the light, we saw two cars pull up behind us. Both cars were driven by teenage boys. They began honking and waving at one another and we smiled at their burst of spontaneous enthusiasm. As we pulled away from the light, the cars raced around us, one on either side. One of us said, "Well, they're young, I hope they'll be okay."

Soon we noticed that their behavior continued to escalate. Their cars began to swerve and weave and one went partially up over the divider.

We then realized they were no longer concentrating on their driving at all, but were involved in throwing tennis balls at the windows of one another's cars.

When we adults see behavior of this kind, we react with wonder that kids would play such dangerous games. Certainly, at best, they must be feeling self-destructive. The adult judges the incident from an experienced and more mature position.

If we could discuss this incident with these young men, we would probably find they were neither dumb nor malicious. They would tell us they were having fun and it hadn't occurred to them that anyone (least of all themselves) was at risk.

Teenagers may look adult, but they are still in the process of cognitive maturation. When they tell us they didn't think it would happen to them, they're speaking truthfully. They haven't fully developed the ability to project into the future. They haven't yet learned the relationship between cause and effect.

Thus we see many young people taking what appear to be foolhardy risks and often suffering serious consequences. We've talked with hundreds of pregnant young women who never thought they'd get pregnant. They had not yet internalized the connection between sex and pregnancy.

Families of these young women and the fathers of their babies are all affected by the decisions that are made. However, few of the young women who become pregnant as teenagers and decide to carry their pregnancies to term ever seriously consider any choice except that of parenting their children.

For a more complete discussion of adolescent development as it relates to early pregnancy, adoption, and parenting, see *Working with Childbearing Adolescents* by Barr and Monserrat (New Futures).

## Adoption Is Difficult Decision

The decision to carry a pregnancy to term and then place the baby for adoption requires a tremendous amount of thought and courage. It may be even more difficult for a teenager because her normal development encourages that she be as much like her peers as possible. This is how she feels she can gain their acceptance.

The pregnant teenager who makes an adoption plan becomes different not only from her non-pregnant peers but also from her sub-group of pregnant and parenting peers because the vast majority of them choose motherhood.

Working with these young women is a tremendous challenge. They're facing some of the most difficult and significant decisions of their lives. They have had little experience in decision-making, and they are at a stage of cognitive development that may not allow them to project into the future.

The pregnant teen is faced with choices about health care, education, finances, and living arrangements. Her most pressing decision will be whether she will become a parent or release her child for adoption.

Susan, now employed full-time in a government job, delivered her child during her senior year in high school. She recalled those months of decision-making:

> *My mom was for adoption but she said it was my decision. She said, "I think adoption would be the best way to go, but it's your decision and you're going to have to figure it out."*
>
> *In the beginning I was real stubborn. I was going to keep the baby and I was going to quit school. I think I was being real selfish because I was thinking about nobody but myself.*
>
> *I had to think about it for a few months. My parents would have supported me if I had kept my baby, but they wanted me to graduate, and I don't think I could have. They might have been able to get me a baby-sitter so I could go to night school, but I didn't think that was fair to them. I didn't want my mom to be stuck as a baby-sitter because she's working too.*
>
> *I started thinking about growing up in a single-parent home. We moved a lot because my mom kept changing jobs so she could support me. I hardly ever saw her, and I didn't want that for my baby.*
>
> *Moving and changing schools all the time was a real pain. Just when you feel like you're getting settled, yank, you've got to move because your mother found a better job. That's hard on a kid. I didn't want Danny to grow up like that.*

## Mother Insists on Counseling

Often a pregnant teenager tries not to believe this is happening to her. She may not acknowledge her pregnancy for several months. Lana followed this pattern.

When she did admit her pregnancy, she insisted she'd parent her child herself. She explained later why she eventually changed her mind:

*I spent the first three months telling myself I wasn't pregnant. Then I spent the next two months trying to decide how I was going to tell everybody about it.*

*My mom finally found out and took me to the doctor. She made me see an adoption counselor too. I came in and told Arleen (the counselor), "You aren't going to tell me anything. I'm going to keep this baby. I don't care what anyone says, and you can sit there and talk all you want. I don't care." I was a real smart aleck.*

*My mom wanted me to see Arleen because she wanted me to realize what options I had, that keeping the baby wasn't the only thing I could do. She was concerned about the depression I had been in, and she thought I needed somebody that understood and wasn't personally involved.*

*My mother also told me if I kept the baby she wasn't going to support me and my child. I had just spent six months sitting around, and I was dying for school to start because I felt like my brain was dead. It was at that time I decided I wanted to go to college, and that was a major factor.*

*Arleen gave me some books to read. Then on the way home my mother and I had a long discussion about how I had a tendency to set myself up to fail. Later I had a big discussion with my sister who is a couple of years older than me. She told me that if I kept the baby I was being extremely selfish.*

*Those things and the books Arleen gave me made me change my mind. Arleen was in total shock two weeks later when I said I wanted adoption. I was firm throughout the rest of my pregnancy, from five months to the day she was born, and now, two years later, I know I made the right decision.*

## Fear in Adoption Planning

Few parents would be willing to trust their child to a baby-sitter about whom they know little or nothing. Indeed, few of us would risk doing so for an hour, let alone a lifetime. Yet, this is exactly what many adoption agreements require of a young birthmother. She is expected to trust an agency to put her child's life in the hands of strangers about whom she knows almost nothing! That is an incredibly fearful thing to do.

Many people have never thought about adoption in this way. They may think adoption is the easy way out for the pregnant teenager. They suggest that it is a selfish act performed by an individual who is unwilling to accept her responsibilities. Consequently, impressionable young women may think they will appear to be weak and uncaring if they consider an adoption plan.

Are these fears justified? Will a birthmother be judged harshly or negatively for her decision? Most certainly she can expect such judgment on occasion. She may be looked down on, be questioned, and have various sorts of pressure that can last the rest of her life.

## Negative Reaction from Peers

Suzi was sixteen and living at home when she became pregnant. During her pregnancy, she transferred from her regular school to an alternative program where she did quite well. She remembers running into strong negative response after her child was born and had been placed with his adoptive family:

> *Three months after I placed Dwayne, this girl found out and she was telling me, "You bitch, you shouldn't have done that. It was your mistake and you should have paid for it." I'd be paying for it? Well, Dwayne would be, too, and that's not what I wanted. I wanted my baby to be happy.*
>
> *This girl's mother even told me I should have kept my baby and she would have helped me. I'm thinking, "Sure, right, for a little while you'd have, and then . . ." I didn't want to have to drag my baby through the mud, no money, no nothing.*
>
> *Sure, I'd have been able to give him a lot of love but that doesn't pay the bills. I don't know where that woman's head was at.*

Marty was pregnant at seventeen while a senior in high school and living at home with both parents. Marty's parents were both seventeen when she was born, and Marty is their only child. She says she spent most of her life trying to be their "perfect little girl" and not disappoint them in any way. Marty shuddered as she remembered the nasty comments she heard during her pregnancy and after her baby was placed with the adoptive family:

> *The kids in high school are malicious, you know. They're mean, really vicious. Most of it was talking behind my back. Like, "I can't believe she'd give her baby up for adoption" or "How could she do something like that? She must not love it."*
>
> *There was one girl who was asking me about my baby, and I told her I was planning to give it up for adoption. She looked at me and said, "That poor little thing. It isn't even born, and already it's unloved!"*
>
> *And I'm like, "You don't understand, because that's not the idea at all. It's not because I don't love the baby. It's because I do."*

## Fantasy of Teen Parenthood

Joan Anderson, counselor, has worked with Options for Pregnancy for seven years. Options is the birthparent arm of WACAP (Western Association of Concerned Adoptive Parents). "I find I learn as much from my clients as they do from me," Anderson commented. "I have tremendous respect for the difficulty of their decision, how agonizing it is, and what a loving decision it is.

"I think the two most difficult things for teenagers are looking ahead and facing reality," Anderson continued. "Once she gets past the initial shock of telling her family, she starts fantasizing about her pregnancy. She tells her friends she's pregnant and they think it's terrific. They can't realize what a tremendous shock this will have on her life. If school has never been interesting or positive for her, the pregnancy may be a convenient out. During pregnancy she may say, 'Oh, I'm too tired. I'm not going to school.' Sometimes this becomes a pattern. It's hard for her to look ahead."

As helping persons, we need to focus on each client's goals. These are important whether she's planning to parent or if she makes an adoption plan. She needs to think about what she's going to do with her life. The ones who have the hardest time with this are those without much success at school and without much family support. The baby becomes the focus of their lives.

## Considering an Adoption Plan Later

This focus on the baby may be short-lived. By the time the reality of parenting hits her, she may think it's too late to make an adoption plan because of her bonding with the child and because of the expectations of other people.

Sometimes a young mother, after a few months or even years, feels she can no longer care for her child. How do you respond?

This is a dilemma for professionals working with young mothers. They're not sure how to respond when a mother says, "I should have released my baby for adoption." First, explore what she means by her statement. Is she simply expressing frustration or exhaustion? Perhaps she needs parenting assistance, economic help, or emotional support.

If she seems to be thinking seriously about adoption, it's important to offer counseling on an ongoing basis. Of course it's difficult to let go of a child one has been parenting. The grieving and loss will be extremely intense.

Perhaps she is unable or unwilling to care for her child at the present time, but is still uncertain about adoption. She may need help investigating alternative arrangements. Is there a family member or friend who can care for the child while she works through her difficulties? Or she may make arrangements for foster care through an agency.

Before tackling such a situation, be sure you know the community resources available to the young mother who may consider an adoption plan for an older child.

Anderson reported having several clients who planned to relinquish their babies at birth, then couldn't go through with it. "Each parented for awhile, then called to say, 'I feel guilty that

I haven't done the right thing in keeping this baby.' Their guilt was not that they couldn't handle the parenting. Rather it was because they hadn't made a better plan. Finally they could say, 'This is not a good situation for my child and it's not going to get better.' So they look again at the adoption plan."

Anderson replies to these young mothers, "You haven't failed at all. Your original plan was made out of love and what you felt was best for your child." Emotionally she couldn't relinquish at birth, but later she realized she was still unable to provide adequately for her child. Adoption again became a positive decision.

"Feeling she failed is a problem," Anderson pointed out. "I usually suggest she place her baby in foster care for a few days to give her a sense of separation. She can get some idea of what it would be like without the baby, some space to make a decision. This happens most often when the baby is less than a month old."

## Sandi Reconsiders Adoption

A social worker described a client whose baby was six months old when she decided to reconsider adoption:

> Sandi is a wonderful mom. Her baby is secure and well-cared for, and they are bonded to each other, but Sandi doesn't feel this is right for her child. She doesn't like the idea of being on welfare, she feels second class, and she sees no future for herself or her baby. She finally is ready to go back to school.
>
> The birthfather wouldn't meet with me before birth, but he came to the hospital. He became intrigued with the baby, and Sandi couldn't go through with the adoption plan because Curtis decided he wanted to be a parent. Sandi had some misgivings but followed his lead. So they played house for a few weeks. Both were sixteen.
>
> Then it wore off for the young father. He no longer seemed interested in the baby. He resumed going out with his friends all the time and leaving Sandi to care

*for the baby. She was disillusioned, felt the parenting
decision was made for her, but she would deal with it.
Then she decided, "This isn't right for my baby. I want
her to have a mom and dad and I want to go to school."*

*I'm moving slowly with this client. I've told Sandi
many times that whatever she decides to do, I know her
baby will be cared for just fine, whether it remains with
her or with an adoptive family. I'm worried about her if
she relinquishes the baby. Sandi wants to be with the
father, but she realizes he probably won't always be
there for her. He's saying whatever Sandi decides is all
right, but she feels he'll pressure her to relinquish. It's a
difficult situation.*

A difficult situation indeed. Sandi's counselor speaks for
most of us who work with pregnant adolescents. We know it's
hard for almost any mother to make an adoption plan and carry
it out. We also know how hard it is for a woman or a young
couple to spend their teenage years performing the monumental
and adult task of parenting. We must do everything we can to
help them face the realities in their own lives and make the best
possible decisions for themselves and their babies.

Making an adoption plan is hard for any birthparent. For a
teenager not yet developmentally able to project into the future,
planning an adoption takes a quantum leap into maturity. The
more you can do to help her look ahead, to understand the
realities of parenting and of adoption, the more likely she will be
able to make the best possible decision for herself and her baby.

# CHAPTER 3

# Agencies
# Stress Counseling

*Betty, my counselor, helped me a lot. I'd see her once a month, and on those days I'd feel real good about myself.*

*Then I'd go back to school. My friends would say, "I think you should keep the baby," and the things I'd planned on doing would get messed up in my head. I'd think about what the people at school were saying about keeping it. Then I'd go back to see Betty and it would be a relief. She helped me understand more about my feelings than my friends did.*

*Sometimes I'd talk to my mom, but it was mostly Betty. I could actually tell her everything without it being told to everyone else. (Connie, 18)*

Individual work is extremely important during the decision-making process. Since many teenagers are fearful of criticism from their peers, they need to be able to talk individually with a counselor on a regular basis. If they are considering an adoption

plan with a licensed adoption agency, they are likely to be
involved in fairly extensive counseling.

Marge Driscoll, birthparent counselor, Holy Family Services,
Los Angeles, stresses the need for those considering adoption to
work through their feelings. "You go sit in a social worker's
office and you're going to have to do this," she emphasized.
"We don't do it because we're sadistic. It's because we know
adoption is a process, not an event.

"A lot of people make up their minds before they call, and
that bothers us. It's better if they see us *before* they go through
that decision-making process. We want to talk with them about
their other options. In fact, only half of those we counsel go
through with adoption," Driscoll added.

## How Agency Adoption Works

Two kinds of adoption services are available — agency and
independent. Independent or private adoption means the birthparents go through the legal process of placing their baby
directly with adoptive parents. This kind of adoption will be
discussed in Chapter Four.

Adoption agencies may be public, private, or sectarian
(church-related). In agency adoption, birthparents relinquish
their child to the adoption agency rather than directly to the
adoptive parents. The agency then places the child with a
carefully selected family. In some agency adoptions, the birthparents never meet the adoptive parents. Birthparents don't
know their baby's new parents' names nor do the adoptive
parents know theirs. More and more adoption agencies, however, are allowing, even encouraging some degree of openness
in adoption.

Families adopting a child through an agency generally have
gone through an extensive home study to determine their fitness
to parent. Families who apply for a healthy baby through an
agency generally must wait several years for a baby. During the
time they are waiting, they learn about the process of adoption.

After the adoptive couple fills out a lengthy application form,
an agency social worker meets with the couple together and
separately, and visits them in their home. The social worker

discusses with them such topics as the adoptive couple's reasons for wanting to adopt a child, the strength of their marriage, their attitudes toward childrearing, their financial stability, and their capabilities for parenting a child born to someone else.

In most states the birthmother cannot sign final adoption papers until after she leaves the hospital. However, she is asked to sign a release form in the hospital stating that someone else can take the baby away from there. If she releases through an agency, she signs permission for the agency to take the child.

As soon as the birthmother and birthfather sign the relinquishment papers, the baby can be placed in his permanent adoptive home. He will be in a foster home until these papers are completed.

If the birthmother and birthfather have made their decision, the father can sign immediately after birth and the birthmother can complete this step on her way home from the hospital. If this happens, their baby can probably be placed with the adoptive parents immediately.

Relinquishment becomes final and cannot be changed when these signed papers are filed by the agency with the State Department of Social Services. When this has happened, the birthparents generally no longer have any legal rights or responsibility for their child.

State adoption laws differ greatly, however. Check the above information with an adoption agency in your area to make sure you are aware of your local law.

An adopted baby has two birth certificates. The first one contains the information provided by the birthmother, and this certificate is "sealed" — filed away where it cannot be seen except by order of the court. A new birth certificate is then prepared listing the adoptive parents as the child's parents.

Laws regarding secrecy in adoption vary from state to state, and some of these laws are changing fairly rapidly. Helping persons need to remain current on this information.

## Finding the "Right" Agency

When you're working with someone willing to look at pregnancy alternatives, encourage her to contact several resources. If

62    Agencies Stress Counseling

the first agency doesn't seem to fit her needs, suggest she call another as Katheryn did:

> My mom and I went to one agency and they were real cold. The worker told me right off all the things I couldn't have. There couldn't be any changes in what they do. I couldn't choose the parents, and she didn't want me to spend time with my baby. There was no "It's your decision." I didn't think I could deal with that.
>
> I had met the counselor at the Options agency before, so we went over there. Joan was totally different. She seemed extremely interested and caring. I saw her regularly, at least once a week while I was pregnant. Any time I needed to see her, I'd call her. She was wonderful.
>
> Now when she has a girl who wants to talk to someone who has been through it, she calls me.
>
> At some point, I want to go back to school to become a counselor.

Katheryn's mother added:

> I have no idea how big Joan's caseload is, but I know she'll always take the time if we need her. At the other agency it was, "You can get me between 9 and 5." But not all crises happen between 9 and 5. I think Joan's response to our needs made us feel we were very important no matter what our decision was. She was not in it to get the baby, and she made that very clear. Whatever our decision, Joan would go through this with us.

"In our program, we work with a lot of young women who don't even think about adoption," commented Joan Anderson, counselor, Options for Pregnancy, Puyallup, Washington. "They want counseling for whatever concerns them during the pregnancy. Sometimes they don't even think of me as an adoption counselor.

"On the other hand, people who call saying they want adoption, then change their minds, don't want to be in touch with us as much if they parent. Perhaps they feel guilty, or, because we've done some adoption planning, they think that's all I'm here for. Part of our role as counselors is to help them link up with resources, especially if they decide to parent at the last minute. They're going to need a lot of information on resources.

"If she comes to me planning to adopt and doesn't want to look at the possibility of parenting, I try to get her to think about why she doesn't think that's possible. We don't leave the parenting option out even if she says, 'I've already decided on adoption.'

"I still ask her to keep that door open. I'm not pushing it, but it's a lot easier to make a final decision if she has kept some doors open emotionally and realistically," Anderson explained.

## Marty Didn't Choose

It is extremely important to help a young woman explore both the adoption and the parenting alternative. If she does decide on an adoption plan, it is imperative that she know this is *her* choice, not a decision made by someone else.

Marty, who released her baby for adoption three years ago when she was 17, feels she was never allowed the opportunity to consider parenting. She explained:

> *I never even considered keeping the baby. I don't know why, but I knew from the instant I got pregnant that I couldn't keep it. I wish I had thought about parenting, but I knew how important it was to my mom for me to go through nursing school. She talked constantly about how when I graduated I would go to nursing school. I was the first one in my family to go to college, and she was so proud of me.*
>
> *I didn't know what would happen when I told her I was pregnant, so I decided to lessen the blow by telling her I was giving it up for adoption. It wouldn't be as bad as if I were going to keep it. So I never considered keeping.*

*I wish I would have. That's the one thing about the adoption that I'll never forgive myself, not realizing that I wanted to keep my baby.*

*I couldn't talk to my mom because I was practically doing the whole thing (adoption plan) for her. I couldn't tell her what I thought I wanted. I never really let myself think about it out in the open even to myself, so how could I talk to my mom?*

*I couldn't tell Lynn (counselor) because, my God, I was in her office telling her I wanted to give my baby up for adoption. I couldn't be going in there and telling her how I felt about wanting to keep the baby. If I wanted to keep it, what would I be doing here in the first place? And I didn't have anybody else to talk to.*

*I thought I was going to be big and mature and very strong about this whole thing and it wasn't going to bother me. I didn't want a baby anyhow, I was going to nursing school.*

*But I didn't want to go to nursing school; Mom wanted me to go. A baby is what I planned on for most of my life. I wanted to go to nursing school to be with babies. Babies are my life, but I never felt I had the option of keeping my baby.*

*I never let myself see the joy in being a parent. I only saw the things I made myself see, you know, changing diapers, taking care of a sick baby, being up all night, not going to school, flunking my tests, the kid crying and my not being able to study. Those were the things my parents wanted me to see. Mom never told me anything good about being a parent. She kept reminding me about all the bad parts of having a child.*

*No one ever discussed with me the fact that it would have been possible to be a parent, no one, not my parents, not any of my relatives, not my friends. No one ever sat down and said, "You know, you could do it." It kills me because I see so many girls and women who are doing it and are doing a good job of parenting. I didn't even get the chance to try.*

It's easy to suggest that Marty never gave anyone a chance to discuss her parenting alternative. She may have seemed convinced that adoption was her choice, but she would probably feel better about her adoption decision today if she had seriously looked at the parenting alternative, too.

Kristi, a birthmother who is now a social worker, stresses the importance of following one's own feelings. She, too, points out that the adoption decision must not be imposed on a birthparent by someone else:

> I tell other women, "Do what you feel is right and don't listen to what anybody else has to say. If you decide on the basis of what somebody else says, forget it. It's not going to work. My parents didn't want me to keep the child, but they said they would support me if I did. They let me make my own decision. That was my child, and it was my life that would be affected by the decision.
>
> I see people now who are making decisions for other people. I see people now being forced into adoption or abortion by their parents, and it doesn't work. You already feel guilty and you want to make it right. People are telling you how to make it right, but it may not be right for you.

Marty and Kristi illustrate the reason most social workers and some attorneys insist on providing counseling for their birthparent clients. They understand the importance of helping pregnant women and their partners look at both parenting and adoption alternatives.

## Training Is Crucial

The more training a person has in the skills of listening, offering support, exploring options and dealing with feelings, the more effective that person will be in alternatives counseling. K.C. Sherrard, ACSW, counselor at the Maternal Health Center, Bettendorf, Iowa, stresses the need for ongoing training for counselors.

"First, it's important to know yourself by exploring your own beliefs and attitudes," Sherrard pointed out. "Counselors work with a diverse group of people, and we need to develop a keen sense of how the values of others may influence our counseling. When a counselor's values differ from those of her clients, then the counselor must assess how best to work with these individuals. We must not push or persuade a client to do what we think is best."

In addition to developing self awareness, it is also important for the counselor to develop good listening and observation skills. "Let your client talk to you, *hear* what she is saying, and *observe* what is left unsaid," Sherrard continued. "Don't ever say, 'Okay, that doesn't sound so bad.' Instead, 'Can you tell me about this?' can be more helpful. Paraphrase back what you've heard your client say to you and ask if you understand her clearly. Clarify issues that are cloudy.

"Often a counselor can interpret what a client says and provide new insight. It's a much easier task simply to tell someone what you think she should do rather than to allow a process to occur where the client comes to her own decision based on the counseling session. However, your goal is for her to make her own decision."

Counselors need to practice obtaining information through openended questions. "Too many 'whys' and 'what for' questions lead to a defensive atmosphere in counseling," Sherrard suggested. "When a client shares her thoughts and feelings, simply ask for more elaboration. Ask 'Can you tell me more about how you're feeling about this?' And, allow for silence!" she emphasized. "Your client needs some quiet time to sort through her confusion. Often counselors jump in too quickly in an attempt to keep a certain pace going in the interview."

Another sensitive issue of counseling discussed by Sherrard centers around working with sad and tearful clients. "When your client is faced with serious decisions and losses, you may encounter some pain and tears," she said. "Ask yourself as a counselor if you feel comfortable working with someone who is letting out this type of pain. Many times counselors want to try to fix it and make it better. Instead, it's important that we assist sad and tearful clients by giving them permission to cry. We need to affirm that this is an okay and natural thing to do."

## Importance of Trust

Brenda is an example of an unproductive counseling relationship. She was never able to develop trust in Ellen, the agency caseworker:

> *I didn't talk much to Ellen at the agency. I thought I wanted to be on my own. I didn't want anybody's help because at that time I thought everybody was after me, and they just wanted to knock me down a couple more times.*
>
> *As far as the agency goes, I didn't trust Ellen at all. I was mean to her which was awful of me, but that's what happened. She was sort of like a robot. She said the things she was supposed to say, but I didn't feel she cared much about me.*

An effective counseling relationship creates an atmosphere where confidentiality exists, where there is acceptance of the client, and where there is the opportunity for open and honest, nonjudgmental communication. From this blooms a trusting alliance between client and counselor.

---

*Training, experience, and time are the keys to becoming an effective counselor.*

---

"After I introduce myself and stress confidentiality, I ask if she needs any services at this point. 'How are you feeling about this pregnancy? Was it planned?' I try to find out a little about the situation before I delve too deeply," Sharrard explained. "I ask about her support system. 'Who's here for you? Who is in your corner? How are they responding to the pregnancy?' Then I pick basic things: 'How is the money situation?' 'Where are you living?' 'Who will help you after the baby is born?'"

It is important to find out from your client why and how she came to you. What services does she want from you and your agency? Let her know your role, then work together to develop mutual goals. If your client wants her significant others involved in the counseling, that's all right.

"You don't have to do therapy to develop good assessment techniques and good questioning techniques. It's important to know what you can handle personally. For example, if someone is talking about long-term mental health problems, I refer them. Don't be afraid to refer," Sherrard advised. "Then develop a good relationship with the people to whom you refer. Get out in the community and meet these people."

Training, experience, and time are the keys to becoming an effective counselor. Our best trainers can be our own clients. Let them know you can learn from them as well.

To find out what training resources are in your community, contact local mental health centers, adoption agencies, colleges and universities, and any other source you're aware of that provides training for professionals.

## Stress Grief Preparation

Grief preparation is extremely important for anyone making an adoption plan, but this is hard. People don't want to think about it. They'd rather think this is the right decision, it's a good decision for the baby. They don't want to think about the pain.

"I hear about this in private placements where the girl is working with an attorney who doesn't provide counseling," a counselor reported. "Hospital personnel sometimes say they can tell if a birthparent has received counseling. If she hasn't, she doesn't know how to cope with the grief, and she may end up keeping the baby. Counseling gives her an opportunity to anticipate her grief."

Follow-up grief counseling is extremely important. Birthparents need someone with whom they can talk. Even a supportive mom may not be able to talk about the baby because of her own grief or because she thinks her daughter needs to move on.

The birthmother's mom may say, "Let's don't open the wounds," but both of them need to talk about it. They need to face the fact, "This happens, this hurts, but I know I made the right decision." Counseling both before and after placement is essential.

A broader discussion for helping birthparents cope with their grief is presented in Chapter Twelve.

## Rethinking the Decision

During the last weeks of pregnancy, it is common for a woman to begin to vacillate in her decision to place her child in an adoptive home. As the birth of her child draws near, the baby becomes more real to the mother. The adoption plan is less and less merely an idea; it becomes closer and closer to reality.

At this time a woman previously firm in her adoption planning may suddenly buy baby clothes, bottles, and disposable diapers. What is the role of the counselor now? *It is exactly what it has been.* The counselor continues to listen to the client's feelings and thoughts.

It may be tempting to try to talk the young woman into sticking with her decision, but surely this is the wrong approach. For her to question when birth is imminent means she understands the significance of her planning. In fact, this may be a healthier step for her than remaining in denial.

Many women complain about the pressures they feel they receive from counselors and social workers. Suddenly they feel pushed and coerced by people who were formerly their support persons. This is not only uncomfortable, but feels like abandonment to them. Birthparents report that these workers never really cared for them — they only wanted their babies.

If a young woman has been firm in her decision to release her baby for adoption, she is less likely to change her mind at this time. If allowed to feel and experience her desires to keep and parent her child, she is again in a position to explore her decision at a new, more in-depth level. The decision she is making is a difficult and painful one. To pretend otherwise is cruel and dishonest.

This young woman has a right to explore all of her alternatives as long as she chooses. It is, after all, her decision. It is her life, her baby, and her family that will be affected. And it is her

responsibility and her mission to be as clear about her final
decision as possible.

This is true, regardless of how uncomfortable or inconvenient
this may be for her caseworker.

This last-minute change of mind may be triggered by seeing a
baby somewhere, or shopping and seeing baby clothes, or
whatever. If you listen to her and support her, you will enhance
her chances of reaching clarification. She *must,* however, be
listened to, cared about, and supported in whatever decision
she makes.

Trudie, twenty-three, who released her son for adoption a
year ago, felt she got this kind of understanding and support
from her counselor:

> *My counselor helped me make my decision. She was
> always there, and she laid the facts on the line. She
> showed me that although it hurt an awful lot to do what
> I did, it was the right decision for me. The most impor-
> tant part of it was she was behind me one hundred
> percent either way.*

Glenna Weith, attorney, Champaign, Illinois, represents
adoptive parents, and she, too, recommends counseling and legal
counsel for birthparents. Weith feels problem pregnancy counseling too often does not include the adoption option: "Planned
Parenthood and other family planning clinics may do an excellent job of helping women know their rights concerning abortion, but I think many young people need more information on
adoption. I'd like to see clinics providing staff training sessions
where those of us in agencies and private adoption explain to
them what we do," Weith suggested.

## Adoption Agency, Clinic Work Together

Many people assume that staff members at an abortion clinic
are not interested in adoption, but this is not necessarily so.
Nova Health Systems, located in Tulsa, Oklahoma, and in six
Texas cities, operates both Reproductive Services (an abortion
clinic) and Adoption Affiliates, a licensed adoption agency.

"We work with birthmothers who come here to have abortions and change their minds, with birthmothers who want an abortion but are too far along, and with people who would never consider an abortion but come here to talk about adoption," explained Sherri Finik, program director of Adoption Affiliates in Tulsa. The Tulsa agency placed eighteen babies in the past year. About half of the women involved in adoption counseling at the agency choose to rear their babies themselves.

"We've been providing abortion services since 1973, and we have always referred women interested in adoption to other agencies," Finik said. "More and more over the course of time, however, we realized some didn't follow up on those referrals. The denial, the fear, the not knowing how to cope with the system combined to keep them from doing so. Sometimes people come to the clinic thinking it's their first trimester of pregnancy, and they find it's the third trimester. There's a lot of denial going on, and it continues after they leave us. Pretty soon they're in labor, and they go home with the baby.

"We thought if we could offer adoption services here, we could do so much more than say, 'Take this phone number and call this person.' If the people came here and felt comfortable with us, we could go ahead and work with them. We have always supported a woman's right to adoption. We did a lot of research about adoption and established our agency.

"It depends so much on the experiences that birthmother has had with her friends and her family," Finik noted. "If she has a friend who is unhappy and is adopted, she assumes it's because the friend was adopted. On the other hand, if a cousin was adopted and it's a good situation, she decides adoption is good. Or if she is an adoptee herself, her view of adoption depends on her feelings about her own situation."

## Agencies Place Minority Babies

Many agencies report difficulty in placing Black and biracial babies because of the lack of Black families waiting to adopt. They are reluctant to place these babies with Caucasian families. Adoption Affiliates has placed several Black and biracial infants. "I tell a Black mother if I don't have any Black families waiting, and I stress that we're actively recruiting these families," Finik said. "If we don't have a Black family waiting when she delivers, is she willing to have her child placed with a Caucasian family? If she says, 'No,' I can't promise her that her baby will be placed immediately with a Black family. However, the young women we see haven't found this to be a problem."

In their search for potential Black adoptive families, Adoption Affiliates runs newspaper ads and talks about the need whenever they are featured on television. Helping in the search, according to Finik, is a young and articulate Black woman who was already involved in the Black community.

The Cradle Society, Evanston, Illinois, is placing more minority babies recently, according to Margaret Svetlauskas, Supervisor of Social Services. While it might take a month or two, they are finding homes for these babies. They place minority babies in Caucasian homes if there is no minority family waiting for a child.

This agency places approximately fifty babies per year, about one-third of whom are minority infants. All were placed in families within two months last year, and most were with their adoptive families very soon after birth, according to Svetlauskas.

## Native American Adoption Law

Adoption of Native American children is subject to the Federal Indian Child Welfare Act. First preference under the Act is to place a Native American child within the extended family. Second choice is to place the child with a member of the tribe, and third choice is with a member of another Native American tribe.

Only after these possibilities are exhausted is a Native American child legally available for adoption by non-Native Americans.

If you are involved in an adoption plan for a baby with a birthparent of Native American heritage, no matter how slight, check the laws carefully before you proceed with the planning. A Native American birthmother will have to understand and deal with this as part of her decision-making process.

## Birthparents Emphasize Need for Counseling

Deanne, a social worker who is also a birthparent, recently commented on the need for adoption counseling:

> *I never got any counseling (as a birthmother), and it's still devastating for me. I was twenty-two and married, and when he learned I was pregnant, he left. I saw an attorney I found in the paper. I don't know to this day whether the family had a home study to determine whether they would be adequate parents. I don't know whether it was black market, and this scares me.*
>
> *I think it is so important to get counseling for your own peace of mind and to help you set up an adoption plan that would be best for you. I still feel my child is better off in a lot of ways, but I think I could have handled it better if I could have talked more to somebody about my plans, and if I could have had help after placement when I was grieving.*

Kristi remembers the almost total lack of counseling she received from the adoption agency which placed her baby five years ago:

> *I never saw the same social worker twice and I got no counseling. I contacted the agency when I was five months pregnant. I filled out their paperwork, and my mom and I spent an hour with a worker who I never saw again.*
>
> *Another social worker came once to my house and stayed fifteen minutes. We never talked about what I wanted in the adoptive family until after my daughter was born.*
>
> *The adoption is completely closed, and I'm trying now to get some information. I need to know she's okay. That's all I want.*
>
> *One of these days I'm going to get into the field of adoption so I can make sure this doesn't happen to someone else.*

Kristi's story illustrates the importance of consistency in counseling relationships. Being shifted from one counselor to another occasionally is unavoidable. Once a productive counseling relationship is established, however, it is important to maintain that relationship as long as needed.

Julie, sixteen when she released her son for adoption, was asked, "How can a counselor be most helpful to a young woman deciding between an adoption plan and a parenting plan?" She replied:

> Don't pressure her into either decision. She's pressured by parents and other adults to release and by peers to keep. She becomes very confused and doesn't know what she wants. The counselor needs to make sure she is well informed about both options.
>
> Ask her what her goals and dreams have always been. Remind her that those should not change just because she's pregnant. She's carrying a child she loves. She knows she's willing to give up things for that child, but in a year she'll still want what she wanted before she had the baby. She needs to remember that her heart wants to take care of her child but her mind has to do what it believes is best. For some, it will be to keep, for others, to release.
>
> Tell her, "Your child deserves the best. You already gave him life. Make sure neither you nor your baby ever regrets that beautiful gift. It's most important that your child have a chance at happiness, and then, so will you."

# CHAPTER 4

# Some Choose
# Private Adoption

*I didn't believe all this secrecy hogwash, and I didn't like the idea of releasing my child to the agency rather than to its adoptive parents. The worker said, "But if anything goes wrong, you don't have to worry about it."*

*That was my child, and I wasn't about to lose control until s/he was with the adoptive parents. I knew I was better able to plan for my baby than any agency, no matter how professional. (Marion, 32)*

Licensed adoption agencies generally offer a strong counseling program for both their birth- and adoptive parent clients. Potential adoptive parents are screened carefully. Legal issues are handled well, and the interests of the birthparents are generally protected.

Yet more babies in the United States are placed through independent or private adoption than are relinquished through licensed adoption agencies. Estimates range as high as seventy-five percent of infant placements occurring through private adoption. Why is this happening?

## Why Private Adoption?

While many adoption agency counselors and other staff members are warm, caring people, agency social workers sometimes have the reputation of being cold and judgmental. Or the agency may be perceived as a middle-class Anglo institution existing to provide babies for adoptive parents. The admirable goal of providing extensive counseling to birthparents may be interpreted as implying birthparents are "bad," "sick," or at least unable to know their own minds. For some people, adoption agencies appear to be too controlling. Being involved in planning the adoption for their child is important to many birthparents. In some states, agency adoption is much more closely regulated than is private adoption.

These are some of the reasons many birthparents turn directly to attorneys for help rather than working with a licensed adoption agency. It may seem easier to call an attorney and say, "I'm pregnant and I want my baby adopted." If she's lucky, she'll find an attorney who is warm, caring, and who insists on counseling for birthparents. She may feel she has some control over the choice of an adoptive family for her baby. If she's interested in maintaining some contact with her child, private adoption may appear a more promising approach.

A birthparent is not allowed by law to receive money in addition to legitimate pregnancy and birth expenses when she places her baby for adoption. Rumors abound, however, of birthmothers profiting illegally from the adoption of their babies if they work directly with an attorney. This undoubtedly happens, but the birthparents we interviewed and those with whom we have worked have not only understood and followed the laws against selling babies, but in no way have they *wanted* to profit financially from their adoption planning. In fact, this was one reason Trisha, nineteen, was put off by the attorney she visited:

*I went to see an attorney. He was ready to go play golf, and the baby didn't seem important to him at all.*

*He told me I could pick the parents. He said they could
be rich, and he told me about back yards, dogs, that I
could have whoever and whatever I wanted. It didn't
sound right to me. He was stressing money too much.*

Trisha next visited an adoption agency. She perceived the
counselor as cold and uncaring, someone who didn't seem
interested in her.

Trisha was persistent. She next called an independent adoption service and talked with a counselor who Trisha felt fit her
needs. Trisha made and carried out her adoption plan with the
help of this counselor. Trisha said:

*Anita is the most loving person. She loves us and she
wants to help. Other teachers and counselors need to
realize a pregnant girl may be alone and need somebody
to talk with. Her family may be completely against her.*

*Anita was helping fifteen girls at once and she cared
about all of us. She'd take me to lunch, then she'd have
to pick up this girl for something and see that girl. She
was always there helping us with our lives.*

*The most important thing she did for me was to teach
me how to hug somebody and not feel weird about it. My
family never hugged much, but Anita used to hug me all
the time. At first I was afraid to hug her because I didn't
know her that well, but she taught me it was okay.*

*If more people took the time she did, followed up, but
never tried to persuade them, I think more women would
consider adoption.*

Independent adoption services are becoming more common
in many areas of the United States. If you have such a service in
your area, visit and ask lots of questions. How much control do
the birthparents have if an adoption plan is made? Most important, is counseling provided, and if so, for how long and under
what circumstances? Who provides the counseling? Does it
continue after the adoption is finalized? What about follow-up
services for birthparents?

Some independent adoption services provide excellent guidance for birthparents, while others appear to be more interested in satisfying the needs of their adoptive parent clients. As a birthparent advocate, you need to be well informed before recommending an independent adoption service.

## Independent Versus Agency Adoption

A licensed adoption agency generally is not involved in private or independent adoption. Independent adoption is legal in most states although several do not allow this form of adoption. It is essential that people involved in problem pregnancy counseling know their state laws. The following information is a starter kit, not a legal brief.

In private adoption, the birthparents sign a "consent to adoption." This names the couple with whom their child is placed. In most states this consent must be signed in the presence of a representative of the State Department of Social Services or its local designee.

In some states the lawyer can take consent from the birthparents to place the child with the prospective adoptive family. This is termed the "take into care" form and is *not* the final adoption paper. The time at which an independent adoption becomes final varies from state to state.

Usually a baby who is independently placed will go home from the hospital with its new family. In some states, the adoptive family is not studied to determine its fitness to adopt the child until *after* the baby has been placed in their home. In other states, a home study is required before placement.

Dan Farr of Seattle, Washington, is an attorney who works with an adoption agency and also handles independent adoptions. Farr commented that if he were a parent, teacher or medical person working with a young pregnant woman wanting to consider adoption, he would probably recommend a good agency. He said, "I think for the majority of birthparents, it's much safer to go through an agency if it's a good one because they screen the adoptive parents more effectively. Besides," he added, "as a birthmother, how do you know what this attorney is all about? With an agency, I'd also have some assurance that she would have pre- and post-adoption counseling and that they will be looking over her shoulder to be sure everything is done properly. Too much nonsense can go on in adoption. You need a team of people who care."

Attorney placements, independent adoption services, and licensed adoption agencies — each of these systems has flaws and each, depending to a great extent on the people involved, may provide excellent assistance to women considering the adoption alternative.

## Some Attorneys Arrange for Counseling

Farr is an example of the increasing number of attorneys across the country who are insisting on counseling for their clients and who are concerned about the welfare of everyone in the adoption triangle.

Farr, who teaches a class on adoption for attorneys, is outspoken about the need for a different kind of law in adoption. He recommends the concept of a group covenant or a group ethic in adoption law.

"All of us — attorneys and judges throughout the United States and law school professors — we see all things in terms of the rights of the individual. If I represent a client, whether it's a murder case or a boundary line dispute, I must consider only my client's rights. I'm not supposed to be concerned about the other individuals involved," Farr explained.

"Unfortunately, this legal concept of fighting for the individual's rights to the exclusion of others also applies to adoption. If I represent the adoptive parents, I'm not supposed to be concerned about the birthmother or the baby."

This is why many people strongly insist that the birthparent must have one attorney and the adoptive parents another. In some states, this is mandatory for birthparents not yet eighteen. Whether or not separate attorneys are required by law, it appears rational to operate in this way. Farr's comment is valid.

If birthparents relinquish through a licensed agency, their rights are represented by that agency. They don't have to be responsible for the adoption legalities because the agency takes care of this part of the adoption. Usually the relinquishment of their child will be finalized before the child is placed with the adoptive parents.

In private adoption, practice varies greatly. There are attorneys who believe birthparents don't need counseling. One flamboyant attorney in southern California said, "My birthparents don't need counseling. They're not sick in the head. They're in a fix and they want me to help them get out of it."

---

*We must feel certain that any resource*
*we recommend puts high priority*
*on the needs of the birthparents.*

---

There are attorneys who profit financially from adoption, people who may be within the law, and others who stray. When there are couples desperately wanting babies coupled with the shortage of healthy infants, the potential for black market adoption exists. It is a reality of which everyone working with adoption must be aware.

We all need to check thoroughly the resources we utilize, whether these be attorneys working independently, independent adoption facilitators, or licensed agencies. We must feel certain that any resource we recommend puts high priority on the needs of the birthparents.

We don't want to recommend private adoption unless we're assured that any needed counseling will be available. We must also ascertain that pressure absolutely will not be exerted on the birthparents to place for adoption if they do not feel this is right for them. Neither do we want to refer to an agency known for its bureaucratic tendencies, or for its lack of warmth and caring for individuals.

If, on the other hand, your community has one or more adoption agencies staffed by well-trained, warm, caring, supportive people, you'll feel comfortable referring students/clients/patients to them. If you have access to an independent adoption service staffed by people who are well-qualified to work in this field and who have the personal attributes so important, you can offer them as an option. You may also know of attorneys who care about their clients, feel adoption is a special kind of law practice, and insist on counseling for those involved in adoption. If your community offers all of these services, your students/clients/patients will have the options they deserve as they consider their alternatives.

## Birthparents First, Says Attorney

Farr continued discussing his thinking regarding adoption and the legal profession: "My whole approach to adoption the last seventeen years is that we approach it wrong. We have to operate on the assumption that what is in the best interest of the mother and baby is paramount.

"If the adoption falls through, that's fine. If adoptive parents aren't willing to look at it in this way, I don't want them for clients. This is in complete violation of the legal ethic, but in adoption, it's got to be this way.

"The group ethic or covenant ethic means a body committed to an idea as opposed to other individual rights. We aren't taught that way in law school, but in adoption, this is how it has to be. So I believe in counseling for the birthmother before and afterward. She's got to have it.

"Adoption is a tough deal, and it's wonderful. Unlike anything else, you're dealing with tremendous grief and pain by the birthmother, tremendous joy by the adoptive parents, and it will affect the infant from then on."

## More Control for Parents in Independent Adoption

"Independent adoption is legal in this state," said Fran Thoreen, adoption social worker, King County Adoption Service, Seattle, Washington. "I believe it is a viable option for prospective adoptive parents and birthparents. It provides a unique opportunity for both birth- and adoptive parents to exert considerable control over planning for their baby's future. It is also for action-oriented assertive folk who want to take charge of a very central aspect of their lives — parenting a child or finding a home for their child. Agencies have eligibility criteria, fees, and waiting lists that don't meet the needs of all people.

"Very often, after months and years of impaired fertility, a couple feels a sense of helplessness over becoming parents.

Likewise, birthparents may feel helpless facing an untimely pregnancy," Thoreen pointed out.

"So these parents, birth- and adoptive, take control of this crisis in their lives and reduce their sense of helplessness," she continued. "They network and find each other. Parents wanting a baby search out or are sought out by parents wanting to find a home for their baby. Both birth- and adoptive parents value the control and choices they believe are available to them through the independent adoption process.

"However, *all* people who wish to build their family through adoption need a professional team," Thoreen stressed. "They need an attorney with expertise and recent experience doing newborn independent adoptions in the county in which they live, and who is sensitive to the emotional issues of both birth- and adoptive parents. They also need an adoption social worker who can help facilitate the adoption in compliance with good social work practice and good child placement practice as well as in compliance with federal law and local court policy. As long as independent adoptions are on the increase nationwide, we have a professional responsibility to reach out to the people involved.

"In the services that we offer we don't promote closed adoptions and we don't promote open adoptions. We do offer consultation and mediation as to the advantages and disadvantages of the various options. We're here to facilitate the kind of adoption that families want," Thoreen concluded.

## Advocate Needed in Private Adoption

If the birthmother chooses independent placement, she may need help in arranging for legal counsel. She'll need assistance in understanding her rights and in asking for those rights.

Most lawyers are not counselors. Even though they may be well-versed in their own field, they may be unprepared to understand and meet the needs of a young birthparent client. She may be intimidated by attorneys. Her lawyer may use words she doesn't understand, and she may be embarrassed to ask for clarification. In such cases, advocacy is crucial.

Independent adoptions can work well, but the lawyer and/or independent adoption service should be carefully selected. Some

young women have been given incorrect or inadequate information regarding adoption and/or their rights. Later they must face
a different reality.

Other attorneys and adoption service staff are well informed
on the adoption process. They seem to understand the implications of such an action for birthparents. More is needed,
however, than knowledge.

When you are researching adoption attorneys and independent adoption services in your area, be alert to their attitudes
toward birthparents. If you sense an attorney feels the birthparent needs nothing but legal assistance and/or if s/he appears
negative toward birthparents generally, watch out. You'll
probably want to look for another attorney.

---

*We must be aware of adoption law
as we work with potential birthparents.*

---

Recently I (Jeanne) was appalled to hear an attorney, speaking at an adoption conference, concentrate on the money birthparents want. The attorney stressed that you can't buy babies,
and of course we agree with her. In doing so, however, she
implied that birthparents tend to want all they can get
financially.

She questioned the legality of certain pregnancy-related
expenses, suggesting that a teenager should not be paid for "pain
and suffering — for not being able to wear a bikini during her
pregnancy." Again, we agree, but assume most birthparents
would be insulted at the implication that they would request
reimbursement for such "pain and suffering." As this attorney
talked, she constantly put down teenage birthparents. Her
approach was cold and legalistic, and she appeared to expect the
worst from these young people.

Perhaps this attorney has encountered difficult situations
involving pregnant teenagers. We must be aware of adoption
law as we work with potential birthparents, whatever their age.
In doing so, however, we do not need to assume that the birthparents with whom we work want to "get all they can" through
this adoption. On the contrary, we must begin by assuming that

our clients want to make the best decision possible for themselves and their babies. We have worked with many
birthmothers and overwhelmingly, this is what they want.

## Attorney Insists on Counseling

Attorney Linda Nunez, Tustin, California, handles independent adoption cases and works closely with Parenting Resources
in the same city. Parenting Resources facilitates Cooperative
Adoption™. "I insist on counseling for adoptive parents as well
as birthparents," she said. "A lot of the birthparents don't want
counseling, but I strong-arm them into it. I think they're afraid
counseling is going to be painful, or they're real afraid to dig
into the deep issues that counseling brings out. The vast majority
feel they'll never do this again, and they want to do it the
right way.

"Sometimes they have other counseling issues to explore, and
I can find a lot of excuses to get them to see a professional. I
have never had a birthmother refuse counseling. I think it is my
place to push."

Nunez does not see many teenage birthmothers. Her average
birthmother client is in her twenties. Nunez feels this is partly
because there is so much peer pressure among teenagers to keep
their babies. "Whatever her age, it's important to provide her
with good neutral counseling from someone who will not benefit
whether she goes through with the adoption plan or not," Nunez
explained.

Nunez usually represents both the birthparents and the
adoptive parents, and she agrees with Farr that this is not an
adversary proceeding. She recommends that birthparents get as
much education as possible on adoption and get it as quickly as
possible. "She should read as much as she can and talk to as
many people as she can, both agencies and individuals. She
needs to decide what kind of adoption interests her, then find the
family that fits that kind of adoption.

"I get a lot of calls from birthmothers who go through the
phone book and pick up pieces of information here and there,
and I like that. If she's looking into the basics, I explain the
difference between agency and independent adoption; I'll give

her the names and addresses of agencies if that's what she needs. I probably work with only about a third of the birthmothers I speak with. I think agencies are more appropriate for some of them. I'm most comfortable with a birthmother who is willing to do some reading and some work," Nunez concluded.

Marion, who was thirty-two and very self-sufficient when she placed her infant, agrees with Nunez on the importance of the birthmother being well informed about adoption. Marion also commented on the need for counseling:

> *I made it a point to be as knowledgeable as possible on adoption. I think you need somebody there to help you work things out. But you need somebody who is empathetic and experienced in what is going on.*
>
> *There are some people who have offered me great emotional peace who have never gone through adoption. That must come first. We're all human beings first, and that's important in dealing with an adoption, whether you're working with the birthmother, the parents, or the child. If that's the center from which all else emanates, you'll have a much easier time of it.*

Another attorney who insists on counseling for her birthparent clients is Deborah Crouse Cobb, Collinsville, Illinois. "Every attorney I know who works in adoption makes counseling available," she reported. "We offer counseling but we can't force it. We have private counselors who don't have a vested interest in the adoption decision. A lot of them are children's counselors who work with teenagers. The adoptive couple pays the counseling fees whether or not the birthparents keep the baby.

"We tell each birthparent she has a right to her own attorney and the adoptive couple will pay for it," Cobb continued. "The birthparent needs to understand up front that she controls her attorney, *not* the adoptive couple. If she changes her mind about the adoption, the adoptive parents pay only the fees up to that point. She may still need legal assistance, perhaps in suing for child support.

"A teenage birthmother can be very skittish. The least little thing can send her into a tailspin," Cobb mused. "It's not bad. It's just that there's so much she may not understand. She needs to know her legal rights well before she delivers — which is partly why we try to get them into counseling. And even though there is no legal requirement to pay for counseling after delivery, I tell the adoptive parents I expect that money to be there up front if she needs counseling throughout that first year.

---

*She needs to be aware*
*she is a legal consumer*
*and she has rights.*

---

"If the birthmother has chosen people she thinks will be good parents for her baby, no one, not her doctor, not her attorney, no one should tell her to think further. This has to be her decision. If she asks for alternatives, you can provide them, but if she comes in with a couple already selected, the attorney has no business suggesting someone else. She needs to be aware she is a legal consumer and she has rights," Cobb maintained.

"She also needs to be aware the attorney cannot give her the world," Cobb cautioned. "She may want legal visitations, but this is still generally not possible, not upheld by the court. She needs an attorney willing to explain reality to her as well as the ideal. She might think she'd like a telephone conversation daily with her child, but it's extremely doubtful this would happen."

Although she offers counseling to all birthparents with whom she works, Cobb has never had an older woman agree to counseling. "They always say no," she said. "But when I'm working with a teenager and she says 'No' to counseling, I feel more compelled to talk her into it. My bias is that a teenager may need more direction."

Whether it is independent or agency adoption, it all starts with the birthparents. They make the decision, and it's a decision they will carry the rest of their lives. They will never forget that baby.

"Our goal is to find a way to allow them to carry that decision with peace of mind and heart. We can't be technocrats as

attorneys, focusing on the legal and forgetting that concern,"
cautioned Dan Farr. As you work with a birthmother, think of
her thirty years from now. How do you think she is going to feel
at that time?"

## How You Can Help

In order to be an effective advocate for your client considering an independent adoption, you can do several things. First, in-
vestigate the lawyers and services doing independent adoptions.
Find out what their reputation has been. From this research, you
can learn fairly quickly who is respected and who is not.

Attorneys can be ethical and they can be unethical just like
anybody else. When you're going to use an attorney, you need
to know who is paying the bill. If it's the adoptive couple, do
they have any control over the services the attorney provides?
What if the birthparent changes her mind? Is the attorney
knowledgeable about and experienced in adoption law? No one
can specialize in everything. It's probably best to work with an
attorney who does adoptions frequently, a person who knows
adoption law.

If you need to refer someone to an adoption attorney and you
don't know anyone, try calling the adoption caseworker at your
county offices. Ask for the name of a good attorney who handles
adoptions, someone who cares for people and who is concerned
for the needs of birthparents.

It's generally best to encourage the birthparents to have a
different lawyer from the adoptive parents. It is difficult for the
same attorney to represent both sides of an issue equally. And
frankly, since the adoptive parents are the paying parties, it may
be tempting to meet their needs first. If both parties have legal
representation, birthparents are more likely to have adequate
counsel.

Be sure your birthparent client understands that it is legal and
typical for the adoptive parents to pay for an attorney for the
birthparent(s).

Independent or private adoption can be a satisfying route for
planning an adoption. The birthparent(s) are generally able to
have more control over the adoption process, but that control

may be there only if she/they insist on it. When an adoption
agency is not involved in an adoption, it is even more crucial
that someone else be an advocate for the birthparent(s). If this is
your role, remember, as always, in adoption *the birthparents
come first*.

# CHAPTER 5

# Openness in Adoption: An Emerging Trend

*Adoption is a unique blend of gains and losses, great joy and intense pain. Pain and loss are realities in adoption, and open adoption is one of the ways we may be able to lessen that pain. Open adoption empowers birthparents.*

*For the adoptive parents, open adoption helps clarify the realities that their child has two sets of parents, and that this is forever. And open adoption gives the adoptee access to the information s/he needs as s/he grows up. (Randy Perin, Director, Adoption Resource Center, Children's Home Society, Seattle, Washington)*

Adoption is changing rapidly in the United States. Closed or secret adoption was the practice in this country for several generations. Many adopted children were not told anything about their origins, or even the fact that they were adopted. While this practice is no longer widely accepted, many people still assume that if a child is adopted, "of course" there will be no further contact with his birthfamily.

In much of the world, however, this has never been the case. In many cultures, secret adoption is practically unknown. When a child is reared by someone other than her birthparents, the situation is openly acknowledged and contact between the two families often continues.

## Adoption Law Changes

The first law to mandate closed records in adoption was passed in 1917 in Minnesota. In 1938 the Child Welfare League of America issued a statement in favor of closed adoption, and many states quickly passed similar laws. Many of these laws still stand, but many adoptees, birthparents, and some adoptive parents are actively working to open adoption records. They feel that adoption as it has been practiced for so many years is wrong, and that babies have been taken from their birthmothers' arms without any effort to consider birthmothers' rights and feelings. Adoption activists feel this has been damaging to adoptees, and that adoptive parents' interests are not well-served by a system built on secrecy.

Adoption began to change in the seventies. First, birth-mothers were encouraged to write letters to their babies explaining why they were making an adoption plan. Gradually birthparents became involved in the selection of "their" adoptive parents. At first the birthmother was merely asked to state her preferences. What religion did she prefer? Would she want her child reared in the city or in a rural area? She was told her wishes would be considered in the selection process.

Some social workers began sharing descriptions of adoptive parents with their birthparent clients, descriptions which included no identifying information. In some cases, the adoptive parents were chosen by the birthparents before the baby was born, and the two sets of parents could correspond if they wished.

In the early eighties, Lutheran Social Service of Texas began meetings between the birthparent(s) and the adoptive parents at the time of placement. Sometimes these birthparents and adoptive parents would continue to meet after the adoption was finalized. Other agencies started to offer more and more choices to birthparents.

Closed/open adoption is a continuum ranging from the completely closed adoptions of a generation ago to the completely open Cooperative Adoption™ pioneered by Sharon Kaplan of Parenting Resources, Tustin, California, and Mary Jo Rillera, Triadoption Library, Westminster, California. Some agencies and private adoption attorneys still feel strongly that there should be no contact between the birthparents and the adoptive families. Others advocate openness to a point — perhaps stopping short of exchanging identifying information. Still others encourage birthparents to interview several potential adoptive couples and to spend time with them in order to be as sure as possible that they choose the "right" family for the baby.

## Variety of Services Available

Your clients/students/patients need to know the wide range of adoption services available to them. They need to be urged to ask questions, and they need to be encouraged to take as much control over their child's placement as is reasonably possible.

In some parts of the country adoptions are still mostly closed. However, some of the agencies not facilitating meetings between birth- and adoptive parents say this is because their clients have not asked them to do so.

Clients probably haven't requested these services because they don't know enough about them to inquire, according to Kaplan. "It's up to the adoption agencies to make it clear there are a number of choices," she commented, "but clients can't depend on agencies to tell them about this variety of services. They need to ask, and sometimes they need to insist on getting the adoption plan they want."

As a helping person, you need to know as much as possible about adoption and its many forms. Only then can you help your clients find the best adoption plan for them.

An adoption worker reported that her agency for many years allowed no contact between birthparents and adoptive parents. Recently the agency changed its policy to allow a meeting at the time of placement. "The reason, off the record," the worker related, "is that we didn't have any clients. Word has gotten around that young women have choices, and this is changing adoption. As a result, birthparents are going more and more toward independent adoption, and agencies are being forced to change.

"Perhaps it's too bad they feel forced into changing, but we need to tailor services to the needs of our clients," she added.

Birthparents should be encouraged to verbalize their desires before making an adoption plan. Some birthparents want to write letters, keep mementos, and see their babies prior to relinquishment. Some feel they could never be peaceful if they met the parents. For others, knowing the adoptive parents is a tremendous source of satisfaction. Some who don't know the identity of the adoptive parents hope their children will search for them, while others aren't sure they could handle being "found."

A teacher described a student who absolutely did not want open adoption. Kandi didn't go to an agency. Instead, she released her baby for adoption through an attorney, and she received no counseling. The teacher reported:

> Kandi's lawyer told her the adoptive parents were well-known, and she should understand why they wanted a closed adoption. After the placement, she volunteered to be part of a panel invited to talk about teenage pregnancy in another school.
>
> As Kandi was sharing her adoption plan with the class, she suddenly broke into tears. She finally admitted she had feelings for the baby. She didn't regret the adoption but. . .she kept talking to those eighth and ninth graders, encouraging them to avoid the kind of decision she had to make. She says she's still satisfied with the closed adoption, but it hurts far more than she expected.
>
> Actually, I think most of the time the girls who choose open adoption, who see and hold the baby and make plans for the baby, are more settled. But they both feel

*that awful hurt. I think open adoption may allow the
birthparent to deal with it and then get on with her life
more quickly.*

Connie, eighteen, lives in a rural area with her boyfriend and
his family. She left school during her pregnancy three years ago
and never returned. She works full-time as a waitress. To her,
open adoption was important:

*People say, "You're never going to get over it. You'll
always wonder where he is." That's why it's so perfect
with me and Steven. They send me several pictures every
month. They write to me, and they sent me hair from his
first haircut.*

*If I didn't know where he lives or what he looks like
. . .when I think about that, I feel empty. Those letters
and pictures make all the difference.*

## Flexibility Is Essential

Because people are so variable in their feelings and preferences, the helping person must be flexible and nurturing. Of
course agency practices and state laws will vary, making some
things more difficult or even impossible to arrange. However, to
the fullest extent possible, it is the responsibility of the support
person to help the birthmother meet her needs.

Cheri, seventeen when Delilah was born, placed her with the
family she selected. Delilah is a year old now, and Cheri has
seen her several times:

*I still see Delilah. The adoptive parents and I write,
we call and we see each other. They come over here and
I go over there. We have a real good relationship
because we're like family.*

*Sometimes I feel a little awkward because Delilah is
my daughter, and yet she's not. Sometimes that's hard. I
know they're good parents, and they're giving her
everything I couldn't. Not that I couldn't have been a
good mother, but I think they're better for Delilah. And*

*when she grows up she'll know I loved her. That's most
important to me. She'll know I didn't throw her away.*

*I can see what a difference the openness makes
because my fiancee is adopted. He sees the way it is
with us and how it is with him. He knows his birthparents' names, but he has never seen them and he feels
unwanted. They had seven children and simply didn't
want another one. There has been no contact, and he
doesn't know where they live. Sometimes he feels
cheated because he'd like what we have. He has his
adoption in the back of his mind a lot.*

Open adoption may not work for everyone just as joint
custody in divorce doesn't always work. The important thing in
open adoption is that there be a good match in the degree of
openness wanted between birthparents and the adoptive family.

---

*Whenever possible, the match is made
according to mutual needs and desires.*

---

Recently one of our clients released through an agency whose
practice is to provide the birthmother with letters and pictures
over the years. They routinely ask the birthmother about her
preferences related to this practice. Adoptive parents are also
asked to state their preferences. Then, whenever possible, the
match is made according to mutual needs and desires.

At the time of her baby's birth, Rose, twenty-one, felt she did
not want to see her baby. After signing adoption papers, she still
felt she did not want contact through letters or pictures. The
agency worker was extremely sensitive to Rose's position. She
did not force her in any way. She supported Rose's wishes.

The letters and pictures are being kept in a file, and the social
worker assured Rose that if she ever wants these things, she may
have them.

## Research Adoption Resources

It's important to know the agencies and independent adoption
services in your area. Visit them and learn all you can about

their policies, practices, and philosophies. If possible, talk with birthmothers and adoptive parents who have used their services. As clients, they will have first-hand reactions to the agency's service provision and philosophy. Once you've learned about the needs of the people you're serving, you'll be able to make an appropriate referral.

Marion is an assertive and charming professional woman who had no intention whatsoever of becoming pregnant at age thirty-two. When it happened, she considered abortion, but decided, as she put it, that having the child would be a minor inconvenience while "killing it" was an ethical problem for her. She continued her pregnancy and made an open adoption plan. She doesn't regret this decision, but "minor inconvenience" is not a particularly accurate description of her experience:

> *I started looking at my finances. How would I raise a child? I travel a lot in my job. I'm constantly on the road — I can't even take care of a goldfish. How could I handle a baby? That was turmoil number two. (Deciding against abortion was turmoil number one.)*
>
> *I figured I could continue my work and hire someone to take care of my child, or I could raise this child myself. If I hired someone, I would exhaust my funds and would probably have to resort to welfare. I wanted a better choice for my child. So I started thinking about adoption.*
>
> *Turmoil number three was finding the right family. I chatted with an adoption agency worker who said they would choose the family for me. I didn't go for that so I called another agency and discovered I didn't live in the right county for them. I was on my own.*
>
> *I found a private group that facilitates adoptions. I also talked to my doctor and I read a lot, although any literature on adoption seemed to be teen-oriented. There was very little I could find for a woman my age and my emotional and mental capacity. I also did a lot of writing my feelings out, and I started investigating all the other places, the attorneys, the doctors.*

*With each one I emphasized that they would not have control of this situation. This was not going to be a situation in which they would put their arm on my shoulder, pat my head, and say I was a good girl. A lot of them resented this. Some said, "Well, these decisions are yours," but when we started talking about how it would be done, they were going to be in control.*

*What irritated me the most was being treated like a teenager. Once I decided on adoption, attitudes became condescending. The pat on the shoulder, the "you poor dear." Don't tell me how I have to feel. I objected to that.*

*Also I wanted to meet the people who would adopt my child, and I wanted to see where they live. These pretty pictures (on the resumes) are fine, but I could take a picture of a raving maniac and you'd never know he had a problem.*

*These things happened mostly during my fourth and fifth months. This was when the night monsters came to life. Those nights were not something I would wish on anyone.*

*One day I was talking to a woman in my office, and she told me about this couple she knew who had been married nine years. The woman had miscarried six times, and they had recently gone through the heartbreak of a failed adoption.*

*I said, "Well, give them my phone number." She suggested I call them, but I said if they want to be parents, they can call me. They did, and we met in a restaurant.*

*A couple of weeks later we met again. I asked them questions I would be skeptical about asking anyone, very personal, very upfront questions. They were very, very open, and they came through my grilling with flying colors.*

*When I came home after a two-week trip, it occurred to me I couldn't find a better couple. So I called them and told them I thought they ought to raise my child.*

*This decision lightened my load considerably. At that point my emotional turmoil dropped amazingly.*

*Then it was time to start the Lamaze classes. Six dozen friends offered to go with me, but the offers dropped off as they realized I needed their commitment to two hours of classes every week. Finally I asked Alyce, the adoptive mother, to go with me. Ric wanted to go too, so the three of us went together. We got strange looks in the classes, but this helped me get to know Ric and Alyce. They were very nice, very gentle folks.*

*We occasionally saw each other at their home and mine during this time.*

*We all had our jobs cut out. First, I had to be sure they were the right people. "What if this child is handicapped? Are you going to change your minds?" And they had to deal with, "Was I going to change my mind? Was I going to come in the night and take the baby?" We had to convince each other this would work.*

---

Why should I have to forget my son?
The whole idea is to have
a stable environment.

---

*This is all well and fine until the baby is born. Then you have to start keeping the promises.*

*Of course I saw my son. Ric and Alyce were in delivery, and we had some nice quiet moments together after the baby was born. We spent most of that first day together.*

*Then I went home, and the baby went home with them. I've visited him a couple of times and I'll continue to do that. People say, "Oh, you have to let go." No, I don't have to let go.*

*Why should I have to forget my son? The whole idea is to have a stable environment. I'm not going to go marching over there to visit him every day. I haven't seen him in about a month, but I'm going over one day next week.*

*It's been a little tough this past month. The mom part of Marion is rather upset. I wouldn't say I went through an enormous amount of grieving because it was more like being at peace. However, I guarantee if you give up your baby, there will be times you'll wish you had the family and the picket fence. When you see a couple with a child, you ask, "Why wasn't I there?" But I don't get off on these tangents so much that when I see a pregnant woman I want to run her down.*

*It's a matter of educating yourself, and if you have education, you have the power. I'm at great peace because my child is well cared for. What I wanted was a couple that I would remain in contact with for the rest of my life, someone with whom there would be no secrets or running away. And someone I could respect and who would respect me.*

*You have to come to terms with yourself.*

## Post-Adoption Agreements Based on Trust

At this time, agreements between birthparent(s) and adoptive parents have no legal guarantee. Until the adoption is final, the birthparents have the power. After finalization, the adoptive parents do. Many people are caring and trustworthy, and open adoption is working for many people today. However, the birthparents may face disappointment. A pregnant minor teacher reported the experience of one of her former students:

*Carole released her baby a year ago to the couple she had selected. She says they agreed she could see her baby occasionally, but each time she called them, they didn't have time. She kept feeling they had lied to her before placement.*

*Last week Carole called. She was very upset because the adoptive family had moved out of state, and she still hadn't been able to visit her baby. She went back to her counselor and learned that they couldn't do much about it once the adoption was final. Carole thinks these people moved to get away from her, but I doubt it.*

*I think it probably was simply a move made because of a better job opportunity.*

*Carole chose them because they were friends of the adoptive parents of Carole's friend's baby. Carole's friend sees her child fairly often, and Carole had hoped to have a similar arrangement.*

*It is an open adoption. Carole has their address, they have phone conversations with Carole, and they send pictures. She feels betrayed, however, because they wouldn't let her see the baby.*

*At this point, I think Carole needs to realize it's out of her control and she needs to get on with her life. She's actively involved in a church, and I suggested she get counseling help there.*

"While arrangements between adoptive and birthparents can't be forced by the court, I tell the adoptive parents not to promise something they don't intend to do," commented Deborah Crouse Cobb, Illinois attorney. "I think this has to be a cooperative effort. If they say they will send a picture once a month, plan on doing it. Some of the literature I'm reading now indicates that it may not be long before some of these promises may become enforceable," she added.

Sandra Musser, a leading advocate for open records and open adoption, relinquished her daughter in a closed adoption thirty-four years ago. "Girls have no idea of the long-range effects of closed adoption, but they're learning much sooner than we did because we had to stay in the closet," she said.

"My personal feeling is that we ought to outlaw closed adoption. I don't think closed adoption is ever good for first-time mothers. No matter what they say early on, no matter how much they bury it, the day is going to come when they have to suffer and deal with the pain. Thirty-four years ago I placed. I've found her and we've reconciled, but I'm still suffering from it. You know it has to have a long-lasting effect. I've had my reunion but the loss is still so great," Musser continued.

"The other thing is they keep worrying about the birthmother coming back and stealing her child, but we have only had experience with the adoptive parents breaking their agreement with the birthparents.

"We'll never have open adoption until we have open records, and we'll never have open adoption until agreements have a legal basis," Musser concluded.

## How You Can Help

Be aware of and advise your counselees of their rights in the adoption process. Clarify with them what they want and encourage them to make these wants clear to their attorney, independent adoption service or agency counselor. It is important to get all these agreements in writing before the birth of the baby.

Once the child has been born and is in the home of the new parents, negotiation will be more difficult. Verbal agreements aren't always enough. Even when everyone's intentions are good, people get busy and find other things which may take priority over the agreement with the birthparents.

Leticia is a good example:

> *Leticia's family strongly favored independent adoption over agency placement because they wanted the baby placed with a family recommended by their gynecologist. Their attorney was a good one, ethical and in tune with Leticia's needs. Leticia said she'd like to have pictures of the baby sent to her after placement. This was not a written agreement, but her attorney assured Leticia that the family had agreed to this plan.*
>
> *Leticia's baby was born and placed with the adoptive parents. Leticia waited for the promised pictures. . .and she waited. Her grieving was painful, and she longed to have the photos so she could be reassured that her child was happy and healthy in his new home. She was upset and feared something was wrong.*
>
> *Finally her school counselor called Leticia's lawyer and explained Leticia's needs. It was a month later that the picture finally arrived — and there was only one. Leticia appreciated the photo but was disappointed to find this was her only contact.*

This need not have happened. If the agreement between Leticia and the adoptive parents had been clearly negotiated and written before placement, the misunderstanding probably would not have occurred even though there is no legal support for such an agreement. After the adoption is finalized, birthparents must depend on good faith that the adoptive parents will keep their mutually-negotiated agreement.

## Value of Letter Writing

Probably one of the most therapeutic activities for a mother considering an adoption plan is writing a letter to her child. This activity does several things. First, it helps her shift her focus from her pregnancy as a condition to the personhood of her unborn child. Equally important, it causes her to ask herself what she wants for her child. And finally, it allows her to consider what the child might want to hear from her.

Initially your client may resist the idea of letter writing. The activity may not seem purposeful when her child is not yet born. She may also feel it would be frightening or painful to put her thoughts and feelings on paper. However, your assurance that this activity will be a useful one is usually enough to move past the initial resistance.

Reading letters written by other mothers is a good start. *Dear Birthmother* by Silber and Speedlin (Corona Publishing) and *Pregnant Too Soon* (Morning Glory Press) are good resources. If the young woman is a good reader, she may want to take some samples with her to read and ponder.

The next step is dependent on the personality type and writing skills of the individual. If she feels insecure about her writing skills, you may need to help by talking out the ideas with her and perhaps writing them out together. Or you might suggest that she "speak" her letter on tape and tell her you'll transcribe it for her. Others may be used to writing and prefer working on their letter alone.

A young woman may experience feelings of inadequacy about what she's written. She may rewrite her letter many times before she feels satisfied with it. It is essential to offer support and reassurance that she is doing a good job of communicating.

---

*The more she can personalize
her letter to her child,
the better.*

---

She may ask you what she should write about. Or she may concentrate on her feelings at the moment. You might ask her, "What do you think your child will want to know?" Talk with her about what may interest adoptees as they're growing up.

Sharon Kaplan, Parenting Resources, counsels with many adoptees as well as birth- and adoptive parents. She commented, "Adoptees often ask, 'Did the rest of my birthfamily know about me? Was my birth a secret or did my grandparents and siblings know? Did my birthparents want to see me again? What was the relationship between my birthmother and my birthfather? Why was I placed in this particular way, this agency or this attorney? How was my adoptive family selected?'

"The more she can personalize the letter, the better," Kaplan continued. "She can say 'This is what was going on between us. This is why I chose to place you this way.'"

You will find that some birthmothers want to write to the adoptive parents. This is a way of establishing a bond with these often unseen people to whom she is entrusting her child. She may find this to be quite meaningful.

The birthfather may also be encouraged to write to his child. He, too, may find it healing to express in writing his love for his child and his reasons for choosing an adoption plan.

The final letters are usually insightful and carry a great deal of feeling. Growth in self-esteem is associated with expressing one's own truth. That self-esteem is vitally important.

## Concern for Birthparent Demonstrated

Michelle was attending a private Christian school when she became pregnant at seventeen. She knew almost immediately that her baby's father would not be around to help parent, so she made an early adoption decision.

Michelle's story demonstrates the riskiness of an open adoption plan for the adoptive parents. . .and the beauty of an agreement based on trust and caring between birthparent and adoptive parents:

> *I decided almost as soon as I had the pregnancy test that I would plan an adoption. I didn't want to raise this child without a father. I don't have family support, and I didn't believe in abortion.*
>
> *I transferred that summer to a teen mother program, and I mentioned right away that I was planning adoption. My baby was due in December, and I planned to stay in the special school until I graduated soon after that. The teacher was concerned that staying there after I delivered might be too hard on me, but I thought I'd be okay because I knew I was making the right decision. I don't have problems seeing mothers with their children. If they have family support and father support, great, more power to them.*
>
> *First I talked to my doctor who has a list of people who are infertile, but I didn't know exactly how he worked it. He didn't explain a lot.*
>
> *I thought about going to the agency where my parents adopted me, but I wasn't gung ho about them either. Then Claire came to class and talked about open adoption, and I knew that was for me. My birthparents don't know anything about me, and I don't think I could get through it if I didn't know where my daughter is. I get pictures every month.*
>
> *So I picked out the couple. We went to dinner a couple of times and we talked on the phone occasionally. They were excited, but they didn't get too emotionally involved then because they knew I might change my mind. I think I'd have felt smothered if they had been too pushy. I didn't want them at the hospital when I gave birth, but I let them come over the next day.*
>
> *My daughter was born the day after Christmas, and she went home with her adoptive parents two days later. I think I did okay during January, but it got harder in February. Finally I called Claire and told her this was a*

*mistake. I should never have given Jessica up, and I*
*wanted her back. Claire told me that was my right*
*because the adoption wasn't final, and that I could meet*
*the adoptive parents at her office the next day. I felt*
*terrible for them, but I wasn't coping well. So I went*
*over and brought Jessica home with me.*

*The adoptive parents told me they were hurting, but*
*that they knew I was, too. They said they realized*
*Jessica was still my child. If I felt she should be with*
*me, they understood.*

*I kept Jessica that night, and nothing went wrong. I*
*fed her and changed her, held her and loved her. She*
*scarcely cried at all. By morning, though, I realized I*
*had made the wrong decision. Jessica needed to be with*
*her family. I called the adoptive parents and told them.*
*Of course they came right over. That's the last time I*
*saw Jessica.*

*I can see from the pictures they send me that Jessica*
*is happy, so well taken care of, and they love her*
*so much.*

Michelle's counselor was with the Calvary Chapel/House of
Ruth adoption ministry in Downey, California. Potential adoptive parents are warned at their orientation seminar that the
birthparent may change her mind. In California, this is possible
in independent adoption for several months after signing the
initial adoption papers. The needs of the birthparent are stressed
strongly throughout the adoption planning at House of Ruth.

The couple who adopted Michelle's baby were sensitive to
this issue. In spite of the heartbreak they would have experienced if they had lost "their" child, they knew Jessica's
birthmother still had a right to raise her and they weren't going
to interfere with that right. If they had been less sensitive to
Michelle's needs, would she still have realized that "Jessica
needed to be with her family"? We don't know. We do know
sensitivity to the birthparents is an integral part of a successful
adoption.

# CHAPTER 6

# Family Support Is Crucial

*My mom went through being pregnant when she was young so she knew what it was like. She handled it (my pregnancy) real well. I know it hurt her. This was her first grandchild and I saw the hurt in her face, like why couldn't it have been at a different time?*

*She said, "The baby would be your responsibility. I'm not going to be your baby's mother." I thought that was kind of cold but it's a fact — because if you're old enough to get pregnant, you're old enough to handle the responsibility or to make another decision about it.*

*My stepdad had a hard time dealing with the fact that I had gotten pregnant, but at the end he said if I changed my mind and kept the baby, he'd help me out. He'd give me a place to stay and help me financially until I could do it myself. But I didn't feel I wanted to impose on him and my mom. My baby really was my responsibility. (Susan, 17)*

Involving the family is another crucial part of the decision-making process. Legally it is the young parent's right to make the decision. However, most young people do not exist in a vacuum. They come from families, groups of people whose lives will be impacted by the decisions they make. When the woman making the decision is still living at home, she is probably dependent upon her parents for food, shelter, and support. Further, these people will continue to be in her life long after her adoption decision has been made and carried out.

Joanne feels cheated because she doesn't think her mother kept her promise to support whatever decision Joanne made:

> *All through my pregnancy my mom told me she would support whatever decision I made, that I could do whatever I wanted. All along I said I'd give him up. Then in the hospital after he was born I told my mom I wanted to keep him. Suddenly she was totally different. She was telling me all these things, everything we'd have to do if we kept him. Then I realized she was just saying she'd support me in whatever I did. It wasn't really how she felt.*
>
> *I think she influenced my decision at the end. When I told her I couldn't give him up, she was different. She said, "Well, how are you going to go to school? How are you going to support him? How are you going to support yourself? How are you going to live?"*
>
> *I didn't want to deal with all that so I went ahead with the adoption. Now I think it was best, but I think my mom should have let me come to terms with myself. I think if she had continued to say she would support me whichever way, I think I still would've given him up eventually. I was in the hospital for four days. We talked about it that first day so I still had a lot of time to decide.*
>
> *I even had him for several days after I left the hospital. I decided I was going to give him up but I told my mom the only way I could do that was to say goodbye to him the way I wanted to. So I took him to my aunt's*

*house and we stayed there. My aunt kept saying while I was in the hospital, "Do what's best for you, do what's best for him, not what's best for your mom or whoever, because you're the one who's going to have to live with your decision the rest of your life." That helped a lot.*

Often family members declare their intentions to support the young woman's decision regardless of what she decides. For some, like Joanne's mother, this statement may originate mostly in the intellect. They may not have the opportunity to work through their own feelings about the pregnancy and planning.

If she's getting counseling, the young woman can work intensely on her decision-making, benefiting from both group and individual counseling. She is faced with an array of mixed emotions, conflicting ideas, and advice. Along with that goes the chance to work through each of these things. If the young woman's parents have not had the same opportunity, they may face an overwhelming flood of emotions and internal conflict when the baby arrives.

## First Appointment Includes Parents

Claire Priester, counselor, House of Ruth, Downey, California, much prefers at the first appointment to see parents with their teenage daughter. She described Nanette and her family:

*The first time I met with Nanette and her parents, I asked Nanette, "Why are you considering adoption?" Nanette pointed to her parents and said, "Because they say I have to." We spent most of that appointment talking about her feelings and her parents' feelings. Of course I didn't push for any commitment from anyone, nor did I tell the parents they had no business telling their daughter what to do with her baby. Sometimes, with a little patience, these things work out.*

*Two weeks later Nanette told me, "I really want adoption. I just didn't want to admit it because they wanted it." When she was given some room to make her own decision, she knew adoption was what she really wanted. If her parents hadn't tried to push adoption on her, there might not have been the initial conflict. Nanette's parents were honest with her that they thought adoption was the best thing. That first month after I started seeing them, however, they were going to let her keep the baby and live with them. They told her, "We don't want to raise another child. We were through when we had you and your sister. This will be your responsibility even though we'll allow you to stay with us." I think that was fair.*

*Lots of times parents are able to help their daughter see reality. If they work through the whole thing with her, she'll probably make a good decision.*

*One thing I'm always telling parents is that the decision doesn't need to be made right now. They say, "My daughter is seven weeks pregnant and she needs to get in there and make some decisions NOW." A lot of parents just need to slow down.*

## Families May Need Help at Birth

If the family hasn't been involved in the process throughout the pregnancy, there is a good chance that one or more family members will need intervention at the time of the birth. Most often this is the grandmother.

If the young mother has been working consistently with her counselor, she has prepared herself for the experience. In contrast, her mother may not be prepared emotionally. The sight of her daughter in labor, the first glimpse of her grandchild, and the other experiences surrounding the birth will draw out these emotions. She may relate this to her own pregnancy and child-birth experiences, or she may be touched by the child's resemblance to a family member. Whatever the cause, the result can be extreme pain and vulnerability.

These emotions are not wrong or bad. They are signs that these family members are experiencing fully what is transpiring. For them, the emotions are a necessary part of the grieving process. If allowed to pass through this experience, the grief will subside and the individual will gradually begin to feel better.

Of course it is preferable to work with families prior to the birth. It is important to learn as much as possible from the pregnant woman about her relationships with her family members. Encourage her to discuss the dynamics of her family with you. Find out who has power, who is supportive, and who is offering resistance. Also, find out which of the family members are important to the young woman. It may be one or both parents, or neither. Sometimes the crucial person is an aunt, a brother, or a close friend.

Once you have learned who the significant people are, you can reach out to these individuals. A phone call may be greatly appreciated. Often that is all that is required to begin a relationship. Offer these individuals your support and invite them to come in to see you. Let them know that you empathize with their situation and that you would like to offer them the same type of support you are providing their loved one.

Such calls also provide reassurance for the family that you are truly a concerned individual. It provides them the opportunity to learn about the services being offered and to ask questions related to procedures and philosophy. Many parents will use these early contacts as a means of compiling information. They may ask questions about the types of adoption available, seek referrals, and learn about procedures.

## Birthgrandparents Need Counseling

When Christine's fifteen-year-old daughter, Katheryn, was pregnant, Christine appreciated the open communication both she and Katheryn had with Joan, the adoption agency counselor:

> *Joan stressed that she would be there for us, and that we needed to know we could call her at any time. We had Joan's home phone number so we didn't have to go through the agency. I think we understood immediately that we could call her whenever we needed to, and that gave us a warm feeling that someone truly did care.*
>
> *Now, three years later, I still talk with Joan occasionally. I've been to a couple of group meetings, and the other day Joan asked me to help with a grandmother*

*support group they're starting. There are some*
*birthgrandmothers who are having a tough time. Their*
*husbands don't want to talk about it — the baby's gone,*
*let's forget it. But they're feeling the loss of that child.*
*They need to know their feelings are genuine and it's*
*okay to feel them.*

Renee's baby was born and placed for adoption the summer
before Renee's senior year of high school. Her mother, too,
talked about birthgrandparents' need for counseling:

*I feel strongly that counseling is important for*
*parents too. A lot of times we tend to think about how*
*we want things to be but we don't know how to be*
*helpful. We may be so personally involved with our*
*anger and our frustration that it's hard to be objective.*
*You can say, "Well, it's your decision, and we'll do*
*what we can to support you." It's still nice to have that*
*third party there because when you have angry feelings*
*about the situation, you can share them with the*
*counselor. Maybe she can convey those feelings to your*
*daughter.*
*The pressure wasn't on at the agency we selected.*
*They spent a lot of time explaining to the girls how*
*their lives were going to change as a result of this*
*baby, whether they were going to keep or choose*
*adoption. They would stress, "Basically it's you and*
*your baby."*

Don't push family members to deal with their emotions
before they're ready and have developed a trusting relationship
with you. Usually these issues will arise naturally during the
course of your conversations with them. It is also important that
you don't cut them loose too soon. Post-natal and post-adoption
counseling may be extremely important because people grieve at
different times and in different ways.

Providing parents with relevant reading materials may be
helpful. *Parents, Pregnant Teens and the Adoption Option: Help*

*for Families* by Lindsay (Morning Glory Press) is written specifically for and to parents of pregnant teenagers considering the adoption alternative. Reading this book will help them understand there are others who have experienced feelings and challenges similar to theirs.

## Involve Grandparents from Beginning

You can also ask the young woman how her parents are doing. Ask questions that will help her clarify her perceptions of her parents' feelings and behaviors. Some teenagers are not yet sensitive to their parents' feelings. Often they misinterpret parental motives and reactions. During these conversations, try to help the young person develop some insight into what this experience might be like for members of her family. At the same time, let her know that she is your primary concern. Teenagers tend to be mistrustful when adults form liaisons with their parents.

Sherri Finik, Adoption Affiliates, Tulsa, Oklahoma, mentioned two adoption plans changed at the last minute because the birthfather's mother decided, in each case, that she wanted the baby. In one, the parents were fourteen, and the paternal grandmother took the baby with the approval of the birthmother.

In the other situation, the paternal grandmother came to the hospital on the day of birth. In an emotional scene, she said she was going to take the baby home and raise it. She had the baby for awhile but things didn't work out. Ultimately the birthmother ended up with the baby, and she didn't appear prepared to raise the baby. Keeping the baby was an emotional reaction on the part of the paternal grandmother. She didn't think through the ramifications of taking the baby home and caring for it herself.

"These two cases made me very aware of the significance of the birthfather's extended family," commented Finik. "When I talk with the birthmother and, if possible, the birthfather, I always ask, 'Do you have a sister who wants a baby? Do you have an aunt who is infertile? Tell me about someone who might want this baby at the last minute.' We need to know that because it's to no one's best interest to plan an adoption and choose a family, then at the last minute an aunt makes an impassioned plea for the baby. At that point everything the young woman has planned goes up in smoke."

Is family adoption a workable solution? It depends on the personalities of the people involved. Some people can't handle having a relative raise their child. It's too difficult for them to see their child on a regular basis and not be able to play the parent role. Others find this to be a more peaceful solution. They like knowing where their child is, seeing him periodically, and being involved in his growing years.

Our role is to learn what people need, then find ways to help them satisfy those needs.

## Birthgrandparents — His and Hers

John Holzhuter, Catholic Social Service, Topeka, Kansas, generally meets with the young woman and her parents on their first appointment. From then on, the birthparent (or birthparents) meet with another counselor and the birthgrandparents-to-be are encouraged to see Holzhuter regularly. Frequently the parents of the young woman and the parents of the young man don't see the pregnancy in the same way. Holzhuter stressed that it isn't his place to decide who's "right" when this happens:

"I have to remember it's not my business to get invested in what happens here. There are two sets of grandparents and two parents. Too often social workers want to do their work with the girl's *or* the boy's parents, but they don't get them together."

A key question in getting both sets of parents together is, "Are the boy's and the girl's parents equally responsible for the pregnancy and the decisions which follow?" If the girl's parents continue to blame the boy for their daughter's predicament, and the boy's parents continue to blame the girl, they are probably going to have difficulties. Negotiation can take place only on the basis of mutual responsibility.

Holzhuter thinks the best solution is to get these two sets of parents of teenage parents-to-be together to process the situation. "I've seen some unusual turnabouts in this," he reported. "Mother and father are ready for an adoption plan for their daughter's baby, but the mother and father of the boy are raising hell and saying, 'We'll take this baby.'

"I encourage them. I say, 'I agree with you,' and support them as they wear themselves out with their pain and their concern. At the same time I say, 'Maybe you need to be saying these things to the girl's parents.'

"I don't remember a time when the teenagers' parents say, 'This is wonderful,' at the beginning," Holzhuter continued. "Often I hear, 'These other parents are no good trashy people.' But there seems to be a redemptive way that people can minister to each other. These people who thought they hated each other always seem to do better when they get in there and talk together.

"This whole area takes a tremendous amount of skill, but professionals need to get these families together in order to help them," he concluded.

## Birthparent Must Make Decision

It is very important to young birthparents that the final decision of whether to place the child for adoption is really their own. Many receive input from their parents, and they are likely to consider that input. If they feel overly pressured, however, or if they feel their parents actually made the decision, they probably will have an especially rough time coping with the adoption.

Karen Sakata, social worker at Kaiser Permanente, Downey, California, commented, "Sometimes the parents are pretty controlling. I tell the teenagers, 'It's up to you. You need to make these decisions for your baby.' I think the parents try to be supportive of the birthmother, but they have to realize she is a parent now and needs to make some of these decisions."

Birthmothers who feel it was their own decision to place their child tend to feel better about the placement and feel more positive toward their parents. Those who feel they have been pressured are more likely to express ambivalence about the decision and about their relationship with their parents, as Lonnie did:

*My parents are the ones who told me what was going to happen. My mom said, "You're going to have the*

*baby and give it up for adoption, because your father
and I have raised five children, and we're not going to
raise any more."*

*So, it was plain that that's what I had to do or I'd be
out of here. I'm still angry and upset that nobody helped
me think it through.*

The teenager needs to be allowed to make independent
decisions for her future and that of her child. Such independent
decision-making appears to assist her developmentally as well as
emotionally.

However, there is an element of difficulty here. Many parents
have strong feelings about how their own futures would be
affected by their daughter having a baby. To present these
feelings as a mandate is likely to impair independent decision-
making. To present the feelings as a means of providing information to assist in the decision-making appears to be more
workable.

## Continue Counseling in Hospital

Although you may reach out to parents and family members,
they may not respond during the pregnancy. This means they
may need more help at the hospital during the vulnerable hours
after the baby is born. If at all possible, make yourself available
to them. A visit with a grieving grandparent in the coffee shop at
the hospital may be crucial to the well-being of the family. If the
family members can get their own emotional needs met, they
will be better able to offer their daughter the support she needs.

Sometimes the grandmother doesn't work through the
process of adoption decision-making. She may simply say, "My
daughter is too young. She shouldn't keep this baby." But if the
grandmother doesn't go back and forth with the decision, she
may change her mind after delivery and influence her daughter
to change her decision.

Young birthparents need to be prepared for the fact that their
parents may have a very difficult time when the baby is actually
born. For some, it will be the first time they have ever seen
members of their families display this type of emotion. When

they see their parents feeling upset or demonstrating love for the child, they may be tempted to change their plans based on fears of upsetting their parents.

One of our counselees did just that. She had a very stoic father who became teary at the hospital. She was so shocked and moved by his emotion that she changed her mind and kept her baby. Unfortunately, her father was not in favor of her keeping the child, but did not verbalize this until after the decision had been made.

## Promote Extended Family Communication

Promoting communication between the young woman and her family during the decision-making process may prevent later problems. Encourage her to question family members about their degree of support for her various choices. If she is considering keeping her child, it is important for her to know exactly how much help she can expect.

A nurse who works in an adolescent pregnancy program reported having a student whose family was against adoption:

> *Donette had assumed she and the father of the baby would be married, but he dropped her as soon as he learned of her pregnancy. Donette's mother ran a daycare center and said there was no problem with childcare. Donette insisted that she wanted to go to college and, without this young man, she didn't want to be a mother.*
>
> *Donette's mother believed Donette would change her mind when she saw her baby. After she delivered, Donette still felt adoption would be best, but she kept the baby to please her mother.*
>
> *Donette's parents, however, did not carry through with their promises. The young mother finally placed her child with an adoptive family when he was three months old.*

Another very young teenager heard her father say that he would help her if she kept the baby. This man, who was

divorced from her mother, had a job which required a great deal
of travel. By "help," he actually meant that he would periodically give his daughter small amounts of money. She interpreted
"help" as meaning he would care for the baby while she went
back to her regular school and resumed her activities.

---

*Some family members*
*may be adamantly opposed*
*to the adoption decision.*

---

Such misunderstandings are not unusual. The inexperienced
teenager often needs assistance in knowing what questions to
ask when clarifying these issues with family members.

Some family members may be adamantly opposed to the
adoption decision. These individuals can cause a tremendous
amount of stress for the young woman who is sorting out her
feelings. While it is important that she continue to work out the
decision based on the well-being of herself and her child, these
dissenting individuals may be important to her. Her counselor
needs to help her clarify these issues.

"The most common reason students at Margaret Hudson
didn't consider adoption was their mothers' attitudes," recalled
Rev. Lois Gatchell, Episcopal Deacon and founding director of
this school program in Tulsa, Oklahoma. "If the teenager's
mother is a strong, controlling person, she can easily stop the
adoption plan because her daughter is still dependent on her.
Sometimes it looks like a form of punishment or retribution. The
grandmother would imply, 'You made your bed, now you must
lie in it,' or she would say, 'Nobody helped me out when I was
pregnant.'

"Another response we saw occasionally was from parents
who would not allow us to do adoption counseling with their
daughter because 'It's a sin to give something away that God
has given you.' It's difficult to discuss when they couch it in
terms of religious beliefs," Rev. Gatchell observed.

One young woman, Gina, found that both her mother and
grandmother were violently opposed to the idea of adoption.
Gina's own mother had been a teenager when Gina was born,

and she felt that Gina's decision should be the same as her own. Gina's grandmother took a slightly different view. She recalled how difficult it had been for everyone when Gina's very young mother attempted to raise her. However, the grandmother was absolutely against the adoption plan because she believed that the child should be reared by someone in the family. This elderly woman was willing to raise the child for Gina.

The decision, in this case, was to go ahead with the adoption. Gina did not see her mother as a stable person, and she felt her grandmother was too old to begin childrearing. Also, Gina did not live in the same town with either of them.

Gina had become independent of the family when she was quite young. She knew she was taking a risk with future family relationships but was in an independent enough position to do so. This decision might have been quite different had she been younger and still dependent upon her mother and grandmother.

The biggest issue between birthgrandparents and the adoptive parents is that they are usually peers, according to Sharon Kaplan, Parenting Resources, Tustin, California. "They're in the same age group and they don't know how to negotiate that relationship," she explained. "You sit down with the birthgrand-parents who are trying to support their daughter, and then they meet the adoptive parents. 'They'll be my granddaughter's parents, yet they're our age,' they tell me. Counselors need to be sensitive to this issue."

## Dealing with Confidentiality

As a helping person, you may be asked by family members to provide information about their daughter or her decision. This can become awkward and uncomfortable. Many parents feel they have the right to know about the services provided for and confidences shared by their minor children.

Several issues are important here. First, find out about your state's laws regulating confidentiality and parental rights relat-ing to minors. If you are not protected by law, it is wise to let the young person know so that she is aware there may be limitations on your confidentiality. There may be regulations in your own setting that require you to provide parents with information.

The best approach is to encourage the teenager to communicate with her parents, especially if you agree that there is good reason for them to have information. You can offer to be present to assist in such disclosures. Sometimes this provides valuable support to the parents as well as the teenager.

If the young person is afraid to give her parents information, explore the reasons with her. Sometimes her fears may be grounded in reality. If there is a history of abuse or neglect in the family, the teenager may have very sound reasons for not wanting to discuss things with her parents. If this is the case, check with authorities to learn the rights of the young person.

If parents call or come in wanting information, often you can give them assurances and generalizations that satisfy their needs without giving details. Many times we have found parents are less interested in detailed information than in knowing that their daughter is receiving good care from us.

## Group Session for Grandparents

Julie Vetica, School-Age Mother Program teacher, La Mirada, California, recently had a parent night with discussion led by Marge Driscoll, birthparent counselor, Holy Family Services, Los Angeles, California. Four mothers and one father of the pregnant teenagers attended the session. "I was kind of nervous when Marge started in pretty heavily on adoption," Vetica admitted, "but they liked it."

At the parent session Driscoll used the "Am I Parent Material?" questionnaire from Lindsay's *Pregnant Too Soon: Adoption Is an Option*. She asked the grandparents-to-be to answer such questions as "Could I handle a child and school at the same time? Would I have enough energy for both?" and "Can I afford to support a child?" in terms of their daughter's readiness for parenting. Driscoll also asked, "Do you think your daughter will be parenting this child? How much of the work do you think you'll be doing?" A couple of the mothers admitted they'll probably have much of the responsibility of parenting the child.

"I talk to the students about the impact their babies will have on their parents," Vetica emphasized. "We talk about how they make the complete decision about keeping the baby but the financial responsibility is their parents'. We make life plans for the next year. If she doesn't make an adoption plan, she needs to make a parenting plan, and her parents are generally an important part of that plan."

When she first meets a potential student and her parent, Marge Eliason, Young Parents Program, Billings, Montana, immediately asks, "Have you thought about parenting or adoption?"

"Oh, we're going to keep the baby," they usually reply.

"I say right up front that Susie will find out about adoption. She will know there is another choice even if she ends up parenting," Eliason explained. "I believe that otherwise she may wake up some day and say somebody sold her a bill of goods. And the parents need to know we're talking about adoption as well as parenting."

Another teacher reported working with a young woman and her mother, but not with her father. "He came to the hospital, held that baby and bonded with it. He said, 'This is it, we can't give this baby up,' and she ended up keeping," the teacher said.

The same teacher also spoke of a student who made an adoption decision, and her boyfriend helped her choose the parents. Her mother had not been part of the decision. Then at the hospital the grandmother said, "We need to keep this baby." The young mother kept the baby three weeks, decided to relinquish, and had to leave her home in order to do so.

## Dealing with Extended Family

Lana speaks freely about her experiences as a birthmother. She is enthusiastic about the impact the whole experience had on her life. She feels her immediate family was supportive but says her pregnancy was hard on her grandmother:

*I was very dependent on my mother, very dependent emotionally. I made my own decision, but she was my main support.*

*I felt like there was a weight on my shoulders, that something was holding me back, that there was some-thing wrong with me thinking I'd parent this child.*

*I'm not super religious, but I do have my faith, I do
believe in God, and when I made my decision for
adoption, something snapped. I said, "Okay, I'm giving
this child up for adoption," and it was like a sudden
swing, like this weight was lifted off me and I felt a lot of
peace. It felt good, and I knew it was the right decision
no matter how much it hurt.*

*My mother's first reaction to my decision to adopt
was, "Are you comfortable with it?"*

*I said, "Yeah, I feel good about it. This is what needs
to happen." I felt by giving her up I was offering her a
chance for a life like I had had. I was spoiled rotten and
I loved every minute of it. At fifteen I always wanted a
little baby to cuddle and to play with, but I also wanted
her to have everything. I couldn't do that for her.*

*My father didn't find out I was pregnant until I was
eight months along. He and my older brothers and
sisters were supportive. One sister who lives out of state
said she wanted to adopt the child because she wanted
to keep it in the family, but she couldn't afford to do
that. I don't think I'd have let her anyway.*

*The only problem was my grandmother. I made my
mother swear she wouldn't tell Grandma. I didn't want
her to find out because she's a fanatical religious
person. To her, premarital sex is a cardinal sin.*

*When I was eight months pregnant, Grandma came
to visit, and somebody had already told her I was
pregnant. I used to walk around barefoot, and I had this
dress my mom and I had made. It was real big, and of
course being eight months pregnant, I looked like a
balloon. Well, my grandmother knocked on the door and
I answered. I thought she was going to die! It was like
total shock to her. She knew I was pregnant, but to see
me was a whole different thing. She had a hard time
with it.*

*She stayed a week. She spent that entire week saying,
"How can you do this? How can you give your child
up? How can you take this child out of our family?"*

> *My mother sat there and listened, and finally she said, "Mom, it takes a hell of a lot more love for her to give this child up than it would to keep it." And Grandma didn't say any more.*
>
> *I felt like telling Grandma, "If you want to raise this child, go ahead. I'm seventeen years old, I have a life to live, and I can't give this child what it needs."*

Counselors, teachers and others working with young people considering pregnancy alternatives generally need to include the young person's extended family in the counseling if at all possible. The decision to release a child for adoption must be made by the birthparent(s). However, the entire family needs to be involved with the decision-making because that family will also have to face the realities of losing the child to another family. They, too, need caring support throughout this family crisis.

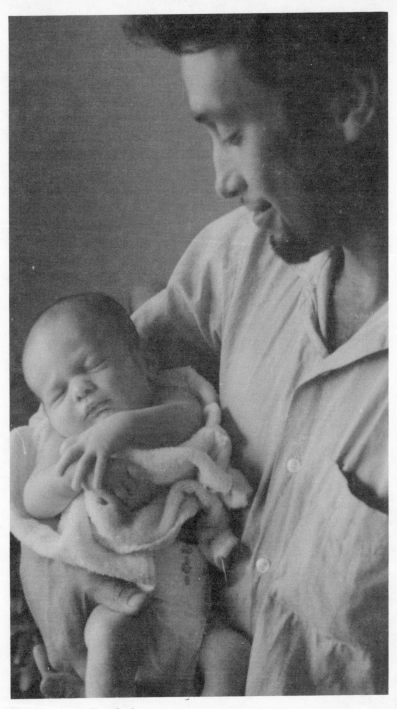

Photo by David Crawford

# CHAPTER 7

# Birthfathers Need Help Too

> *The fathers should get as much counseling and attention as the mother. I think that's extremely important.*
>
> *They grieve and they mourn too. A lot of them think, "Oh, I'm too macho for that," but they do. Some of them need special groups because they may not be willing to go with the birthmother to her support group meetings. (Katheryn, birthmother)*

The birthfather has the right to the same kinds of counseling and intervention as the birthmother. He deserves to be included in the decision-making process if he so desires.

Unfortunately, the fathers aren't often actively involved in the process. Service providers frequently complain that they would like involvement from the baby's father. They are concerned about working closely with the young woman while the young man is obviously absent.

For the young father's sake and for the sake of his future family formation, he needs to be helped to understand both the gravity and the joy of parenting decisions. He needs to experience the skills involved in responsible decision making.

"I don't know how a young man is ever going to develop into a responsible parent if he's left out on the first go around," exclaimed Rev. Lois Gatchell, Episcopal Deacon and adoption agency board member. "He's likely to repeat the same behavior because he hasn't received any help."

Even if you experience little success in reaching young fathers, it is important that you continue to attempt to do so. Make your services available to them. Provide opportunities for them to come in, opportunities as unthreatening as possible. Let them know you're interested in them and you're available if they want to talk.

## Father Has Powerful Role

The father of the baby has a powerful role in the decision. If the young woman makes an adoption plan, the father may be able to stop the adoption. Having the father's support, whether in favor of releasing or parenting, may be extremely important to the birthmother.

Dealing with the baby's father is a good issue to discuss in alternatives groups. Regardless of their circumstances, most young women have feelings, thoughts, and concerns about the father of the baby. Their feelings won't be alike, but interest in the topic is almost universally shared.

Three years ago Trisha placed her baby daughter with a family she selected. Trisha continues to be in contact with the adoptive family. She receives letters and pictures regularly, and she sees her daughter two or three times a year.

When asked about the negative effects of her daughter's adoption, Trisha singled out the baby's father's behavior. As a result, Trisha feels quite negative about birthfathers' rights generally:

*Nothing real negative happened to me after the adoption except for getting the papers signed by the*

*father. I had to beg him to sign those papers. He was in
another state at the time, and the adoption wasn't
settled for nearly a year. That was so hard for Betty
and Carl (adoptive parents). I think they trusted me, but
for a whole year they wondered, even though I kept
reassuring them.*

*I don't think the father should have any rights
because generally he isn't there. I can't say that about
all of them, but some of the girls I talk to, the guys don't
care for the babies like the mothers do. The guys don't
have to agree to an abortion. Why should they have to
sign for an adoption? The woman should have the right
to place the baby for adoption without the father's
consent. It should be okay to let that baby be raised by a
loving family.*

## Fathers' Rights Vary

Fathers' rights vary from state to state, and may be altered
periodically by legislation or interpretation. It's important to be
current on these laws.

Many years ago, the father of the baby had almost no rights.
The mother could choose the fate of the child without involving
the father. Today that pendulum has swung far in the opposite
direction. In many states, fathers have equal rights to the child,
but most of these laws do not attempt to balance the rights of the
father with his responsibilities.

For example, in New Mexico and California, children are not
generally placed unless the father either signs the adoption
papers or denies paternity. What this means in practice is that
the father can stop an adoption without having to come forth
with child support or any other plan for the child. This has left
many young women in bad situations.

If the young mother chooses adoption so her child can have
the security and stability of a two-parent home, she probably
won't like the idea of releasing the child to the father, particularly if she feels he can't provide the stability she wants for their
child. When this happens, the mother may keep the baby
because she is convinced she can parent her child more

adequately than can the father. Unfortunately, many of these young women never receive monetary support from the father.

If we really believe the young man should accept responsibility for the child he refuses to release for adoption, we should offer him the help in finding resources and gaining job skills that we offer young mothers. We must continually search for ways to provide these services.

We also need to remember that when the child is placed for adoption, the father is likely to grieve the loss of his child. His family may also be grieving. So often he and his family are left without resources for dealing with their grief.

Stephanie and Ralph were no longer dating when they made the adoption plan for their baby. Having Ralph involved in the decision-making process was important to both of them:

> *He was there for me the whole time. He went to counseling with me, and I feel we made the decision together. I was fortunate to have him there. I know a lot of fathers take off.*
>
> *The adoption decision was probably harder on him than it was on me. He was nineteen and I think he felt more ready to be a parent.*

Humberto Jimenez, counselor in the Teenage Pregnancy and Parenting Program, Davenport, Iowa, mentioned two young men who, rather than release their babies for adoption, are rearing the children themselves. Dwayne, twenty, had no personal contact with the baby's mother after she realized she was pregnant. She told him, "Just give me my space." After the baby was born, the lawyer contacted Dwayne and said, "Sign these papers."

Dwayne said, "No, I won't do that." He and his child are doing fine, according to Jimenez. They live with Dwayne's parents who care for the baby while Dwayne is working. Otherwise, he takes responsibility for his child.

The other young man who took custody of his child is having a problem forming other relationships, Jimenez noted, because he doesn't want to father any more children. He's twenty, and says one child takes up all his time.

## Connie and Eric's Story

Connie has not been with her baby's father during her pregnancy or since. They have had occasional contact, and Eric willingly signed the adoption papers. The experience was hard on Connie but she appears peaceful about her child's adoption:

*I was seeing the father about three months before I got pregnant. It was my first time and I was only a freshman. Eric was a junior, and I'd do anything, get drunk, whatever, to be with him.*

*We broke up when Eric learned I was pregnant because he didn't want his mom and dad to find out 'cause then he wouldn't get his new car. Actually Eric didn't want to break up with me because he thought that if he did, his friends would think he was a jerk. So he made me feel so miserable I couldn't handle it any more so I broke up with him. Then Eric started seeing my best friend which was pretty hard on me. He's still seeing her, and I still care for him, but not that much any more.*

*I'd see Eric during the pregnancy once in awhile when I was walking back from work, and he'd stop and talk to me. I'd be so embarrassed because every time he'd see me, I'd be bigger.*

*One time I went to the hospital because I was hurting, and one of Eric's friends was there in the hospital. After I got home, Eric called and wondered how I was doing. I told him I was fine, that everything was okay.*

*Eric came to the hospital when Troy was born. He was at a keg party when I went in that Saturday night, and his friends rushed over there to tell him my labor had started. I didn't call him. He was there the next day when Troy was born, and he sent a couple of pictures of himself for the adoptive parents to keep for Troy. Since then we've been friends, "Hi" and "Bye," but not enough to say, "Hey, how are you? What are you up to?" I still feel uncomfortable around him.*

*Eric didn't have anything much to do with the adoption decision. He wrote me a couple of notes*

*saying, "Well, Connie, it's up to you. Whatever you*
*want to do, I'm behind you." He knew I wouldn't give*
*the baby to him, so he pretty much agreed with my*
*decision.*

Of the sixteen birthmothers I (Catherine) interviewed for my
dissertation, only three said the child's father had been involved
in the decision-making process in a meaningful way. The other
thirteen felt they were responsible for the decision-making.
Either they didn't think the father wanted to be involved, they
were afraid of the type of involvement he might want, or he was
simply not available.

For many, making the adoption decision on their own seemed
obvious. They didn't see the father of the baby as wanting or
needing involvement.

## Father Is Absent During Pregnancy

Jeni and Sean dated a few times when she was sixteen and he
was twenty. A year later they started dating again, and she spent
one night with him. She didn't see him again, and she assumed
he wouldn't want to know about her pregnancy or the adoption.
She managed to place the baby without Sean's signature, a risky
way to go:

*I was living with my girlfriend. Sean told me that*
*night that if I got pregnant he didn't want to know about*
*it. He knew I wasn't on birth control and he didn't care.*
*He said, "If you get pregnant, don't tell me." So I didn't*
*tell him until three months after the baby was adopted.*

*When Lisa was three months old I called Sean and*
*left a message with his mother. She didn't like me so she*
*refused to give me his phone number or tell me where he*
*was living. He called her the next day, and she told him,*
*"This girl called and here's her phone number."*

*Sean called me, and I told him. He said later he had*
*a feeling that was what I was going to say.*

*I got the adoption through without his signature. I*
*lied. He could have gotten custody easily that first year*

*because I lied about him being the father. I named
somebody else and didn't give a last name. I told them
this guy Russell did it at a party. I knew they wouldn't
be able to find him and they didn't. They put this notice
in the paper but they couldn't find him.*

*So when Sean called and I told him, he said, "Well, I
guess everything turned out for the best." I don't think
he cared anyway, but I thought he needed to know. It
was time for him to know he had a daughter, and I don't
think I cared how he felt about it.*

## Birthfather's Support Is Crucial

Rev. Fred Trevino, United Methodist Church, Tucson,
Arizona, says generally young women with problem pregnancies
don't want to tell him the identity of the fathers, and he honors
their wishes. He added, however, "I'd love to see them both
being involved. That would be healthier for them and for the
future of their child. But so often the girls say, 'I don't want him
involved. Forget it. It's done.'

"Once, however, two kids in our youth group had a baby.
They didn't get married, and they placed the baby for adoption.
The father was involved, but the relationship didn't develop
beyond that.

"In his own immature way that young father was concerned,
and he needed a way to express that concern. I think he learned
some things about reality, about responsibility, something about
fathering. He and the young woman knew that baby was something they did together whether or not they continued their
relationship," Rev. Trevino pointed out.

As you work with women who are positive they don't want
the father involved, do everything you can to help them realize
the importance of getting the father's signature on the adoption
papers. Having the adoption broken by a father stepping in
months after the child is placed is not what she wants for her
child. The careful plans she is making for her baby's future are
too important for that kind of disruption.

Reassure her that you aren't expecting her to be the sole
contact with the father. Can you, as a helping person, contact

him? If you meet with him and explain the options available through adoption, and that he can be a part of the adoption planning, he may cooperate. Too often we assume that because some fathers refuse to cooperate, all birthfathers must be bad, not worthy of consideration. In fact, when one attorney was asked, "How do you work with birthfathers?" he facetiously replied, "I carry a gun!"

In the state in which this attorney practices, it is legal to take the father's consent before the baby is born, and he explained that he often does so. "Generally I have talked to the birthmother first, and I have a feeling as to whether the father will be cooperative. If he isn't, he can sign a document which states, 'I deny being the father but in case I am, I give my consent to the adoption,'" he explained.

---

*Some birthfathers need as much caring*
*and assistance in their decision-making*
*as do birthmothers.*

---

The "right" thing to do in working with birthfathers is sometimes difficult to determine. Asking a birthmother to sign away her rights to her child before that child is born is illegal for good reasons. She needs to make her adoption/parenting decision all over again after her child is born. If she doesn't have a chance to do so, she is likely not to have positive feelings about the adoption. She may grieve more intensely and for a longer period of time than she would if she felt the final decision was truly hers. Does the same concern apply to the father?

This, of course, is the reason behind the equal parenting laws. Some birthfathers care as intensely as birthmothers. They need as much caring and assistance in their decision-making as is offered to birthmothers.

Joanne kept her baby for a week after he was born, then released him to the adoptive family she had selected. She has pictures of her child. She talked about her child's father:

> *We had a good relationship, but I was afraid to tell*
> *him I was pregnant. I thought he'd hate me and say it*

*was all my fault. I figured he'd think I did it on purpose*
*and I was real scared. Then one day he hugged me and*
*said he'd figured it out by himself.*

*At first he wanted me to have an abortion because he*
*was scared to tell his mom, but I was already five*
*months pregnant and it was too late. Anyway, I didn't*
*want to do that.*

*Finally he said whatever I wanted was okay He was*
*there through the whole thing. We went to Ginny's*
*together for counseling. He thought adoption was best*
*but he said it was up to me. We were both in school so I*
*figured it was the best thing for all of us.*

The birthfather may have trouble deciding what his role is. "Whether the mother chooses adoption or parenting, one of the issues we deal with regularly is helping the birthfather design his role with the child," explained Sharon Kaplan, Parenting Resources.

"Over and over we find the birthfather trying to discuss his relationship with his child in a letter to that child. He tries to explain how he feels about being a dad, but he really doesn't know where he fits.

"This is an important area to explore with a counselor. I think a lot of fathers disappear out of guilt and shame. He isn't able to provide for his child, and he doesn't know what to do. I think it's a crucial counseling issue," Kaplan concluded.

## Some Birthfathers Don't Seem to Care

It is a reality, however, that some birthfathers appear not to care. They don't want to be involved. The birthmother may make an adoption plan because she wants her child to have a different kind of life than either she or the child's father can provide at that time.

Tammy's son, Ricky, was born three years ago when she was seventeen. Doug, the baby's father, ignored Tammy throughout her pregnancy. As a result, she distrusted all men for a long time. Tammy still grieves heavily for her child and reports having difficulty getting on with her life:

*Doug and I were together for three years. He
started talking about marriage as soon as I'd get out of
high school. That's when I finally decided this was not
the man I wanted to spend the rest of my life with. This
was my last year of high school, and I was getting
scared. I thought I'd better do something now so I broke
up with him. A couple of weeks later I found out I was
pregnant.*

*Doug didn't believe it was his baby for the longest
time. A few weeks before my due date I told him the
baby was going to be born soon. He never called back,
never tried to get in contact.*

*A month after Ricky was born I finally decided to call
and tell Doug I'd had the baby. He came over and I
showed him some of the pictures. He flipped through
them and threw them on the coffee table. Then all of a
sudden he wanted to get back together with me. I was
like, that takes a lot of guts, buddy, after what I've been
through. You're nuts, you're crazy, you're history!*

*Finally I had the adoption papers ready to sign, and
we got together and signed them. Doug kind of tried to
get back together then, but my mom told him to leave the
house. She said, "She has to do her homework now.
Please leave." She didn't want him there, she didn't
want us back together, and I'm glad she did that.*

*I didn't really want Doug back, but at that point I
might have taken him 'cause he would have been
security.*

*By then I was pretty turned off on men. I was never
going to get together with any man, I was never going to
have sex, I was never going to fall in love again. I was
never going to trust another man, ever. I thought all
men were jerks. I thought all men tried to do was get
you in bed, then leave you high and dry when they'd had
enough. I had no respect for them at all, none.*

*My dad didn't even seem to care that this guy had
gotten me pregnant. I'd given my baby up for adoption,
and then Doug had tried to pick me up again even*

*though he'd wanted nothing to do with me before. My
dad was still buddies with Doug. That really really
threw me off because I thought, "Hey, my dad should be
doing everything in his power to protect his little girl."
That made me feel like dirt, like, "Thanks a lot, I'm glad
I mean so much to you."*

## Contact with Birthfathers Is Important

The attorney quoted earlier as saying he carried a gun actually feels fairly positive about birthfathers generally. "For the most part, they haven't been a problem," he reflected. "Some are potential problems, and they may delay things. Many of the fathers, especially if it was a one-night stand, could care less, yet the Supreme Court gives them equal rights.

"I'd say ninety percent of the fathers in adoption cases are indifferent," he continued. "All he signs is a consent to adoption. If the adoption doesn't go through, the paper means nothing. If there is no adoption, he is still responsible for child support."

Joan Anderson, Options for Adoption counselor, commented, "I try to be in contact with the fathers, but often they are totally out of the picture before I get involved. I always try to keep that door open because these guys are scared, and they don't know what they ought to do. If they've broken up with the birthmom, they think they can't be part of the planning. I try to work with them."

Linda Nunez, attorney, tries to contact birthfathers by letter "just to bring them into the fold." She encourages counseling for the birthfathers too, and said most of the adoptive parents would be delighted to meet him along with the birthmother. The birthfather meets with the adoptive family in about twenty percent of her cases, Nunez said, and he may get letters and pictures separately from the birthmother's letters and photos.

"If the birthmother doesn't want the father involved, her concern often is that she has to do something, that it's her responsibility. That's usually a big piece of it," Nunez observed. "I find once the birthmother is committed to the adoption, has found the adoptive family, and has gotten the education and the counseling, she usually understands, even if she's mad at him, that he's a part of this baby. When I take the responsibility of seeing him, that's reassuring, and I like to do this as early in the planning as possible."

When she explains to a client the importance of naming the birthfather, Sherri Finik, Adoption Affiliates, Tulsa, Oklahoma, said she loses some clients. "I explain as carefully as I can why that's so important," she said. "I want them to know why it's essential to get the father's consent." About half of the birthfathers in their adoption cases have not been locatable, and have not been seen since the conception, Finik said. "Whenever we can, of course we work with him. If he's known and he's locatable, we certainly encourage him to come in for counseling," she continued. "Some of our birthmothers, perhaps one in seven, have continuing relationships with the father. Of course he should be involved."

David, twenty-one, was part of the adoption planning. Perhaps this is why he feels his grief has been manageable:

> I was overwhelmed when Meghan told me she was pregnant, and I was relieved to learn she had already told her mother. That meant I wouldn't have to do it. Only my parents knew, and they were fairly supportive. My friends were amazed at how well we handled the situation. I think they respected us for what we did. Several said they couldn't do adoption if that happened to them.
>
> I wasn't thinking about adoption at first, but Meghan and her mother thought that would be best. And I was convinced that would be the best decision in the long run.
>
> The day the baby was born was one of the happiest days of my life. I didn't have to pretend any longer, and I felt like a ton of bricks had been taken off my back. I think I had been prepared, so when it was time to release the baby, I was happy.
>
> The first two or three weeks were the hardest in terms of emotional problems for Meghan, and I supported her. Basically everything has gone smoothly

*since then. We met the parents twice before the baby*
*was born, and they send us pictures each month.*
*Meghan and I open the packages, throw the paper*
*aside, and look at the pictures. Then we read the letters.*
*We can't get enough of them.*

Radonna Tims, R.N., Tulsa, Oklahoma, knew one young
birthfather who was allowed to room in at the hospital with the
mother and the baby. Other family members were involved. The
young mother called Tims and said, "I need you here." Her
mother didn't want her to place the baby, other family members
didn't, and the father wasn't sure about the adoption.

---

*The birthfather hadn't worked through*
*the adoption decision prior to the birth.*

---

"He wanted her to keep the baby and stay home while he'd
go off to college. She went through a lot of agonizing, and she
would have made it either way," Tims recalled.

When the social worker came to take the baby, the father
said, "No, we're going to keep it."

"No, we're not," the young mother said.

Tims suggested to the couple that they let the baby go to a
foster home for ten days rather than signing papers immediately.
"They weren't equipped to take the baby home, and they agreed
to do this," she said. Ten days later, both signed the adoption
papers. The birthfather hadn't worked through the adoption
decision prior to the birth. Being included in the counseling and
planning from the beginning might have made the final
decision-making a little smoother for both of them.

Teacher Bev Short, Carmichael, California, doesn't have
birthfathers enrolling at her school, but she encourages contact
with them. "We try to get them to come to our group sessions,"
she said. "Sometimes a girl will take a videotape home to share
with him or they read some of our adoption books together.
Occasionally a birthfather has been part of a panel going to
another school to share experiences. We try to include him as
much as possible."

"Birthfathers have a lot to deal with and they don't have many services available," teacher Julie Vetica pointed out. "I don't see pressure from the father for abortion as much as the pressure to keep because of the flesh and blood thing. They don't realize the ramifications for them of keeping this baby if they haven't finished high school, have no job skills, and no parenting plan."

## Joe and Angela Change Their Minds

Joe and Angela made an adoption plan, but they didn't talk about it much. Angela chose the adoptive family and met with them once.

Joe was totally uninvolved in counseling during the pregnancy, and Angela saw the adoption counselor only twice. After the baby was born, Joe and Angela decided to parent their son themselves. Joe related:

> *For six months Angela and I didn't know she was pregnant. When she found out, she immediately said adoption was her choice. I was thinking adoption, too, but I didn't see the counselor and I didn't meet the parents Angela chose.*
>
> *I was for adoption because I was in college and wanted to continue, and Angela, a senior, had planned to attend college out of state. I didn't want us to have to change our plans.*
>
> *Inside I think I wanted to keep our baby, but I kept thinking of my career and my education. Most of my friends thought adoption was a good idea.*
>
> *Then at the hospital these feelings got stronger and stronger. When I saw him, I knew I wanted to keep him. Angela made the same decision while she was in labor.*
>
> *Angela lives with her mother and I was with my parents, but that first week I fed the baby, I changed him. I have several friends who haven't accepted the responsibility of being a father, and I felt I should accept the father role. I wanted to be involved rather than just being the father out there somewhere.*

*I feel I had a choice, and I would suggest other
couples consider all their options. We didn't really do
that. I thought my life would be ruined if we kept the
baby. I thought I'd have to get a job to support him, and
I couldn't get my education. But once he was born, we
started thinking about how to work things out.*

At this time, six months after the birth of their child, Angela
attends a local community college while Joe attends a college
fifty miles away. He's involved with his child on weekends.

## Larry Still Grieves

Larry epitomizes the birthfather who cares deeply about his
child, but who received no counseling before or after Breanne
was born. He agreed to the adoption throughout most of the
pregnancy and afterward because he knew neither he nor
Breanne's mother was ready to parent. At the same time, he
wanted desperately to father his child, to be responsible for his
family. He and Rachel are still together and will probably marry
after they graduate from college. Throughout the interview,
Larry obviously had difficulty talking about their situation. A
year after Breanne's placement with the adoptive family, he still
grieves intensely, still has had almost no counseling, no professional assistance in dealing with his feelings:

*Rachel and I met the summer before my senior and
her junior year in high school. We were in the band
together and we started dating. We got more and more
serious, and we exchanged class rings early that fall.
When we started having sex, we both felt guilty. Rachel
is from a deeply religious family, and at that time I was
considering going into the ministry.*

*Most of the guys at school would joke and brag all
the time about having sex, but nobody knew about the
relationship between Rachel and me.*

*I learned about the pregnancy as soon as she missed
her first period. Being the supportive boyfriend, I went
with her to speak to a counselor. I took her down to*

*Birthright for the pregnancy test, and then to see
a doctor.*

*For three months we kept it a secret from other
people. In fact, in my family, only my parents know
about it to this day. We didn't tell any of my aunts and
uncles, not even my brothers and sisters. I'm the last of
six children, and I'm ten years younger than the rest.
My parents didn't want anybody to find out.*

---

## Her parents said either we married or we placed the baby for adoption.

---

*When we first learned she was pregnant, abortion
was not an alternative. I didn't force Rachel into having
the baby. She agreed that abortion was not right. We
talked with her parents and they mentioned adoption
right away. Rachel at first thought it was the cruelest
thing anyone could say. How could her parents suggest
this?*

*Finally it came to an ultimatum. Her parents said we
either had to be married before the baby was born or we
had to place the baby for adoption.*

*My parents didn't want any part of it. They didn't
want me to marry Rachel. They hadn't offered to pay my
college expenses before, but suddenly they decided they
could pay for college if we didn't get married. Talk
about pressure!*

*I offered to marry her. We started to make marriage
plans. We looked at wedding rings — here's a girl five
months pregnant and we walk into a jewelry store. The
guy's eyes light up and he says, "Oh, you want to look
at wedding rings? Have I got a deal for you!"*

*Rachel made the decision for adoption.*

*Some of my friends said, "Are you sure it's your
baby? It's probably not yours. You could just walk
away." I knew it was my child. When Rachel suggested
adoption, however, I tried to think maybe it wasn't
my baby.*

*Rachel's adoption plans came between us. For a while I turned my back. I walked away from her because I never accepted the adoption. Up until the time our son was born I had visions of raising the child, of standing in the hospital and taking him away to raise myself.*

## "I Was There When He Was Born"

*I was there when he was born. We had two lawyers, one for us and one for the adoptive parents. After the baby was born they said to me, "Now comes the difficult time. Now is when you must convince her the decision is right." In my own mind I hadn't accepted it, but I had to be the one to say, "This is the best, this is the best."*

*I went through everything a father goes through. I went to the Lamaze classes, I sat in the waiting room. I didn't get to be with her through labor and delivery because she was in labor only two hours, and I was an hour away at college. By the time I got there she was already starting to push and they wouldn't let me in the delivery room.*

*As soon as he was born, I walked in and went over to Rachel. They cleaned up the baby, then gave him to us and we both held him. They gave Rachel a sedative so she could sleep, and they took the baby back to the nursery. That's when I was left completely alone. Rachel's parents had talked to me for a few minutes. My parents never knew anything except he was born that day and he was a boy.*

*I was alone in that hospital for several hours. Finally a counselor came to get some information, and once again I was told, "This is the time you need to be strong and tell her adoption is the right decision, that this isn't the time to change her mind." So I had to lie to Rachel about how I felt. I said, "Adoption is the best thing, it's the only way we can do this."*

*Finally that night I went over to a friend's house. By then it was almost midnight, and we walked in that cold December night until 4:30 in the morning.*

## *Larry Agrees To Talk About Adoption*

*It wasn't until three or four months later that it really hit me and started to gnaw at me. By this time, Rachel was speaking openly about adoption. She was part of a team from her school, and they would speak to students at other schools. They asked me to go and give the male side of the story. Up to that time I had pretty much blocked it out. I had gone back to school, and I saw Rachel only on weekends. I had no contact with anybody back home except for seeing Rachel.*

*I went with the school panel a few times. Talking about your problems is supposed to help, but it didn't. Each time I'd come back, I'd feel worse and worse. Reliving the memories and dealing with the kids' questions, "How could you give your child away?" was tough. They didn't realize how much it hurt when they asked those questions.*

*Finally it was to the point where the time for me to be the strong one was over. By that time I hurt, I ached, I felt so bad. It was time for Rachel to be the strong one. She was the one who always had the counselors around, the social worker calling and checking up. I had no one like that.*

*About six months after the baby was born I talked to a counselor at school. He asked, "Do you love Rachel, or are you just around because of the baby?" That question hurt. I think it's been asked a lot by my parents, by about everybody except Rachel and her parents. It frustrated me, it angered me, and it turned me off to that counselor. I almost decided not to go on any more panels because of that question. I couldn't see why he would ask that. But now that I think about it, I think it's a fair question, and I think everybody needs to be asked it.*

*Nobody at college knows about our baby — except a friend or two from home. And one of them told my best friend here without my knowing it. But that was good because this friend and I can talk about it now, and we do occasionally. A week ago another friend said to me, "Well, it's been almost a year." All I said was, "Yes." He was the one who walked with me the night the baby was born.*

*One thing that always upset me during the whole thing was the way people treated me, the way they talked to me. They assumed that once the baby was born, I wouldn't stick around.*

*I did stick around. I guess that's where the major guilt feelings come in. I stayed, but we didn't get married. I'm not supporting my family. While Rachel was pregnant I got a job as a door to door salesman but it didn't work out. I'm still feeling guilty, and I keep saying to myself, "I couldn't support my own family."*

*I do care about Rachel, and we plan to be married in two years when I finish college. Rachel will have another year of college, and we both know she'll finish too.*

*Now I honestly believe adoption was the best choice. There are things I've been able to do that we couldn't have done if we had a child. Rachel is in college now, a small private college. She always wanted to go there. That was her dream. I'm glad she's able to do that.*

*It's a completely closed adoption. It was a private adoption and we don't know where our son is.*

*I don't think the male issue was ever presented at the school program for the mothers. There was nothing, no help ever offered to the male until after Rachel dragged me in to see them.*

*When we're married, we plan to stay some place here in the middle west, the heartland of the country. I can't think of a better place to raise our children. And we will raise our other children together.*

## Birthfathers Need Services Too

Larry's story, his heartbreak and his anguish, are important for us to remember as we help young people work through their pregnancy alternatives. Some fathers may be fathers only because they provided the sperm. Some may not care about the resulting child. They may not want to be involved.

Others may try to stop the adoption although they appear to have no workable parenting plan.

There are others like Larry, young men who care a great deal about their babies and about the mothers of their babies, young men who may consider an adoption plan because they do care. These young men need caring, they need someone to help them look at their options. If they carry out an adoption plan, they need follow-up counseling from someone who will help them deal with their pain.

The wise and caring approach is to assume, with each birthfather we encounter, that there is a Larry inside, a young man who cares about his family and who needs help.

# CHAPTER 8

# Teachers Discuss Alternatives

*We don't talk about adoption because no one's interested. (Pregnant Minor Program teacher)*

*I went to this special high school where you have to take a parenting class if you're pregnant. We had a lot of speakers — they talked about first aid, breast cancer, all sorts of things, but nobody mentioned adoption. We had an adoption film once while we had a substitute teacher, but nobody paid any attention to it and we didn't talk about it afterward.*

*The teacher didn't even offer any reading about adoption until I told her just before I left that class. She acted shocked when I mentioned adoption, and she said, "Why are you doing that?" (Lilia, 16)*

Lilia's instructor was a good one who cared about her students, and the program was excellent. Infant care was provided on campus, and the young mothers enrolled at the school were learning to be good parents.

Providing guidance in active parenting must be a crucial part of any program for pregnant adolescents. If any — or all — of these young people are going to parent their children, they need help and encouragement to become good parents.

Years ago this was not a goal in some pregnant minor programs. In 1972 a principal in an alternative school in Orange County, California, was organizing a special program for pregnant students.

When asked about the possibility of providing child care, he was indignant. "Absolutely not," he exclaimed. "These girls are too young to be parents, and they should release those babies for adoption. I won't even have a baby bathed at this school. We aren't encouraging children to become parents!" Sadly enough, this large school district still does not provide child care for babies born to school-age mothers. Consequently, most young mothers drop out of school in that district and join the army of undereducated and unskilled young parents.

Twenty years earlier, this man's decision not to provide child care might have been rational, since at that time the majority of pregnant teenagers released their babies for adoption. Even then, however, surely those who were keeping their children should have had help in parenting. Perhaps our priorities are a little mixed up when we provide driver's education for everyone but do not get involved in helping young people become good parents.

## Should We Talk About Adoption?

The teacher who says, "We don't talk about adoption because no one's interested," may also be inadvertently neglecting some of her students.

If even one young woman in the class is considering an adoption plan, she, too, needs support. To assume nobody is remotely interested in this choice is thinking for someone else. And that's not fair.

Phyllis, unhappy mother of a two-year-old, offered some suggestions for people working with pregnant teenagers:

*You could explain that they do have an option. It wouldn't work to say, "I think you should put your baby up for adoption because you're not ready for it," but you could point out how it will be with a child — there are too many responsibilities, so many things to take care of, especially when you don't have a father to help.*

*When you're so young, you don't realize what you're getting into. And you can't depend on welfare to support you all your life. You can't do that because you're not going to get anywhere on welfare.*

*I think more people should talk to the girls about adoption. Everybody seems to put people down about adoption, and I think that's why a lot of girls don't do it. A few girls are strong enough, but a lot of them couldn't handle it.*

*Get someone to come in and tell the girls about the bad parts of being a parent. Get somebody to talk to them. Tell them it's tough to be a mother, especially if you're trying to raise a kid by yourself.*

How much should we talk about adoption in classes for pregnant teenagers? I (Jeanne) asked this question of a group of Teen Mother Program alumnae. Almost all of the approximately one hundred young women who returned the questionnaire were parenting their children. Thirty-seven percent said we should talk about adoption a lot. These young mothers had attended a program which offered a periodic unit on adoption in the pre-natal health class, yet nineteen percent of the respondents said there had not been enough discussion about the topic. In fact, one young mother wrote, "You avoided it. You should let the girls know that it's *all right* if they give up their baby."

## Minority Adoption

Conventional wisdom in some areas is that ethnic minority birthparents never consider adoption. This is not necessarily true. For example, students at New Futures School, Albuquerque, New Mexico, who released babies for adoption included Black, Hispanic, Native American and Caucasian teenagers.

No matter which ethnic group(s) you work with, you want to know something about each individual's cultural background and, above all, develop respect for these differences. However, it is not wise to prejudge a person on the basis of the ethnic group to which she appears to belong, i.e., to assume that because she is Black, she "of course" will keep her baby.

Teachers sometimes say, in speaking of their students in schools in predominantly Black areas, "None of my students would ever consider adoption. It's not part of their culture." This may be true of many of their clients, perhaps most of them. You may work with one hundred pregnant teenagers who "know" they'll be parenting their children, but if you have one student who, after deciding against abortion, isn't positive she's ready to be a mother, that student needs your help.

She needs to realize she does have another option. She isn't trapped into too-early motherhood because she's pregnant. She, too, has the option of adoption.

## Alternatives Discussed in Young Families Program

Marge Eliason, teacher in the Young Families Program, Billings, Montana, was astonished to hear that a teacher in a pregnant minor program might not talk about adoption. She talks with her students often about choices, and Eliason shared with us her approach with her prenatal health students. She tells them:

"We're going to talk — you need to know you have choices. You need to know you don't parent just because you're pregnant. One doesn't necessarily follow the other. Abortion is not the issue. We're already past that. But I want you consciously to make a decision to parent. I want you to tell me what that means to you. When you've decided for something, you've decided against something else.

"We'll discuss adoption. I wouldn't have you buy a car and only show you Buicks. I'd take you out and show you the whole array of what's available. And adoption is one of the things available to you. I don't want you waking up in two years madder than hell and saying, 'I didn't know that was a choice I had.' I don't want a bunch of angry kids coming back here and saying, 'I didn't know I could do that.' I don't want you to drift along like a leaf on a stream just because you're pregnant."

"I really think a lot of kids do that," Eliason explained. "They become pregnant and they don't stop to think they still have a choice. They talk about if, when they had sex, did they think that might be a baby? They all agreed, 'No,' but they thought they might get pregnant. They don't take the next step — that being pregnant means having a baby. So then we talk about the reality of the baby, of how that's different from being pregnant.

"'Being pregnant is. . .' and we go on with the responsibility thing and what they want for their kids, that there's no easy choice. I have a girl right now who is due in about two weeks and she's choosing to adopt. She talks about it in class. She lives with her boyfriend and they're poor as church mice. She's afraid of the boyfriend's temper, and she's afraid of not having any money. She really has bare to minimum parent support. But she's eighteen, she's not fourteen. It's harder for fourteen-year-olds to look ahead and plan an adoption."

Eliason's students who have chosen adoption have had open adoptions. The class is so supportive of each other's decisions that two birthmothers, before their babies were placed in their adoptive families, brought them back to school to tell the other girls goodbye.

---

*She brought the baby over*
*to Young Families once or twice*
*before the adoption took place.*

---

Eliason especially remembers one student, Verna, who worked long and hard on the adoption issue because she felt in some ways she was pushed into it by her parents. She also wanted better things for her baby than she saw the other students' babies getting.

Working through Catholic Social Services, Verna selected the family. She named her baby, and the adoptive parents kept part of the name. Verna's mother and dad were at the hospital, as was the baby's father. He was involved and his family was supportive.

Verna took the baby home for a few days as she had planned. She brought the baby over to Young Families once or twice before the adoption took place. At the end of the week the adoptive parents came to her home to pick up the baby.

"The other kids in the program were really supportive," Eliason commented, "except for one girl who was kind of a pain in the fanny about it. I finally pulled her aside and told her to let Verna alone. I said the little innuendos had to cease, the 'Oh, I could never do that to my baby.' I told her she could think whatever she wanted but she couldn't say it, and she quit. Verna has come back and shared with my students why she did this, the communication that continues with the adoptive parents, the pictures, etc.

"I saw her last spring and she's off to college now. Her baby is two. She and the baby's father, apparently by mutual agreement, are not together anymore. They split about six months after the baby was born."

---

*We have to think parenting is right, too,*
*for young people who make this decision.*

---

Eliason mentioned one student who started school with them in the fall. She was planning adoption, but she couldn't handle being with the other young women who were planning to keep their babies. "When she first came, I said, 'This may be hard for you here, or it may cement your decision because you'll see how hard parenting is.' After a few days she came to see me and said she couldn't take it. I suggested she stay for another day and tell herself, 'I'm here to help me make the decision.' She stayed two more days, then didn't come back."

If you teach a group of pregnant and parenting teenagers and nearly all your students keep their babies, your class may not be a good place for some young people making adoption plans.

"The fine line we walk," commented Eliason, "is if we make adoption seem like *the* right decision, those who are parenting will say, 'She doesn't think we made the right choice.' It has to be that we think parenting is right, too, for those young people who make that decision."

## Angela Decides to Parent

We also have to think it's right, must trust her/their decision, if the adoption plan isn't carried out. We must always remember that the decision needs to be made all over again after the baby is born.

Angela didn't know she was pregnant until she was six months along. She was a cheer-leader whose periods were irregular. When she finally faced reality, she and her boyfriend had been apart for a couple of months. She called to tell him about her pregnancy, and they agreed adoption was the only possible solution.

Angela selected an adoptive couple, and from that time on, seldom saw her adoption counselor. She enrolled in her school's Teen Mother Program.

When she was in labor, Angela decided against adoption. She and the baby's father decided they could parent their child and keep their goals of going to college. A year later both were in college and their child was in the high school's child care center.

One of the teachers talked to Angela recently about the lack of discussion she and Angela had had concerning her adoption plan. "Was there anything we might have done to help you with your decision?" she asked. Angela replied:

> *I think it's kind of hard not to push either way. You give your own opinion and we all have biases. With me, I didn't want to talk about it. When I started talking about it I'd start crying. I didn't even like talking about it with my boyfriend. I guess it depends on the person. I had been with my boyfriend a long long time. Adoption seemed like the best thing to do at that time, but we couldn't do it when the time came.*
>
> *My doctor was telling me before I went into labor, "We aren't going to let you see him. It would be best if we just took him. We'll tell you what he is, that he's healthy, and that's it. Otherwise you might change your mind." You have to decide all over again after he's born. I changed my mind while I was in labor. I thought, "This hurts, no way. . .I'm keeping him."*

While she was pregnant, Angela apparently did not consider parenting her child. She "knew" adoption was the best plan. She made an intellectual decision and says neither she nor her boyfriend seriously considered keeping their child during that time.

If Angela and Joe had had weekly appointments with a good and caring counselor who insisted they look at both their options, they might have gone into parenting with a little more preparation. If they had been more aware of the pain which inevitably follows the release of a baby, might they have waited a few days before making a final decision?

That decision may still have been to parent, but we wonder about a life-changing decision being made by a woman in labor. This is an extremely vulnerable time for any woman. If Angela had been able to talk about her alternatives during pregnancy, her decision to parent might have come before the crisis of delivering her child.

The question definitely is not "Are Angela and Joe 'good' parents?" They probably are. However, those first two or three months were difficult for them, more difficult than they might have been if these young parents had had a little more help in looking at their alternatives before their baby was born.

## Periodic Adoption Unit Offered

In the Teen Mother Program, Cerritos, California, we offer a three- or four-day unit on adoption every two or three months in the prenatal health class. At first I (Jeanne) thought a two-week unit each semester would be good. I planned the unit carefully. I would help them understand the changes occurring in adoption today. I would schedule several speakers and a good video on adoption. We'd discuss, and we'd have reading and writing assignments. I thought I had planned well.

The first two days worked beautifully. The students were interested and responsive, and I didn't sense that they thought I was trying to talk them into anything. The third day was okay, and we got through the fourth day, but I heard a few students commenting, "Adoption again? Why do we always talk about that?" I had enough sense to turn to another topic the next day.

Because our class has open enrollment with new students coming each week, I decided to cut my carefully planned adoption unit into smaller segments. I didn't quit talking about adoption. Actually I started to bring up the topic more frequently, but for shorter periods of time.

I began by explaining, "We all probably know someone who is adopted or who has adopted a child, and some of us may know a birthmother. It's important we all know something about adoption. We need to know some reasons people may consider an adoption plan for their child, and we need to know something about adoption law in this state. In fact, it's as important to be educated about adoption as about the Civil War — and all of you have to take U.S. History and learn about the Civil War."

The Civil War comparison may help put the study of adoption in perspective, that it isn't only the individual considering an adoption plan for her child who should know about adoption. Those who are themselves adopted need to understand that adoption is a different but normal way to build a family.

They should know they were not throwaway babies. Their birthparents made the difficult decision to release them for adoption because they cared so much about them.

## Check Adoption Attitudes

You may want to utilize a questionnaire to learn something about your students' current attitudes toward adoption. A simple questionnaire is included in the Appendix, page 239. Respondents are asked about their feelings about adoption and whether they know anyone who is adopted, has adopted a child, or released a child for adoption. How does their family feel about adoption? What about the baby's father? How do they feel about continued contact with the adoptive family?

After completing the questionnaire, students are likely to be interested in hearing about open versus closed adoption. Be sure you are well informed on resources in your community. If no one in your area is willing to offer much openness in adoption, you may decide to be low-key about this possibility — or you may choose to advocate for a student wishing to make an open adoption plan.

Ask your students for possible reasons someone might consider an adoption plan for her baby. Then ask them to suggest some negative things about adoption. Keep track of their responses on the chalkboard. If someone has a negative "reason" which no longer applies to adoption ("She can't see her baby after she delivers," for example), you'll want to explain later that this is no longer true.

How do your students feel about fathers' rights? Again, be sure you know the law in your state. In most areas, the father's signature is required for the adoption to be finalized. If he can't be found, it may be possible to go ahead with the adoption, but an attorney or an adoption agency counselor should be consulted. Stress to your students the importance of getting the father's signature to guard against the adoption being broken later because the father initially was denied his right to be involved.

You will also want your students to know about agency versus independent adoption, and if private (independent) adoption is legal in your state. Presently all but six states allow private adoption.

In the first session of a brief adoption unit, you'll probably need to focus on students' feelings toward adoption. You might ask them to respond quickly to the question, "What word do you think of first when you hear the word adoption?" As you write their responses on the board, you'll gain insight into their preconceived notions about the topic and perhaps their lack of knowledge of adoption as it is practiced today.

## Prepare Your Speakers

Next you may want to talk about the changes in adoption during the past generation. Or you may decide to invite an adoption counselor to speak to your class on this topic.

As you invite speakers, it's wise to remind them they will be talking to pregnant teenagers, most of whom will be parenting their children themselves. These students don't want to hear all the reasons they should consider an adoption plan — and if an attempt is made to do so, the young people are likely to turn off and hear very little of the presentation.

I remember with horror the two men from the local adoptive parents association who came at my invitation to speak in our prenatal health class. One of them actually thanked the young women for "providing us with babies to adopt." Needless to say, the students were indignant, and rightfully so.

An adoption counselor who spoke to the class had a much better approach. When the teacher asked the counselor how she wanted to be introduced (knowing the class would include some young mothers who tended to be outspoken against adoption), the counselor responded with a smile, "Just tell them I don't want their babies!" She had no intention of implying the young mothers "should" make adoption plans. She was there to provide information and to offer support to anyone interested in looking at alternatives. She knew that most of the young mothers' interest in adoption was vicarious, not personal, and that they would be insulted if she implied they should not be parenting their children. She also knew any student considering an adoption plan would be able to contact her through the cards she would pass out to the entire class.

## Discuss Birthparents' Grief

Describe to your students or have a birthmother describe the grief that follows placement of a child. They need to understand that adoption is not the easy way out of unplanned pregnancy. They need to understand that grief is likely to continue for months. For some, it may continue for years after the adoption is finalized. Explain to them the need for after-placement follow-up, and that this is one reason many people recommend working through an adoption agency or an independent adoption service which will provide counseling during this period.

A birthparent's story can be extremely helpful in showing the realities of adoption, both the negative and positive effects.

You may also want to mention the difficulty birthgrandparents may have in losing their grandchild through adoption, and the fact that they, too, will grieve their loss.

Pregnant teenagers also need help in understanding the grief they will face whether they make an adoption or a parenting plan, according to Sharon Kaplan, Parenting Resources. "They don't usually receive help in understanding that, if they parent this child, their loss of freedom and the life style they know will also cause grief," Kaplan pointed out. "Either way, they will give up something from their lives. Many birthparents see it as either/or. 'I'll keep the child and everything will be fine' or 'I'll give it up and I'll grieve.'"

If you're teaching an adoption unit, at some point you might break your group into twos or threes. Give each group a different vignette describing a pregnant teenager. Ask each group to pretend they are the young person in the situation described. If they were, would they consider an adoption plan? Why or why not? Give them five or ten minutes to discuss, then share together among the groups. Sample vignettes are on page 240.

Perhaps the most important goal for students involved in learning about adoption is to be able to empathize with the feelings and the needs of birthparents. Discussion at this point would center on how young mothers and mothers-to-be can best offer support to a friend or classmate considering an adoption plan. Ask each participant to imagine that she is that classmate. How would she want the others to act toward her? How could they help her?

You may want to ask each student to write a paragraph suggesting what she and her classmates can do to support the student who is making an adoption plan.

Offering extra-credit reading assignments will encourage some students to learn more about adoption. *Pregnant Too Soon: Adoption Is an Option* and *Open Adoption: A Caring Option*, both by Lindsay, and *To Keera with Love* by Kayla Becker are good choices. A study guide is available for each of these books, and all are available from Morning Glory Press. Another excellent resource is *Dear Birthmother: Thank You for Our Baby* by Kathleen Silber and Phylis Speedlin (Corona).

## Respect for Others' Decisions

It is essential to create an atmosphere in which a variety of decisions can be made. Nancy Minor, Instructor/Counselor, Newport-Mesa School-Age Mother Program, Costa Mesa, California, shared her philosophy:

"In my school we develop a respect for everybody's choice," Minor explained. "That's our first step, respect for others. Everybody's decision is different, and you don't decide on the basis of what someone else has said.

---

*Our students become*
*a support group for one another*
*in spite of their different decisions.*

---

"Our students get a lot of respect here for independent thinking. We back that up with group counseling.

"Our students become a support group for one another in spite of their different decisions. They learn that this is just another decision that impacts young people. When it comes up that so and so is making an adoption plan, someone may say, 'How could she do that?'

"We say, for her, 'How could she not do that? Does she love her baby less? No, perhaps she loves it more.'

"Yesterday we saw the film, "I Want to Keep My Baby." Afterward we wrote a list of what that young mother had going for her and what she had going against her. I never put any shoulds in something like that, but what came out of our discussion was that she had so many things going against her. Because of her love for her baby, my students agreed, the baby would be better off with the new family.

"I don't say, 'How does this apply to your own life?'" Minor continued. "We don't need to do that — they do it themselves. Too often we teachers do too much of that. Instead, we use examples from newspapers and books, and we talk about how this girl came to this decision.

"I always say if you haven't considered keeping, you probably aren't making a good decision about adoption, and if you haven't considered adoption, you probably aren't making a real decision. You need to look at both sides.

"The groundwork is fostering support for each person's decision. When you say, 'How could anybody marry that creep?' or 'How could anybody adopt?' you're being judgmental. And we don't need that."

## Alternative School Was Supportive

Barbara, fifteen when she released her baby for adoption, had pregnancy-related problems at her home school. She found that changing to an alternative school helped:

*"Do you know Barbara? She's pregnant," and they'd all stare. I was in ninth grade, and the upper-classmen — it was kind of frightening what they were saying about me. That's how our school is . . .everybody talks about everybody, and if somebody's pregnant, you know the whole school knows. You might as well announce it in assembly.*

*That's mostly why I changed to the alternative school. There were other girls there that were pregnant, and I had a lot of good friends there who supported me, almost like my church friends did. I really liked it there.*

*Right away they asked me what I was going to do. I said, "Well, when I got pregnant, the first thing I thought about was adoption."*

*They said, "If that's what you want, then that's good." They were helping me out a lot. One girl whose baby was two months old said, "I wish someone had told me about adoption."*

*I got to talk to the class several times after my baby was placed with the adoptive family. They were willing to hear what I had to say, and that made me feel good. I like to talk about it to people because I know I made the right choice. When I see his pictures, it makes me happy to know he's all right. At the time I couldn't raise him, and the family I picked was older and had the environment I wanted for him.*

Lana, seventeen when her child was born, was also pleasantly surprised at the support she got from her classmates:

*I was in the teen parent program, and everybody I knew was keeping her child. I was the only one adopting and I was kind of nervous about letting anyone know. So*

*I didn't tell anybody, and they signed me up to work in
the daycare center because everyone in the teen parent
program is supposed to work there with the children.*

*I spent one day there, and I went to my counselor and
said, "I can't do this. I'm giving this child up, and I
can't do that. I'll do anything else you want me to do —
I'll help people, I'll set up daycare schedules, I'll be
Teacher's Aide, but I can't work in daycare." She said,
"That's fine, we'll work it out."*

*Finally I told everybody, and I was amazed at the
support I got. Both in the teen parent program and
outside of it, students and teachers were supportive. One
girl had a two-year-old daughter, and she told me she
wished she had been strong enough to make an adoption
decision. She said, "It's real hard and I've been having
a difficult time."*

*Then I started working hard at my schooling, trying
to make up for some of the time I'd messed around
before that.*

Unfortunately, this is not always the case in alternative
programs. Sometimes comments get out of hand and birthmothers experience a tremendous amount of pain. Joanne,
fifteen when she relinquished her baby three years ago,
remembers lots of negative feedback at her school:

*People who criticize giving him up for adoption —
they need to understand how you feel and that you're
doing what you think best for you and the baby. It's
hard when people are saying you shouldn't do that, you
did wrong. It doesn't make you feel good, and then you
start wondering, well, maybe I shouldn't have done that.
I wish the people at school had understood and not
made it a bigger deal than it was.*

## Adoptive Parent Letters Used in Class

One program has begun to increase awareness of adoption by
using resume letters received from families wanting to adopt a

child. Teacher Julie Vetica uses these letters for a class
assignment.

---

*You write a letter to your baby.*
*Explain why you want to adopt*
*and how you will parent your child.*

---

Early in the day Vetica puts the letters out on a table in the
classroom. Students ask, "Why are you showing us this stuff?"

"Just wait until parenting class," Vetica replies. At that time
each student reads one or two of the letters. Then Vetica asks,
"Which letter do you like best? Which couple would you pick
and why?"

"Generally they choose letters illustrating good parenting
plans. Then they discuss the importance of money versus good
parenting skills. Two points I make," said Vetica, "are that
parenting skills are more important than money, and that people
want different things for their children. Some want siblings,
others want pets. . ."

After the discussion, Vetica says to her class, "Okay, you
write a letter to your baby. Explain why you want to adopt and
how you want to parent your child."

Each student is asked to bring a photo of herself, and this is
included with her resume letter. Almost always someone says,
"Well, I'm just a teenager. Who would ever choose me?"

Vetica hopes somebody will say this, and she says some get
depressed because they don't think they have anything to offer
their children. "But it helps to get them going. If they're on the
border of considering adoption, they may get some counseling
help, perhaps make a plan. If they're keeping, they also need to
make a plan, a parenting plan," Vetica pointed out.

"When they come in I ask the girls to please support each girl
in her own decision," Vetica said. "Also I tell the girls who
choose adoption not to make the others feel wrong if they
parent.

"There is tremendous pressure to keep in the school, and
more and more thinking that abortion is better than adoption.
That floors me but I guess it shouldn't when you think about

how teenagers feel about pain. They wonder why they should go through this for nothing.

"I try not to do as much counseling as I used to. I try to get the kids to the professionals. I think that's real important for teachers and ministers. I think it's important to realize when you're out of your league. It's also important to get the family involved in the counseling, whatever the decision will be. I think the most successful adoptions have been when the counselor involved the whole family and the teen father as soon as possible."

## Help from Home School

Some parents are concerned that their daughter may be pushed out of school if she is pregnant. If she is attending public school, this would be illegal. If she is attending a private school which receives some funding from the Federal Government, it would also be illegal to expel her because of pregnancy or marital status. If it's a private school which receives no government funding, she and her parents should check with the administration. She needs to be in school throughout her pregnancy and afterward. If no pregnant girl has stayed in that school until her due date, perhaps it's time to push for a change in policy.

Special school programs for pregnant and parenting teens often provide special support, but not all pregnant students choose to attend such programs. Susan was a senior when she was pregnant. Although there was some pressure from the administration for her to attend an alternative school, she remained in her regular school throughout her pregnancy:

> *I think what pushed me to finish high school was when we signed up for classes. I was talking to the Dean of Students and he said, "I think it would be better if you'd go to this other school because there are a lot of other pregnant girls there. I think you'd probably be happier there."*
>
> *And I went, "Right, I don't know anybody there, I'm going to be happier there?" I think his attitude about pregnant girls going to a normal high school and how*

*that wouldn't look good to other students pushed me to*
*stay and finish high school there instead of buckling*
*under and going to the alternative school.*

*My counselor was a big help. I put that woman*
*through everything, up and down. I'd go into my little*
*session and immediately go into, "God, I can't believe*
*what they did in school today. I can't believe what*
*they're doing to me."*

*My counselor at school helped too. She wasn't there*
*all the time, but she'd send me encouraging little notes,*
*and she seemed to know exactly when I needed them.*
*Just when I was ready to quit, I'd get a note, "Hang in*
*there, Susan." She had ESP or something.*

This one sensitive counselor made all the difference in
helping Susan remain in school. Without her support, Susan
might not have made it through her senior year.

Teachers who have only an occasional pregnant student may
also want to mention the adoption alternative periodically.
Noelani stayed in her regular classes, but she received absolutely
no support for her adoption plan:

*In the Home Ec classes they don't say a word about*
*adoption, not one word. They talk about keeping your*
*baby or having an abortion. That's why my friends*
*thought it was real weird that I did what I did. That's*
*what everybody does where I go to school now — you*
*keep your baby.*

Kim is a high school Home Economics teacher whose
daughter released a son for adoption three years ago. In her
Family Relations class, Kim says they talk about teenage
pregnancy and the different options. She wants to help her
students understand that adoption can indeed be a loving option:

*Kids say, "How could I give away anything inside of*
*me?" or their parents say, "How could we give up our*
*flesh and blood?" I tell them it's a sign of maturity.*

*That's how I can look down the road and say I want
Elaine's child to have more than we could give him.
    Over and over I've had pregnant students who
would consider adoption if their families would let them.
It's not an option, according to their parents. I feel
strongly that we need to talk about this alternative.*

## How You Can Help

Whether you teach in a comprehensive high school or in a
separate program for pregnant teens, don't assume your pregnant student is going to rear her child herself, and don't assume
she is making an adoption plan. Either way, you'd be thinking
for her. Instead, if you talk about teenage pregnancy, mention
the adoption option. If you're teaching a parenting class, build in
a unit on adoption as a parenting decision. Not only will you be
helping potential birthparents in your class, but the more you
can normalize the discussion of adoption, the more likely your
adopted students will feel good about being adoptees.

Chance comments from caring teachers were reported with
appreciation by several interviewees. Judy Glynn, Axtell, Kansas, mentioned one of her daughter's teachers telling Glynn and
her daughter that his sister had been pregnant at sixteen. He
knew how hard it was on a family, but he assured them they'd
live through it. "Somehow, that helped," Glynn commented.

If you are a teacher or other staff person in a school, you have
a wonderful opportunity to be supportive when you work with a
pregnant teenager and/or her partner. Whether she's making an
adoption or a parenting plan, she needs to stay in school, she
needs good prenatal care, and she may need to alter her diet and
her lifestyle to increase her chances of delivering a healthy baby.
She also needs to consider her alternatives.

Most teenagers know little or nothing about adoption. Few
adults know the agencies available in their area, the pros and
cons of agency versus independent adoption.

A flyer containing this information can help a young woman
become informed. List the public and private agencies in your
area. Describe the services available from each one, and include
the name and phone number of a contact person for each. Also

describe services available through independent adoption and, again, list a contact person who can give your client more information.

You are supplying this young woman with information and support as she faces the most difficult decision she may ever have to make. Should she become a mother to the baby with whom she is bonding throughout pregnancy, and face the highly probable result of too little education, never enough money, a life irretrievably changed because of her early entry into parenthood?

Or should she release her baby for adoption and face the grief she will feel at losing her child, grief that may linger for a long time?

A hard decision for anyone to make and to a fourteen-, fifteen- or sixteen-year-old, it can seem insurmountable. If you work with one or many pregnant adolescents, your responsibility to help each make her own decison is a mind-boggling challenge.

We must always remember that whichever decision she makes, she is a mother who cares deeply about her baby and who undoubtedly wants the best possible life for her child. Many young women feel they can provide that "best possible life" for their children — but others need to be assured they indeed have the option of adoption.

# CHAPTER 9

# Support Through Alternatives Group

*The thing I liked about the group was the sense of caring, taking time out to help and reaching out to people in tough situations. (Lorna, 21)*

*Everyone shared their feelings. No one seemed embarrassed about anything and everything was kept in the group. (Joy, 16)*

*I liked the group most of all because everyone cried together and laughed together. (Katy, 14)*

*I never opened up such sensitive and deep feelings before. I always kept everything to myself. It made me feel good, like I really was worth something when I talked. (Francene, 20)*

Peer acceptance is extremely important to most teenagers. Healthy, normal adolescence means less involvement with the family and more with peers.

Pregnancy and parenthood often affect peer acceptance. A pregnant teenager experiences obvious physical differences and less obvious emotional and psychological differences that may separate her from her peers. The demands of motherhood change her ability to relate. After childbirth, young mothers often report a sense of feeling different from their peers.

Because of her need for peer acceptance, a young woman may do whatever is necessary to gain acceptance from her peer group. If she's part of a program with other pregnant and parenting teens, she's likely to find acceptance there.

If she's considering an adoption plan, she still has the same needs. She, like all teens, wants the acceptance of her peers. She is vulnerable to their comments and alert to their choices. The fact that she's considering a different choice places her in a different category from the others. Her peers who are keeping their babies are likely to point out these differences. Their remarks may be quite innocent and non-malicious and may change to support if a dialogue occurs. Occasionally, however, remarks may be intentionally cruel and, regardless of the intention, they may alienate. If this happens, keeping one's baby may appear to be the key to acceptance in the "in-crowd."

It is highly advisable to form another sub-group of expectant teenagers, a group consisting of young women who are serious about consciously exploring their alternatives. They don't all need to be making adoption plans; rather, they should be a group with a common desire to work through their decisions and be willing to support each other in that process.

The importance of peer group support cannot be over-emphasized. In addition to the supportive aspects, the group can provide one another with the opportunity to gain information, give and receive feedback, and form close friendships. Such a group provides a young woman an oasis in which she can be genuine.

## Starting an Alternatives Group

An alternatives group can respond to the need for peer support. An alternatives group is different from an adoption group. In fact, the word "alternative" is not a particularly familiar term to many teenagers, but that's all right. By the time they've been coming to the group for awhile, they'll understand that word at many different levels. If you don't like the term "alternative," another label will do, but it should reinforce the concept of choice.

Weekly meetings are best. Regardless of the number attending, it's important to set aside a regular time period devoted to the exploration of alternatives. If there are times when only one or two girls attend, they should always get the same quality of attention as does a larger group. Only minor changes in the format are necessary when the group size changes.

---

*They don't have to agree
with the other person's decision.
Only support is necessary.*

---

Before beginning an alternatives group, it is important for the leader to clarify the purposes of the group. For example, is it primarily for decision-making or will other issues be discussed? Regardless of your specific focus, the group should provide participants with the opportunity to think, to feel, and to share. The format should provide for safety and support.

Two agreements are crucial in this kind of group. First, participants must commit to supporting the decisions of other group members. Regardless of what another girl chooses, her peers in the group are committed to giving her complete support for her decision. They don't have to agree with the other person's decision. Only support is necessary.

Confidentiality is the second essential. Each group member must commit to keep information shared within the group sacred to the group. This is difficult for some teenagers, especially those who have found peer acceptance through talking about one another. Participants in alternatives groups, however, are likely to keep the confidentiality agreement. This level of commitment raises the trust level rapidly and develops group cohesiveness.

Alternatives groups can be formal or informal. The pulse of the group can guide your planning. Some meetings can be devoted to exploring specific content, such as agency versus

independent adoption. Guest speakers can be planned for other
sessions. Once group cohesiveness has been established, leave
some sessions open, allowing for in-depth sharing among
group members.

If you decide to form an alternatives group, who will participate? Perhaps all program participants will be involved in this
decision. In some settings, it may be wise to make the alternatives group available only for those who are actively involved in
the decision-making process. If you choose to limit group
participation, perhaps you'll interview potential participants
before they attend the group. In this way you can screen people
and learn about their motives for wanting to participate in such
a group.

Often the program participants themselves are referral
sources. Young women who never mention an interest in
adoption to staff members may learn about the group through
their friends. Others, of course, will be referred by other staff
members.

Group work can also be done in a classroom setting. It won't
be quite as intimate or personal, but the same issues can be
raised with a mixed group. The agreement for confidentiality
will not be as strong nor will the sharing be as deep, but this
approach offers some advantages. First, it provides a mechanism
for raising issues concerning alternatives. It also provides the
opportunity to establish a policy of mutual support.

Suggestions for facilitating an alternatives group are listed in
the Appendix beginning on page 242.

## Handling Disagreements

An issue of disagreement may occasionally arise in a group
like this. Mary Lou and Tasha are an example. They participated
in an alternatives group together for several months. In addition,
they lived in the same maternity home:

> *Mary Lou was eighteen and quite mature. Tasha was
> only thirteen, far less secure, and unhappy about being
> away from home and family for the first time in her life.
> Mary Lou became a model for Tasha. Despite their age*

*difference, the two offered one another mutual support
and they developed a close and loving friendship.*

*Mary Lou had a well-developed ability to project into
the future and to visualize the potential outcomes of her
decisions. She became very clear about the fact that she
could not offer her child the kind of life she wanted
for him.*

*Tasha had a tremendous amount of turmoil in her
personal life. Her parents were going through a nasty
divorce while she was living in the maternity home. She
felt as if all that had once been secure in her life was
crumbling away.*

*Although Tasha was extremely intelligent, her
cognitive development was age-appropriate. The added
stress made projection even more difficult for her. As a
result, it was hard for Tasha to visualize what her life
and the life of her child might be in the future.*

*Tasha eventually made the decision to keep her child.
When she shared her decision, Mary Lou was upset and
heartbroken. She was worried about her beloved young
friend's future. She disagreed strongly with Tasha.*

*Tasha and Mary Lou were allowed to disagree in
group. They were encouraged to discuss their differences openly. Both cried throughout the entire process.*

*It was an honest, open, and deeply touching inter-
action, but underlying it all was that original agreement
to accept each other's decision. Not only was that
crucial to these two friends, but it was also important
for the rest of the group as well.*

*As a result, Mary Lou and Tasha were able to remain
close and to give each other the support each needed
when her baby was born.*

It is usually threatening when one's peer makes a choice
markedly different from one's own. It can promote doubts and
insecurities regarding the validity of one's own choices. Teenagers may be especially threatened because they rely so heavily
on the validation of their peers. They need help in dealing with

these feelings of differentness. The concept of mutual support is vital.

## Evaluation of Alternatives Group

We asked participants in one alternatives group to discuss their experiences. They felt strongly that the sessions met a unique need. Their comments reflected the various types of benefits they had received. When asked why they had attended, they said:

> *I attended group because it relaxed me, made me feel more like one of the others. It also gave me a chance to really open up. (Hillary, 15)*

> *I needed support and I received it from the group. (Evelyn, 17)*

> *I attended because I was going to give my baby up for adoption. During group, we talked about keeping the baby and giving it up. It really helps to talk about what we're feeling instead of keeping it all inside. (Alicia, 18)*

> *I attended because I got to see both sides of the decision I would make very soon, and I wanted the best for my child. (Janice, 15)*

The young women were then asked, "Did attending Alternatives Group help you make your decision about you and your child?" Among the responses were:

> *Attending group was very helpful. Just being able to talk about feelings I had was help enough. I went from adoption to keeping and back again. (Kathleen, 17)*

> *Group helped because we talked about both keeping our babies and adoption. Looking at both sides makes you realize which is better for you and your baby, and makes it easier to make a decision. (Jeni, 16)*

*Yes, group prepared me for what to expect and the best way to go about handling problems. (Allie, 18)*

*Yes, because I heard girls who had already made their decisions talk about them. (Shawna, 16)*

*My mind was pretty much made up, but group helped me deal with what was ahead for me. I found it wasn't so bad, and that I wasn't alone in my decision or my feelings. (Nora, 17)*

*Attending the group helped me to understand that the decision I made was best for me and my child in the situation I was in. I'm glad there was a group like this to attend. (Lucia, 18)*

## Choices Group Provides Support

Bev Short, Director of Sierra Nueva, Carmichael, California, calls her alternatives group Choices. When a young woman enrolls in this school program, Short discusses scheduling, then comments, "We have a little group called Choices. Are you thinking about keeping your baby or are you considering adoption at all?"

Usually the student says, "Oh no, I'm keeping."

Short sets the tone by replying, "Well, you know a lot of the students are planning on keeping, too, but there are always a few students who consider an adoption plan. Because there aren't many of them, it's important we give them lots of support.

"It's my observation over the years that although adoption is a difficult decision, it's probably one of the most loving and unselfish decisions a person can ever make," Short continued. "It takes a lot of courage for a girl to do that, and we need to give her as much support as we can.

"If you ever want to consider alternatives, or if you'd like just to sit in on the group each week when we talk about that option, you're welcome. If you don't want to be scheduled there all the time, I want you to know that at any time you're welcome to come in and visit."

Usually only a few students wish to be included in the Choices group, Short says. Participants include not only the young people who want to consider adoption, but also others — those who may not want to do anything else that period and those slightly interested in adoption. The only requirement is that each participant be accepting of the others and that they maintain confidentiality. "I tell them this is a very special group and we need to be very supportive," Short concluded.

Short's "Strengthening Support for Birthparents in a Teen Pregnancy Program: A Guideline for Helping Professionals" is an excellent resource for teachers presenting the adoption option. It is included in the Appendix beginning on page 245.

Another group activity at Short's school is the weekly peer counseling and panel training session. According to Short, ninety-one student panels were presented to more than three thousand students in the district's high schools last year. Most panels include a birthmother so the panel training exposes the entire group to adoption.

At this training session, several students form a panel which is videotaped. The rest of the students play the role of the high school classes they will visit. "They get to know each other well because they ask each other questions as they play the roles. Their questions are wonderful," Short explained.

## Adoption Awareness Week

When I (Catherine) was a counselor at New Futures School, we became interested in providing adoption information to all of our students. We decided to devote a week to adoption awareness.

Some of the staff were concerned that such an activity might create some unpleasant feelings. Knowing the negative feelings that many young women express about the idea of adoption, they feared there might be a rebellion among some of the students. They also wondered if there might be repercussions for the girls considering adoption plans.

At the same time, we agreed that it was the responsibility of the staff to set the tone. So, after much deliberation, we decided to proceed with caution. We called the project "Adoption

Awareness Week" because we felt this title would not be threatening. As with Rape Awareness Week or Career Awareness Week, we did not expect the topic to apply specifically to everyone. Rather, the focus was to be on information and attitudinal change. We didn't want our students to get the mistaken idea that staff was pushing for adoption planning. Rather, we wanted to help students learn more about adoption as the way some families are formed.

The outcome of the first Adoption Awareness Week was fascinating. We did not have the full scale rebellion we had feared. In fact, there was *no* rebellion at all. There was *no* anger. No one got upset. When the adoptive parents came to speak, some girls came to hear them more than once — and not just the pregnant students, but also teen mothers. The most popular speaker was a former student who had placed her son ten years earlier. The most obvious result was that students showed more understanding and support of those considering adoption.

---

*Many issues relating to adoption are also pertinent to teenagers planning to parent their children.*

---

The activity was repeated the following year with even more success. Since this is a school program, we used classes to integrate the adoption theme. We began by asking which staff members would like to participate. A few were interested in becoming involved. Each then began to explore what s/he could do in his/her particular portion of the program.

Some very creative ideas were generated. For example, in World Issues class, there were speakers on international adoption. In the Your Community course, adoption agency personnel spoke. In Civics, a lawyer discussed legal ramifications of adoption. The activities were planned to fit into the regular school day as much as possible.

Many issues relating to adoption are also pertinent to teenagers planning to parent their children. These students asked questions about guardianship and the issues involved in allowing their parents legally to adopt their babies. They were also interested in the possibilities of future husbands being able to adopt their children.

Surprisingly, a few staff members were quite ambivalent about these activities. Some admitted they were afraid to deal with the prospect of grief and loss in the students. A few did not believe in adoption. In order to deal with this sensitive topic, the staff needed help in dealing with their own feelings. Another component was developed, an in-service on adoption awareness for the staff.

One word of caution: If you plan an adoption awareness activity, screen the guest speakers carefully. It is essential that their focus match yours. They are not there to coerce the young people or to convince them that adoption is the best choice. Their purpose is to educate and to assist in expanding the students' awareness.

Students tend to be accepting of what the staff feels is important. If we truly believe that awareness of alternatives is important, we will convey that to the young people with whom we work.

CHAPTER **10**

# The Church's Role In Adoption Planning

*His compassion toward the situation, talking through the various choices with me meant a lot. I guess what he did was give me the tools to work with. He helped Katheryn and me know how to look at the pros and cons of keeping and adopting, not only for Katheryn, but for the baby and for me.*

*He also helped me go through the grief process again. You need to understand that the birthfamily is going through a grieving process in the beginning, grief for what might have been. Then when the adoption plan is made, you face more grieving, this time for the child you are losing. (Birthgrandmother)*

Traditionally, people have turned to their clergy for help when they face crises in their personal lives. When there's a birth, a wedding, illness, or death, many of us call our priest, rabbi, or minister.

Does this reliance for help from one's church or synagogue extend to those facing problem pregnancy? The answer is mixed. One suburban minister said he hasn't seen a pregnant teenager in twenty years, while a pastor at a church in the same general area operates a full-fledged adoption ministry through his church.

## Religion and the Public Sector

Helping professionals in public schools and other public agencies are generally sensitive to the issues of church and state separation. This does not mean they have to deny the helpful role churches can play in crisis situations with families who have a religious orientation. For these families a problem pregnancy can be a spiritual crisis as well as a physical, economic, and emotional trauma.

A direct way to get at it is to ask the family, "Do you have a minister (priest or rabbi) with whom you can share your feelings?" "The answer I dread most," observed Rev. Lois Gatchell, Episcopal Deacon, Tulsa, Oklahoma, "is, 'We wouldn't want people in the church to know about it.' There is something wrong with a congregation whose comfort level is measured by a lack of human problems. I think churches were meant to be helpers of lost souls, not clubs for the righteous.

"Most clergy would respond in love to families experiencing a difficult pregnancy, but many times they feel inadequate," Rev. Gatchell said. "The public information efforts of agencies can help them. Clergy need to be assured that the problems they face constantly, i.e., grief, guilt, denial, hopelessness, are the same with the problem of unwanted pregnancy as with other human ills. If religion offers comfort, forgiveness, hope, faith, and love, then it has immense resources for a family in crisis. It is not a quick fix. It takes effort and time on all sides, but the church or synagogue can be very useful in problem resolution."

Because the family often sees their clergy person first, the church or synagogue plays an important role in problem pregnancy decision-making. "Often they go in the direction their clergy sends them," commented Sharon Kaplan, Parenting Resources, Tustin, California. "Some families are welcomed, but others feel rejected. When rejection happens, we must deal with the birthmother who feels she has lost not only her boyfriend and perhaps her family, but also her religion.

"I often call on the clergy to help a young lady heal," Kaplan continued. "I always ask her what her religious beliefs are, and often I hear she hasn't even been able to pray because she is so ashamed of what she has done to her family. There are churches which have been very castigating and haven't welcomed back someone with an untimely pregnancy. I think the clergy often are the real players in whether this birthmother comes out of this feeling okay about herself, and whether she will stay connected with her family and her religion.

"I don't know many counselors who talk about religion in their counseling, but I think this may be crucial. I don't know that anybody can make a decision about a baby without taking into account their basic belief system," Kaplan concluded.

## Some Churches Aren't Involved

Many churches don't appear to be much involved in problem pregnancy counseling. One minister said, "Sometimes we tend to say we don't have the problem here. . .we don't have a divorce problem, we don't have problem pregnancies in our congregation. Of course, when we say that, we're sticking our heads in the sand."

"Twenty years ago there was a tendency to keep too-early or single pregnancy quiet, but I hope that's changing. Some of the more rigid churches appeared to 'cast these women out' — not literally, but it might have seemed that way because it brought shame on the group," Rev. Elwood Wissmann, United Methodist Church, Dana Point, California, pointed out. "The pregnant women and their parents tended to be quiet about it because they didn't know what their church would do. We can't be supportive if we aren't aware there's a problem.

"Beyond professional counseling, there needs to be a support community which is broader than just counseling. Hopefully the church can be that support community," Rev. Wissmann added.

Rev. Dennis Adlof, St. Luke's United Methodist Church, Enid, Oklahoma, observes that generally in the case of teenage pregnancy, the family decides to care for the baby. "I think being supportive is the main thing," he said. "They're going through enough guilt, enough feelings of failure already. I'd try to understand their situation and attempt to answer whatever questions they have. Usually they'll come up with the questions, their own points of concern, if we listen carefully.

"I've heard others try to place a heavy theological and ethical system on people dealing with problem pregnancy. I don't think that's helpful. We need to be supportive, lay out the options, and help them make their decision," he suggested.

A minister whose daughter became pregnant at sixteen reported the rejection they faced at the Christian school she had been attending. The administrator said she must check out of school but her parents felt she needed to continue her education at that school. "I've had a tough time with this," her father reported. "I met with the superintendent. I asked to meet with the school board and was brushed off several times. Finally my daughter said, 'Daddy, it's not worth it. Let's drop it.'

"I called the superintendent. I thought this would touch him, but instead, he was pleased to learn he no longer had a problem. The interesting thing is that when his son was in worse trouble, they managed to get him back in school. My whole family was hurt by this school's rejection."

## Minister Expresses Strong Opinions

"Unfortunately, some ministers perpetuate the myth about adoption — 'You fooled around and got pregnant. Now you ought to do the right thing and keep the baby,'" said Rev. Don Mohlstrom, Associate Director of Circulation and Marketing, *United Methodist Reporter,* Dallas, Texas. "That's unfortunate," he continued, "because ministers who feel this way don't think of the needs of teenagers. They believe the American myth that every woman wants to be a mother."

Rev. Mohlstrom has worked in a problem pregnancy clinic in California and has taught problem pregnancy counseling classes through University of California, Riverside, extension service. He stressed that any minister with a youth or singles program in the church must deal with problem pregnancy eventually.

He's concerned about "the terrible ignorance about adoption procedures" that he feels exists among the clergy. "They want her to do the 'right' thing and place the baby within the congregation," he said.

Illustrating Rev. Mohlstrom's concern is the birthgrandmother who reported mentioning to her pastor that her daughter was making an adoption plan. His response was, "My brother wants a baby." The birthgrandmother reported:

> *I said, "Okay." But my daughter wanted contact with the adoptive family, and I started thinking how ignorant some people are about the birthmother's feelings. I knew Hilary would be going through depression later. I wanted her to be able to pick up the phone and say, "How is my baby?" although I realized she might not have that close a relationship.*
>
> *I had these questions, but our pastor was really busy at the time. . .we went back to the counselor we'd been seeing who had time to talk with us. She helped us choose a family.*

"When we had the clinic, we referred only to established agencies," Rev. Mohlstrom continued. "I think that's important, rather than placing the baby with a family within the church. Agencies are the experts, and we need to call on them for help.

"I got called to the hospital once when a young mother who had planned an adoption changed her mind. Her minister was there with her saying, 'But this couple has already paid your expenses.' The guilt he was pouring on her. . .I think a lot of people don't understand adoption loss and don't know how to deal with it.

"Any minister who feels there is something wrong with the girl for being pregnant in the first place should refer her to someone else," Mohlstrom added.

## Clergy Wants to Help

Rev. Linda Pickens-Jones, Program Director, Los Angeles District, United Methodist Church, commented, "The frustration

is that so often people don't want the minister to know anything.
People tend to be protective of the minister on all kinds of
issues. They don't talk about their problems. I wonder how we
can set a climate for people to feel open, especially about
problem pregnancy. People are so fearful of being judged.

"At least from the mainline clergy, I don't think people are
going to be judgmental. They really want to be present in the
struggle, in the decision-making with families. They want to
listen, to give feedback, to be a safe place to come to, a place to
get referrals."

Rev. Pickens-Jones continued to express her frustration.
"When you get to real-life issues, people can't seem to figure
out how the church has anything to do with it. They think if the
church gets involved, it will be judgmental. They haven't sorted
out that religion is all about love, forgiveness and whole life.
The whole issue is a love issue, not a shame issue. They can't
quite figure out why a minister would be involved. So ministers
have to find some way to be available without being pushy.

"Ongoing education is important. We already have programs
and discussions, and some of them should deal with these
sexuality-related issues. This can help set an atmosphere of
concern and caring."

## Priest Supports Adoption

Rev. John P. McAndrew, Associate Pastor, St. Irenaeus
Catholic Church, Cypress, California, acknowledged that some
priests may come from a sexually repressive background and
can see sexuality only in terms of sin. He commented, "Coming
out of that background they may see any deviation from the
norm as sinful. People are hurt by these attitudes, and I don't
think we as a church should support this kind of thinking."

Father McAndrew feels that adoption is the decision most
clergy would support. While the church used to push marriage
when a young couple became pregnant, more often now they
will say, "Don't get married just to give the child a name."
When Father McAndrew talks with a pregnant teenager or an
older woman with a problem pregnancy, he offers the support of
the church and suggests ways of meeting her various needs such

as housing and counseling. "I can be a minimal support, but they don't often look to the clergy for much help," he admitted.

---

*If we come off as condemnatory,*
*we lose, everybody loses.*

---

"In talking with the clergy, it's important that the teenager and/or parents find someone with whom they are comfortable," Father McAndrew advised. "You don't have to go to that person who seems judgmental and not very helpful. The general stance of the Catholic Church is that we need to be pastorally available for support. If we come off as condemnatory, we lose, everybody loses. We take people where they are, not where we think they ought to be. If I can take them where they are and allow them to answer their own questions and find resources with them, then I might be able to help."

Judy Glynn, a birthgrandparent who received counseling from an adoption agency, mentioned the different ways two priests dealt with her daughter's pregnancy:

> *One priest never mentioned it and never came to see us, but we felt he spoke to us from the pulpit. His message was, "You're okay, you're loved no matter what is happening in your life."*
>
> *The other priest came to our church two weeks before our grandson was born. We stayed after church his first Sunday and my husband said, "Father Dennis, are you aware our daughter is pregnant and about to deliver?"*
>
> *After Scott was born, Father Dennis came down the aisle that Sunday with his hand out, a big smile on his face, and said, "Congratulations on the birth of your grandchild." It took me back a little, but it also gave me the message that this was something to be excited about. I appreciated that.*

Glynn also mentioned a Protestant minister in her small town who found an opportunity quietly to tell the birthfamily that he was praying for them and that he admired their courage. "That was one of the nicest things, because it is so easy to doubt yourself at that time. Just a simple comment can do so much," Glynn commented.

"The response of the people in the church makes a big difference," she observed. "Generally those people who don't say anything don't know what to say. They can still go out of their way to express support, perhaps just a touch, or talking with us."

Lois and Brad were horrified when their fifteen-year-old daughter told them she was pregnant. Lois described the help they received from a priest:

> We talked and talked and talked with Elise and Jimmy. At first they wanted to get married but we felt they were entirely too young.
>
> The kids agreed to talk to an outsider, someone not caught up in all our turmoil. Brad has a friend who is a priest, although neither of us is Catholic. They've been friends for a long time and Brad has a lot of respect for this man. So we all went to see him, the kids, Jimmy's parents, and us.
>
> The priest talked to all of us, and he talked with the kids individually. He gave them the pros and cons and asked what they thought would be best for the baby. He helped them see they weren't ready for marriage or the responsibilities of parenting.
>
> That was the first time Elise and Jimmy considered adoption. And that's what they did. Now, two years later, Elise feels it was a good decision.

An example of a concrete way a clergyman can present the adoption alternative was described by a sixteen-year-old birthmother. She reported feeling extremely negative when her parents suggested adoption. She changed her mind after spending several hours with a birthmother who had recently released her child. The two met through their church at the pastor's suggestion. "That evening made all the difference in the world to me," said the young woman who, four months later, released her daughter at birth.

## "Don't Ask Questions!"

Rev. Fred Trevino, United Methodist Church, Tucson, Arizona, offered realistic advice to clergy people: "First step is to keep your mouth shut and try to discern what's happening on a feeling level. Don't ask questions because that might be interpreted as being judgmental. If the person is carrying any kind of guilt feelings, they'll emerge, but first you need to build trust with that person. Listen to what's going on, no judgments.

"Part of that listening is dealing with the alternatives. If she doesn't raise the alternatives issue, we need to. That's part of it. I feel I must bring up adoption as one of the options. Adoption needs to be understood."

Rev. Trevino mentioned baptizing a fourteen-year-old's child recently. "Her parents brought the young woman in to see me soon after they realized she was pregnant. She was scared to death," he recalled. "First we talked about what choices she had. She said, 'Well, I want to keep my baby.'

---

*Who will care for that child?*
*There has to be some reality.*

---

"'Why do you want to keep the baby?' I asked. I was very clear about raising possibilities about what it would mean to her, her lifestyle, what it would mean to her education and to the baby. Then I had a session with the parents. If you're fourteen, you can't make that decision realistically without your parents' input. Then we all met together. That was a long and painful session. What it came down to was that she did want to keep the baby. So I felt it was my responsibility to deal with the parents. They have agreed to do some things and she has agreed to do some things. I hope it works out.

"Sometimes grandparents get clobbered in terms of their long-term commitment to this issue," Rev. Trevino continued. "If the kid can't make it alone, is going to school, has to get a job, who will care for that child? There has to be some reality.

There's a lot of emotion involved in knowing that's my body, my baby, my decision. Somehow we need to deal with that lovingly and creatively. If you have to raise those grandkids, okay, but what if you don't want to?"

## Youth Group Offers Support

Young women sometimes report they feel out of place at their church during their too-early pregnancy. Connie, however, found the greatest support among her friends at church:

> *Mostly I do things with church people because I feel more comfortable around them. And that didn't change while I was pregnant. They weren't embarrassed being around me.*
>
> *That scared me a lot at first. What if they wouldn't want to take me out because I'd be big and I couldn't do everything? But they didn't care. They helped me a lot, my youth pastor and other people in the church. They gave me a lot of support and that made me feel good.*
>
> *It wasn't like at school where everybody, when they talk to you, they stare at your stomach instead of talking to your face. At school I wouldn't walk by the main lounge where everybody sits at lunch because if I did, everybody would stop talking and stare at me.*
>
> *At church, it was different.*

Several of our interviewees mentioned appreciating the peer support they received in their church groups, groups composed basically of non-pregnant teens. It appears that the youth group leader encouraged an attitude of acceptance and support for these pregnant teenagers. This gave them a place to participate in activities with age mates without having the pressures they found at school.

## Importance of Updating Resource Information

Several ministers recommended that clergy keep an up-to-date resource listing of adoption agencies and other people involved in alternatives counseling. Knowing as much as possible about these resources and these people is important. Which adoption agency seems most tuned in to the needs of birthparents? If she prefers independent adoption, which adoption attorney in your community insists on counseling for birthmothers? Is there a good independent adoption service in your area?

What degree of openness is encouraged in your community? Does the agency or private adoption service permit the birthparent(s) to choose the adoptive parents? Are arrangements usually made for exchange of letters and pictures after the adoption is final? How about other continuing contact between birthparents and adoptive parents?

Asking these questions does not imply that every client wants a specific kind of adoption, or that you would tell each one what she should do. It simply means that clergy will be better able to provide the kind of help she wants and needs if they know what's available in their community.

"The more informed clergy are on current practices and resources regarding adoption, the more help they can be in counseling birthparents and their families. Periodic seminars held jointly by agencies serving parenting teens and those offering adoption services (if they aren't the same) would ultimately improve the role of churches in the process," according to Rev. Gatchell, founding director of the Margaret Hudson Program for pregnant and parenting teens in Tulsa, Oklahoma.

"We're starting to reach out to the clergy and help sensitize them to adoption issues," reported Kathleen Silber, co-author, *Dear Birthmother*, and Associate Director, Independent Adoption Center, Pleasant Hill, California. "Many churches are generally opposed to abortion. They may offer no option other than parenting the baby when the mother may not be financially or emotionally prepared to do so. If the pastor has any knowledge of adoption at all, it is usually of traditional adoption.

"It's important to educate the clergy about some of the dramatic changes that have occurred in adoption so they can present these alternatives to women who come to them in crisis," Silber continued. "We're educating clergy about open adoption both from the standpoint of birthparents and infertile couples. Generally the image in the community is that there are no babies, or that it will take years and years to adopt a child. Yet most of our families have babies within six months."

Silber has a long history of working with clergy, having done so for ten years as Regional Director of Lutheran Social Service, San Antonio, Texas.

## Pastor Offers Counseling Suggestions

Pastor Norman Cluck, Lighthouse Christian Center, La Mirada, California, described his response to problem pregnancy calls: "Almost always it's the teenager's mother who calls me. They'll come into my office and we'll talk and cry together. When she calls, the first thing I do is pray. Then I make sure I have the resource information they may need.

"How can I comfort these people? That's what they need right now — comfort. They need me to go over there and be their pastor. They don't need a heavy, somebody coming in and saying, 'Oh, the Jones have been wanting a child for years.' No, they need reassurance at this point. The young woman needs to know you don't reject her as her pastor. Your opinion of her hasn't changed.

"That first visit would be a time to give reassurance and support. Then as I'm leaving I'd say, 'Let's get together real soon. Why don't you call the office and make an appointment? Let's talk about it a little further, talk about your plans.'

"If she comes in again, whether with the whole family or by herself, I say, 'What have you been thinking? How do you feel we ought to work through this situation? What is the best possible scenario for this baby?' I always bring up adoption in a positive way. If they don't consider adoption, however, we need to help them work out a parenting plan. Who will be in charge? There are a lot of questions to ask at that point.

*There is no substitute for love,*
*whether you're her pastor,*
*her parents, or her friend,*

"This might take several sessions, and at no point should we cut ourselves off from them. We need to keep the door open."

Pastor Cluck also gets calls concerning problem pregnancy from young women who are not members of his church. "We need to handle all of the children of God with the same care whether they are church persons or not," he commented.

"When you're working with a woman who is trying to deal with her problem pregnancy, there is no substitute for love, whether you're her pastor, her parents, or her friend," he concluded.

## House of Ruth Ministry

House of Ruth is the adoption ministry branch of Calvary Chapel, Downey, California. It's an independent adoption service focusing on open adoption. Needs of the birthparents are paramount.

Karyn Johnson, wife of the Calvary Chapel pastor, started the adoption ministry in 1979. A birthmother herself, Johnson was — and is — convinced that closed, secret adoption doesn't serve the needs of the birthparents or anyone else in the adoption triangle. Birthparent clients at the House of Ruth may look through as many adoptive couple resumes as they wish, and may interview several of these couples until they find the "right" parents for their child.

Karyn and Jeff Johnson are fairly young, exude charisma, and are extremely enthusiastic about their adoption ministry. The church sponsors sheltering homes for single pregnant women, and they are building an apartment complex for single mothers.

"We say House of Ruth is an adoption ministry, but adoption is the last thing we'll share with the girl," Johnson commented. "First of all, we want her not to abort. Then we want to work with her. Can she keep the child? Can the father take the child? Is there anybody who could have this child within the birthfamily? If not, then we talk about adoption.

"Often I think the clergy are too opinionated," she continued. "They're likely to say to a girl, 'Why don't you just put your baby up for adoption and go on with your life?' But adoption is not for everybody. It's not a pat answer. It's tough on everybody emotionally.

"It's not something that naturally happens like having a baby. It's something you work through, and there is a need for it now. If you're going to deal with the abortion issue, you've got to deal with the adoption issue."

Counseling is a crucial part of the House of Ruth ministry. "We try to get the younger ones to understand this is a long-term thing," Johnson explained. "We have very few who break the adoption, probably because we always ask first what we can do to help her keep her baby. Does she need money? Food? A place to live? Our work is not to push adoption. Our birthmothers are so well informed of their rights that I tell them, 'You'll know more about adoption when you leave House of Ruth than do most attorneys.'"

Rev. Jeff Johnson sees the adoption ministry as an obvious one for the clergy. "Once you take the step to get involved in adoption, it's neat because you're going to go all the way with that family. You're going to work with the mother, with her parents, with the baby, and with the adoptive parents. Who is better at doing this than a pastor? That's his job, to look after his flock, to lead people to solutions."

To reinforce their insistence that birthparents come first in adoption, Pastor Johnson related, "We tell the adoptive parents right up front, 'We know you don't want to hear this because you'll bond with your baby immediately, but there's something you must never forget. In California birthparents may change their minds several months after the baby is placed with the adoptive parents. Until that adoption is final, you are baby-sitting, and you might lose your baby. It could happen.

"If it does, it will hurt a lot but you'll live through it. Most of the time this doesn't happen, but in any case, being sensitive to the needs of your child's birthparents is part of parenting."

## Rabbi Stresses Love and Support

"Placing a baby for adoption is a real act of love and nobody should ever lay a guilt trip on the mother. This is something clergy need to know," Rabbi Michael Gold, Pittsburgh,

Pennsylvania, insisted. Gold is the father of two adopted children and author of *And Hannah Wept* (The Jewish Publication Society). He writes (page 224), "We must tell society that every adoption placement begins with two acts of love. It is an act of love when a birthmother places a baby and an act of love when strangers accept that baby into their home and hearts."

"It's very very important for any clergy person to avoid any message of judgment. It's done. Now how do you help that young woman?" Rabbi Gold asks.

## Church Ministers to "Churchfamily"

Orangethorpe United Methodist Church, Fullerton, California, uses the term "churchfamily" to signify the caring concern members have for one another. What better place could a woman find for discussing her problem pregnancy and looking at her alternatives than within her churchfamily?

Pastor Cluck of the Lighthouse Christian Center, who offered the counseling suggestions on page 184, faced the problem pregnancy issue very personally when his seventeen-year-old daughter told him she was pregnant. He recalls that he said nothing for nearly an hour after she told him.

"When I finally got my thoughts together, I assured her of my love and of my support. I said that whatever we were going to do, we would do as a family. Whatever the consequences, we would go through it together."

That seems an appropriate response for the clergy to make to any woman's concern about her untimely pregnancy — assure her of the love and the support of her churchfamily.

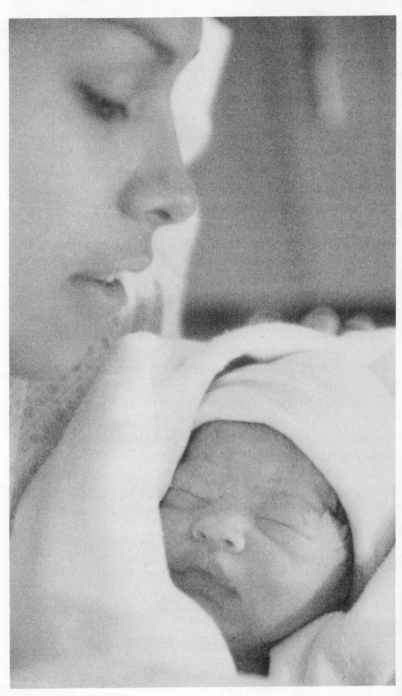

Photo by David Crawford

# CHAPTER 11

# Hospital Staff —
# How to Help

*Several years ago Shauna made an adoption plan.
She didn't think she wanted to see her baby so they put
her in the surgical area. A few hours later she decided
she'd like to see her baby after all, but she wasn't
allowed to. The nurse said she couldn't because she
wasn't in the maternity wing. Shauna said she would
walk over there, but they wouldn't allow her to do that.*

*So she kept the baby. Perhaps she would have
anyhow, but I feel she might have gone through with the
adoption plan if she hadn't felt she had completely lost
control of the situation. (Julie Vetica, teacher)*

Hospitals may need help from adoption specialists to clarify
their roles and establish procedures which will support rather
than inhibit the adoption process. Nurses may not know about
adoption agencies. They may not realize the changes occurring

in adoption practices. Sometimes hospital staff may view social workers as bad people coming in to take birthparents' babies. Adoption agency personnel and other adoption facilitators need to provide in-service on this topic.

## Pressure from Hospital Staff

Pam Peevy-Kiser, R.N., formerly with the Margaret Hudson Program, Tulsa, Oklahoma, worked occasionally in a local hospital's post-partum ward during the years she was the nurse at Margaret Hudson. "I'd talk to the people at the hospital, and then the next week I'd be back with one of our students. I was appalled at some of the things going on.

"Things were happening, such as not allowing the birth-mother to see her baby, not because they were deliberately hurting the patients, but because that was the way it had always been. For example, 'No show, no report' was a blanket label they'd give birthmothers as they came in.

"If someone asked for the birthmom, the staff said she wasn't there. 'No show, no report' told the staff she was placing the baby for adoption."

Kristi delivered her baby six weeks before she graduated from high school. She went on to college, and graduated last year. Kristi is now a social worker in the state of New Mexico. She remembers the "No show, no report" times:

> I got a lot of pressure while I was in the hospital. I had an emergency C-section. An hour after I was out of delivery and in my room, the hospital administrator called and asked when I would sign the papers.
>
> The baby was early, I wasn't with it, I was bonkers. I wasn't scared, not upset, just not there. At that point I threw the phone at my mom. She told him, "Just leave her alone."
>
> I remember the nurses in the hospital being real bad. I told one nurse I wanted to go downstairs and feed him, and she said, "You can't." She was real cold, real callous. She said if I wanted to feed him, I should be in the maternity wing.

> *I also had a problem with the way the hospital
> handled people who came to see me. It was all hush
> hush, and I didn't even exist in that hospital. My best
> friend had trouble finding me, and they told her she
> couldn't come to see me. My mom had seen her outside
> and brought her back to the room. Because of all this, I
> decided to keep him, but a few hours later I decided to
> go ahead with the adoption.*
>
> *At the time I was so vulnerable. Those things made it
> a bad experience, those stupid, petty little things.*

Radonna Tims, R.N., worked several years in labor and
delivery at a Tulsa hospital. Now she is the nurse in the
Margaret Hudson School in Tulsa, Oklahoma. She remembers
knowing very little about adoption when she was at the hospital,
and she feels strongly that hospital staff play a crucial part in the
birthparent's hospital experience.

"One very young birthmother had lots of emotional problems, no family support, and she was very immature," Tims
recalled. "She made an adoption plan and appeared to be at
peace with her decision. The day after delivery, she was waver-
ing, and we talked about it. Then I talked with the head nurse
and realized she thought Jeni should keep her baby. If Jeni did
relinquish, she should be placed on a different floor at the
hospital and she shouldn't see her baby, according to this
woman.

"Her attitude had affected her staff. They resented taking the
baby out of the nursery, and at the same time they couldn't see
how Jeni could give up her baby.

"After we talked, the atmosphere improved somewhat. Jeni
spent time with her baby, and she carried through with her
adoption plan."

Now Tims often coaches students through labor and delivery.
"At least two of our students have decided against adoption
because of something said at the hospital," she reported. "Pati-
gayle, for example, was sixteen and a little rebellious. When she
was told, 'You don't see your baby,' she knew that wasn't right.
So she decided not to place her baby."

The mother of course has a right to her baby while she's in the hospital. That baby is hers and she is the only one who has any say until she signs adoption papers. This is not always clear to the staff because they tend to do only what the doctor writes.

"I know now how much we needed in-service on adoption when I worked in labor and delivery," Tims concluded.

Sometimes a woman comes in for labor and delivery who has received no prenatal care. Tactfully mentioning the adoption alternative at this point might be helpful. One nurse brought up the subject with a woman in her twenties who obviously had been denying the fact that she was pregnant. When her labor started, she could deny it no longer.

When the nurse asked if she had considered an adoption plan, she said, "I've thought about it and I've thought about it, but nobody ever mentioned it to me before."

The nurse immediately called the hospital social worker who explained to the woman the social services available for her and her baby. In addition, the social worker suggested she might like to call an adoption agency counselor. The woman did so, and the next day decided on an adoption plan for her child.

## In-Service for Hospital Staff

"I've been doing in-service in several of our hospitals," Peevy-Kiser reported, "and one of the first things I discuss is that we can't say anyone is definitely going to place her baby for adoption until six months down the road when it's final. We say 'She is considering adoption.'

"If she's told "No show, no report" is an option for her, she may choose it and she may not. The important thing is that she be in charge."

Peevy-Kiser described one situation in detail, a situation which almost changed the outcome of a young woman's adoption plan:

> *Penny was a senior, a bright girl, very goal oriented. She probably called me six times within the twenty-four hours after her baby was born, changing her mind with each call. She was going to keep the baby, she was*

*going to place him. . . I visited her, and each time she
made a different decision, I'd say, "That's fine, Penny.
This is your decision."*

*Penny wanted her baby to room in with her and that
raised a fuss among the nurses. Then she decided to
breastfeed her baby while she was in the hospital, and
that upset the nurses terribly because they "knew" this
would make her change her mind. I sat down with the
nurses and talked for a couple of hours. I tried to help
them understand that if Penny did change her mind, she
probably would have anyhow, and we'd better find
out now.*

*The next morning Penny, who had decided the night
before to keep her baby, changed her mind again. She
called me and said, "I have decided to place him for
adoption. I'm very tired and I'm ready to go home." She
also told me the attorney was there (it was 7 a.m.)
together with a hospital administrator, and they had told
her she couldn't go home until she had signed the
adoption papers!*

*I said, "Penny, give me 15 minutes and I'll be there."
I pulled on my jeans and rushed over. There were these
two guys sitting there, and Penny said, "I have changed
my mind. I'm going to sign the baby over to you"
(meaning me).*

*I took the attorney and the administrator out into the
hall and I said, "Tell me what legal grounds you are
basing this on, telling her she can't be discharged from
this hospital until she signs those papers."*

*They didn't say anything so I continued, "You know
this is illegal. You can't do this. I know you can't and
Penny knows you can't." I turned to the attorney and
said, "Let me guess. I'll bet you have the adoptive
parents out in the waiting room. Do you?"*

*He sullenly replied, "Yes."*

*I said, "What a cruel thing to do. And you know that
when Penny is in front of the judge and she tells him this
happened, this adoption will break down. You're about*

*to lose this baby, but I don't think you will if you back
off and give her time to make decisions. If you don't,
she's going to walk out of here with her baby, not
because she wants to, but because she needs to be in
control of the situation."*

*They said, "Okay, you work with her."*

*I went back in the room and said, "Penny, why don't
you go home and get some rest?" She did, and the baby
stayed in the hospital.*

*Three days later she called me and said she was
ready to go to court and sign the papers. She went to
court and she was okay. She simply needed to be in
control of her situation.*

Penny's counselor was assertive enough to help Penny
through the hassle she was getting from the attorney and the
hospital administrator. Penny's story, however, demonstrates the
need for a birthmother to have her own attorney. The attorney
described above certainly was not working in Penny's best
interests.

Peevy-Kiser feels this sometimes happens because hospital
staff may pay too much attention to what the attorney says rather
than listening to the birthmother. "Everybody needs to remember the birthmother is in control at this pont, not the attorney,"
she cautioned.

---

*She needed to bond with her baby
before she could let him go.*

---

Hospital staff who remember the days of totally closed
adoptions, the time when birthmothers were not supposed to see
their babies, may find it difficult to understand a birthmother's
need to spend time with her baby, possibly to have rooming-in
and to breastfeed.

Nurses with this philosophy might feel that Penny was in
turmoil because she spent so much time with her baby. We
suggest that she needed to bond with her baby before she could
let him go.

"We have the same situation when an infant dies," Peevy-Kiser commented. "If you don't let that mother bond with the baby, she is never going to be able to release it and let it go. We have to remember that everybody's bonding techniques are different in terms of time and physical closeness, the actual activities that may be involved. This birthmother needed time with her baby. That was part of her working through the bonding so she could get to a place where she could release."

Perhaps hospital staff need to be reminded how vulnerable a woman is during labor and delivery and immediately afterward. She is likely to take seriously everything said by the doctor and nurses. "I don't know how you could do this" or "Adoption must be really hard. I could never do that" may be said in a caring and compassionate way, but the birthmother's interpretation is, "This must be wrong. If she couldn't do it, how can I?"

Comments like this coupled with the shame the mother may be feeling at this point can be so intense that she may decide adoption is wrong. Adolescents' immediate response to pain is to take it away, to fix it. Would keeping the baby fix it?

Julie Vetica spoke of a student who was making an adoption plan: "She saw her baby at birth, then left the hospital the next day. A day later her mother took her out to lunch. The young mother started feeling the grief, and her mom said, 'Would you like to go back to the hospital and pick up the baby?' And they did.

"That's the crucial time when the counselor needs to help her make her decision all over again, encourage her to wait a day or two to see how she'll feel. Sadly, this mother later lost custody of her baby to the father who was married to someone else. She had made no parenting plan, and things went awry," Vetica reported.

## Decision Remade After Delivery

No matter how good the prenatal decision-making is, it's merely preliminary. It's a lot easier to make that decision when she doesn't have the baby. Once the baby is here, she has to go back to zero, all the way back to where she was before she made the decision. She decides all over again after the baby is born.

This puts a lot of responsibility on hospital staff. They may not be prepared to support the patient as she makes her decision. "I think most of them feel they must protect her and they should give her input. That's not what she needs," Peevy-Kiser remarked. "What she needs is someone to listen to her.

"As nurses, we usually have answers for patients. When this young woman lies there and says, 'What should I do?' the nurse thinks she should have an answer. But you can't have an answer. You have to turn it back and say, 'I can only help you look at realistic things that may happen if you make either decision. This is real hard, but it's got to be your decision.'"

## Older Mothers Need Support Too

Everything the adolescent is experiencing is likely to be experienced by the older birthmother, perhaps even more intensely. Hospital staff may have even more trouble accepting the adoption plan of an older mother. First, they may think she should have known better than to get in that situation, and second, why doesn't she get a job and take care of her child? She needs the same caring concern so essential for adolescent birthmothers, although she may have built in a little more self esteem than is typical of younger mothers.

Marion, who was thirty-two when she released her infant for adoption, was quite outspoken about her hospital stay:

> My child was born and we spent some nice quiet moments together, the adoptive parents, the baby, and I.
> I don't like hospitals. I hate nurseries. I told them I wanted that baby in with me as much as possible and I didn't want the lights on. By 7 p.m. that night, we were gone. The baby went home with his parents and I came home here. What were they going to do at the hospital? I was going to bleed and sleep in the hospital or I was going to bleed and sleep at home.
> If it hadn't been for one nurse who came in and chatted with me, I wouldn't have known what was going on. She explained what was happening to my body. I never saw my doctor again until my six-week check-up.

*I had a birth plan everyone at the hospital was supposed to read. I wanted all of the hospital staff to mind their own business about this adoption. I wanted them to do the best possible medical job they could do, and I didn't want to hear any superfluous comments about this.*

*My attorney witnessed the birth plan. I highly recommend the use of a birth plan for anyone considering adoption. They may need it.*

## Insensitive Nurse Causes Pain

Hospitals are like any institution. A variety of personalities are involved in working with patients. Usually most of the staff are well-intentioned and supportive of the birthmother. A few staff members, however, may feel justified in letting their negative feelings reign, and will be insensitive toward their patient's needs:

*Tawanna, thirteen, had worked hard on her decision throughout her pregnancy. She decided to place her child for adoption for several reasons — her youth, her educational goals, and her family situation. The thought of losing their grandchild was painful for her parents, but they were supportive of her decision.*

*When Tawanna's son, Adam, was born, she still was certain adoption was the best plan. Her family felt extremely sad over their loss, but agreed on the proposed adoption.*

*I (Catherine) visited Tawanna Saturday, the morning after her son's birth. Tawanna and her mother, Mrs. Jacobson, wanted me to see Adam, so Mrs. Jacobson and I went down to the nursery to visit him. We knocked on the nursery door, and were greeted by the nurse. Mrs. Jacobson said she was Adam's grandmother, that I was Tawanna's counselor, and that we wanted to see Adam.*

*The nurse suddenly became stern and responded coldly, "Are you the biological grandmother or the*

*adoptive grandmother?" Shocked and flustered, Mrs.*
*Jacobson responded that she was Tawanna's mother.*
*"I'm sorry," the nurse snapped, "but only the adoptive*
*family is allowed to see this baby!"*

*I explained that no papers had been signed, and that*
*Tawanna legally was still the baby's mother. The nurse*
*relented enough to bring Adam to the window for a*
*moment. She then walked away with him in her arms.*
*Tawanna's mother was hurt and shaken. She began to*
*cry and said, "If this is the way they're going to treat us,*
*we'll keep this baby!"*

*And they did.*

*Although they love Adam dearly, the situation has*
*been extremely difficult for Tawanna, for Adam, and for*
*the rest of the family.*

When people are hurting and vulnerable, they can't defend
themselves easily from such behavior. Because of her insensitiv-
ity, this nurse adversely impacted the lives of two extended
families, the baby's birthfamily and the adoptive family who had
hoped to love, care for and parent Adam.

Fortunately, insensitive treatment of birthfamilies was not the
pattern in this hospital. In fact, the in-service director was extremely concerned and supportive when she learned of
Tawanna's pain. With her help, we staged that scene and
videotaped it for use in staff training.

Offering in-service training for local hospital staff is an
excellent approach. Especially important is including panels of
birthmothers who will share their thoughts and feelings with
the staff.

Many people simply haven't thought much about adoption. If
they have, they may either think the idea of placing a child with
another family is absolutely wrong — or they may think
adoption is the "solution" for all pregnant teenagers.

You, of course, want them to understand that adoption is an
extremely difficult decision. Help them work out a supportive
approach to their patients, an approach which *must* include
respect for the birthparents' decision.

## Nurses and the Grieving Process

Hospital nurses are trained to administer treatments and medication to relieve suffering. Generally they will tend to have the same empathetic reaction to the birthmother.

If they find her in the pain of grief, a natural reaction is to intervene. Nurses need to understand the healthiness of the grieving process so they can support her during this time without interfering.

Judy Glynn, a nurse at a small hospital in Axtell, Kansas, remembers clearly the day her fifteen-year-old daughter gave birth and released the baby for adoption:

> *The baby was born at the hospital where I work. Two weeks before she was due, I put out the grief chapter from **Pregnant Too Soon** because I wanted the staff to be aware of what my daughter would be going through. Up to this time in adoption cases, the baby had been taken out of the delivery room with the mother never seeing the baby. The curtains were pulled so it was a non-baby as far as the birthmother was concerned.*
>
> *Nurses can be most helpful by not avoiding a birthmother's room, first of all. She'll appreciate a simple "Is there any way I can help?" and then being listened to. We need to walk in and acknowledge her pain. It was one of the maids who made my daughter feel special. She brought in some flowers from another room and arranged them for her. Sometimes the maid is the only one who has time to talk with a patient, so it's important to include maids in hospital in-service.*
>
> *Having material available for the staff to read is important. It made a tremendous difference to the staff that they were able to read that chapter on grief before we got to the hospital.*
>
> *It's probably best for the doctor to write ahead that the birthmother may see her baby. Of course she has that right, but having it written on her chart might stop a potential hassle caused by someone who doesn't understand.*

## Procedures Vary with Open, Closed Adoption

Hospital staff may also have strong ideas for or against "open" adoption. One nurse commented, "We could deal more easily with adoption when I started working here fifteen years ago. Then the guidelines were clear. We knew the birthmother and her family would not see the baby. The birthmother would have few if any visitors. Her name wasn't on the board and her room wasn't listed in the directory. The birth was not announced."

Today's hospital personnel are in more of a bind. They aren't as certain about what to do and how to carry out procedures because today adoption practice varies greatly. Sometimes the whole process is very open and involves many people in the birth- and adoptive families. Another adoption may be carried out with the secrecy so common twenty years ago.

Charlene delivered her baby in New Mexico several years ago. If she had not been assertive, she would have been a victim of the old practices:

> *He was born at 4 a.m. At 7:00 when I asked for my baby, the response was, "That baby can't come out. That baby is being adopted."*
>
> *I said, "That's my baby and I haven't signed any papers yet." I kept him in my room from then on.*
>
> *I especially appreciated a nurse who came into my room late at night and talked with me. She was very supportive, and she made my hospital stay a good experience after all.*

Sometimes at Swedish Hospital, Seattle, the adoptive parents and the birthparent(s) have already met, so the adoptive parents may visit as much as the birthmother permits. If they have not met, but the birthmother gives her permission for the adoptive parents to visit the baby, they may do so when the birthparent is not with her baby. They must have positive identification from the agency or attorney that they are the adoptive parents and that the birthparent has given them permission to visit. Someone on the hospital staff must be with them while they visit the baby.

Mary Ghiglione, R.N., talked about staff support in open adoption situations at Swedish Hospital. It takes a little more time, she pointed out, to arrange to have the adoptive parents, the birthgrandmother, and perhaps others in the labor room, but for the nurse, this is only a day or two. For the birthmother patient, these memories will last the rest of her life. "Open adoption is growing, but it needs a lot of preplanning, a lot of counseling," Ghiglione cautioned.

Swedish Hospital's Open Adoption Consent form and Open Adoption Policy are included in the Appendix on pages 251 and 254. The hospital also has a formal "Adoption Procedure: Nursing Care of Families Choosing Adoption" which is distributed to all staff members. It states clearly that the birthmother is in charge until custody is granted to the adoptive parents. Included on the policy sheet are phone numbers of Seattle adoption agencies and the name of the pediatrician used by each agency. Procedures for circumcision consent, visitors to the baby and mother, and discharge procedures are included.

## Patients Make Birth Plan

Obstetrical patients at Kaiser Permanente Hospital, Bellflower, California, are often discharged twenty-four hours after delivery, according to Karen Sakata, clinical social worker at the hospital. Those who are making an adoption plan are encouraged to go over their hospital preferences well before their due date. "We go over with them what to expect when they come into the hospital, whether they want to see the baby, and if they want to be on the maternity or surgical floor," Sakata explained. "We ask if she has a son, does she want him circumcised?

"Sometimes she'll say, 'Whatever the adoptive parents want,' but she still must sign the consent. Or she may not sign because she doesn't know what they want. Certainly while she's in the hospital, it's her decision.

"We go over the hospital release form and the information they will need to complete it," Sakata continued. "We emphasize that this is not the adoption form. Here in California she can't sign the adoption papers until after she leaves the hospital. We also ask if she wants the adoptive parents to see the baby."

It is important for the birthmother and her family to approach hospital staff before delivery to discuss procedures. Will the potential adoptive parents be involved in the birth? Will they be allowed to see, hold, feed the baby? The birthmother makes these decisions because, until she signs the adoption papers, she is clearly the baby's mother. It is her right to decide who may visit and care for her baby.

Before delivery, a young woman making an adoption plan should discuss her choice of rooms with her doctor. Can she afford a private room if she wants it? If she can't, or if she doesn't think she'll want to be alone, would she prefer being with other young mothers? Or would it be less hurtful to be in a different ward?

One usually has very little choice (none, in fact) in hospital roommates, but an empathetic nurse can help create a positive atmosphere for the birthmother who is releasing her baby. It is usually best for the nurse to explain the situation to the others in the room as tactfully as possible.

Each birthmother at Swedish Hospital is encouraged to write a birth plan. She is advised to include who she wants involved in labor and delivery with her, who she wants as her coach, and the involvement she wants after delivery with her child and with other people.

She needs to state in her plan that she has the right to change her birth plan at any time. A sample birth plan is included in the Appendix on page 252.

If the birthfamily plan to be involved with the adoptive family, the hospital personnel should be notified so they can act accordingly. Otherwise, confusion is likely to occur at a crucial time.

Who is responsible for policies and procedures in the hospitals in your area? Sometimes a hospital social worker can facilitate the adoption process and act as an advocate. In another hospital the head nurse may be the best resource.

## "Can We Have Your Baby?"

Barbara Gant is a clinical social worker at Northwestern Memorial Hospital in Chicago. Formerly she was a social worker with the Cradle Society, an adoption agency in Evanston, Illinois. Gant counseled with birthparents and feels her experience with the Cradle Society helps her work harder to meet the needs of birthparents delivering at Northwestern.

Gant shared some horror stories of nurses going into a patient's room after delivery, trying to persuade her to keep the baby. "After delivery there's a lot more trauma anyway," Gant observed. "Some of it was pretty upsetting. People would come into the room and ask a lot of questions. 'How could you do this? How could you give your baby away?' There was often confusion on the part of the nursing staff as to what the rights of the mother were when an adoption was being planned. We had to advise them that the mother had complete parental rights until she signed the adoption papers — which would not be done in the hospital."

---

*Someone in the hospital said*
*they had a friend who*
*wanted to adopt a baby.*

---

A social worker in an adoption agency in a large metropolitan area reported that they discovered over a period of time that every woman delivering at a local hospital ran into the problem of the nursing staff making negative remarks about placing their babies for adoption. "Out of ten birthmothers who delivered there," she said, "only one surrendered her baby for adoption. All of them had seriously planned to do so. We complained to the hospital social worker, and she said she had repeatedly talked to the nursing staff, telling them this was not their role. Nevertheless, the problem persisted, so we quit making referrals to that hospital."

Several social workers reported that women considering adoption are often approached by someone in the hospital who tells them they have a friend who wants to adopt a baby. In one case when a young woman entered the hospital in labor, she said she wanted to place her baby for adoption. She immediately saw someone in the social service department who put her in touch with an agency.

However, she still was approached by her anesthesiologist who told her he had a friend, and couldn't they adopt the baby? She got phone calls from the people who wanted the baby. She was harassed.

The anesthesiologist and the hospital administrator in charge of policy concerning adoption were reprimanded. Nevertheless, this young woman had a very difficult situation. To have this happen in addition to what she was already struggling with was unnecessary and unprofessional.

Beth, seventeen, had an especially negative hospital stay:

> *I stayed in the hospital only two days. That was not a good experience. Because I was relinquishing him, they didn't take me to the maternity ward. That made sense, I guess, but they put me in a room with three old women who had undergone surgery.*
>
> *First, they couldn't figure out why, if I had just had a baby, I was in there with them. So I told them why. They immediately asked how in the world I could "give up a precious baby." I didn't need that and I started crying.*
>
> *I knew I had made a good decision, but those days immediately following birth are the hard ones anyhow. I didn't need that kind of hassle. I cried for several hours.*
>
> *When my doctor came in, he talked to me and told me what a great thing I was doing. That helped a lot.*

Another woman who was working with an adoption agency was put, at her request, on the gynecological floor. Because she felt lousy after delivery, the hospital social worker and the agency counselor simply pulled the curtain around her bed and talked with her in her room. Apparently her roommate overheard the conversation. After the social workers left, the other patient told the birthmother about her infertile daughter, what wonderful parents she and her husband would be, and couldn't they please have the baby?

The young woman was clear about saying no, that she was sorry but she was working with an agency. She felt good about her decision and about the adoptive family selected for her child.

Her roommate went home. The next day the birthmother had a visit from the infertile daughter who made a plea about how much she wanted the baby. The birthmother handled it well by giving the woman the name and phone number of the agency which was placing her baby. However, she should not have had to cope with this additional burden.

## Working with Patient's Counselor

What can a nurse do to help? The hospital staff needs to understand that, especially if she is working with an agency, the birthmother has her own counselor who is working with her in sorting out her decision.

It's not the nurse's job to do that. The nurse's job is to attend to her medical needs and to be supportive in whatever way she needs support. That does not mean sitting down with her and counseling her or making comments about whether her decision is right or wrong.

Nurses need to be aware of the emotional implications of surrendering a baby for adoption. It's hard for some people to understand that a mother may have a real wish to have the baby with her and to be a mother, and at the same time make a rational decision about her plan.

"People often think a woman making an adoption plan must be very unfeeling and cold," Gant pointed out. "Or if she shows any interest at all in her baby, then she is not going to follow through with adoption. I think that's where some of these remarks come from. People think that to do such a thing, she must not have any feelings."

Gant described situations where social workers have actually stalled at taking a relinquishment because they thought if they waited long enough, the mother would take the baby home. She recalled one instance in which the mother was employed, had two other children, and lived with the father of all three children. Why would she consider adoption?

"Well, she told me and everyone else that she wanted what was best for her children. Another child right now would mean she couldn't do what she wanted for any of them. She felt they would be neglected because of her working long hours. She wouldn't have enough time for her other two children if she raised this baby, too," Gant explained.

"The social workers didn't think this was a good enough reason so they slowed down on the adoption process. The mother went home, but she came back to the hospital to visit the baby," Gant continued. "They thought this meant she wanted to take the baby home. What she wanted was for him to be nurtured. She cared a lot. They couldn't understand it.

"I had talked to her for quite a while, and it was clear to me that emotionally she wanted to take him home, but she was convinced this wouldn't be best for him. I had to coach her as to what to say so she would have the right words to tell them what she was doing.

"During the time I worked with the Cradle Society," Gant concluded, "I worked with about three hundred birthmothers and about half surrendered their babies. I can truthfully say I never met a mother who didn't have some desire to keep her baby, even those who probably couldn't have handled it."

## Birthmothers' Advocates at Seattle Hospital

Mary Ghiglione, R.N., and Kathy Anderson, Coordinator, Maternal-Newborn Patient Services, Swedish Hospital Medical Center, Seattle, Washington, provide well-organized and caring services to their birthmother patients. They act as liaison between birthmothers and adoptive parents.

"While she's in the hospital, I'm pretty much the birth-mother's advocate to see that she gets what she needs from the attorneys, adoption counselors and hospital staff," Ghiglione explained. "I think it's important to know ahead of time the kind of counseling our patient has received. If she comes in and simply says, 'I want to adopt my baby out,' nurses need to assess where she is in her decision-making."

When a woman with an adoption plan enters the hospital, generally Ghiglione or Anderson meet her during labor and delivery. At that point, they assure her that her first task is delivering her child.

"Labor and delivery nurses need to realize that patients with an adoption plan still have all the choices with labor and delivery that any other mother has. I think nurses sometimes have a problem when birthmothers want to be involved with their babies. Because she is relinquishing doesn't necessarily mean she wants no involvement or that she wants a lot of involvement. It's her choice."

Recently a birthmother wanted to breastfeed her baby for three days, Ghiglione related. The nursing staff generally felt this was not a good idea because they thought this would result in too much bonding. The young mother, of course, needed to make that decision, then be supported by the staff.

Valerie, eighteen, described her feelings while she was in the hospital with her baby:

> *When I decided to release I was sure about it. Then when he was born, it was a very high experience. He was just the greatest baby. I thought he was incredible.*
>
> *I had rooming-in with him for three days and really enjoyed being with him. But I also felt I was on a clock that was ticking away. It got harder and harder each day because I knew it was going to end. But I don't think I really wavered. I knew adoption was the right thing.*
>
> *When I left the hospital I didn't want to leave him. I took him to the agency myself and told him goodbye.*

## Suggestions for Doctors

The Adoption Awareness Initiative Group, Seattle, Washington, is part of a statewide steering committee on adolescent pregnancy. Anderson and Ghiglione are active members of this group. One of the group's goals is to educate doctors on adoption, according to Ghiglione. "We're putting out a fact sheet on adoption to see what they know," she explained. "From there, we'll offer a training program. We'll have people from independent and agency adoption, one or two people from hospitals, and perhaps someone from the clergy. We'll offer a one-hour training in physician's offices."

Laurie Cooley, caseworker, Nebraska Children's Home Society, expresses appreciation to the doctors who are supportive of her clients. She writes them a personal letter:

*Dear Dr. _____:*

*I want to take this opportunity to thank you very much for coming in on a very difficult situation with Cindy. I know she appreciated your positive support through her prenatal care and delivery.*

*I also was very pleased to see how wonderfully supportive the nurses in labor and delivery and newborn nursery were. Your support and understanding as Cindy's physician was extremely needed and helpful to Cindy.*

*Thank you on behalf of Cindy and Nebraska Children's Home Society. I look forward to working with you again in the future.*

*Sincerely,*

*Laurie A. Cooley, Caseworker*

The form used with potential birthparents by Bergan Mercy Hospital in Omaha is included in the Appendix on page 249.

## NAACOG Offers Birthparent Seminar

Professional organizations are beginning to become concerned with the birthparent issue. The Nurses Association of the American College of Obstetrics and Gynecology (NAACOG) presents periodic seminars for nurses. These seminars include a session on working with birthmothers. The sessions are offered because so many nurses have said, "I don't know how to help birthmothers. I don't know what I should do. This is a real emotional issue with me."

Hospitals are intimidating to many of us. When you combine the hospital and the legal system, it can be scary, especially if you're already feeling submissive as you lie in a hospital bed. We need to help the birthmother maintain control of her life and make her own decisions. We must never attempt to take control away from her.

# CHAPTER 12

# The Grieving Continues

*The hardest part was handing her over to her new parents. My boyfriend was with me and we were cuddling. He was crying and I was crying. It was non-stop from the minute I woke up that morning until they left.*

*I went right back to school and got along there all right. Night time was the worst, going to bed and thinking about her.*

*I saw Tanya for counseling once a month afterward. Even if you didn't want to say anything, she'd get it out of you. Sometimes she made me mad, real mad. The first time I was mad and I didn't like her at all, but we've become friends since then. She'd make me start crying and then everything would come out. I don't think she meant to. It was just the way it would happen. (Cindy)*

The grieving process related to adoption planning and the subsequent loss of a child often is intense and painful. We need

to understand that grief is a healthy, normal response to loss.
The grieving process is one that moves the individual toward
healing.

We need to be concerned about those individuals who move
through the experience of loss without ever feeling the pain
associated with it. This is probably denial and means that the
feelings are being repressed. Failure to work through one's grief
has the potential for unhealthy outcomes, both emotional and
physical.

## Include Grief in Adoption Planning

Helen Magee, long-time birthparent counselor with Options
in Pregnancy, Seattle, Washington, feels strongly that grief is
interwoven throughout all of adoption: the grief of adoptive
parents over their infertility, the grief of birthparents and
birthgrandparents, and the grief of the adopted children.

Magee focused on several aspects of working with those who
are or will be grieving. She stressed that separation anxiety, loss
and grief are realities of making and completing an adoption
plan. Awareness of and assistance through loss and grief are
vital components of a successful pregnancy counseling program,
no matter what alternative is chosen.

"When clients are dealt with honestly, can identify what has
and will happen and know how to ride out the storms, they can
make it. They can come out of it whole. They can realize
personal growth from it, as can those around them," Magee
commented.

"Before an individual makes a commitment to an adoption
plan, it is vital that she be aware that grief will occur, and she
needs to have information on the grief process," Magee
emphasized.

"Awareness of the losses she has already experienced such
as change in her body shape and in herself, and parental, peer,
and partner rejection is an important stage. So is going through
anticipatory grief work regarding loss. This may alleviate the
mourning process, but it certainly does not eliminate it.

"Support persons also need preparation in order to avoid such
harmful comments as 'Forget it, put it behind you,' 'Get on with

your life,' Don't talk about it,' 'Don't correspond with the adoptive family,' 'Don't keep pictures,' 'Forget the birthfather.' These support persons also need some TLC," Magee reminds us.

## Allow for individuality in grieving styles

Make space for grief in your approach to adoption planning. It should be treated as one aspect of the total process. Educate and prepare your clients for their grief experiences, just as you would educate them for the other aspects of the adoption process.

Allow for individuality in grieving styles. During your work with a young woman, find out as much as possible about her own grieving style. Learn about the approach her family or significant others take to the process of grief.

Staff at Lutheran Social Service, San Antonio, Texas, have a series of "grief" questions for their clients to work on during pregnancy. An adaptation of these questions is included in the Appendix, page 256. Suggest that your client answer these by her/himself. The answers can be discussed in a private session or in group.

This exercise can produce several benefits. First, it provides the client with some self-awareness regarding her own grieving process and that of her family, so she has some idea of what to expect. Second, it makes the concept more real. Third, she is warned that this will probably occur for her in relationship to adoption so that she is somewhat prepared for it. Finally, it prepares *you* to deal appropriately with her grieving process. You will be better able to provide support if you have some idea of the normal grieving process for that individual and for her family.

There is a wide range of grieving styles. For some people, withdrawal is common. A young woman may choose to do her grieving alone, locked in her room out of sight of other people. In other families, it may be customary for everyone to be involved in loud crying and outbursts of pain. No style is more appropriate or "healthier" than another.

The timing of the grief also seems to be an individual matter. For some birthparents, the grieving process begins once they have decided on adoption. For others, the sadness surfaces toward the end of the pregnancy when the baby is becoming more of a reality. Still others feel very little in the way of grief until after the birth when they have seen and held the baby.

The finality of signing the papers often brings on the experience of loss. There are those whose grief is delayed for days or even months after the birth. In most cases, timing can be viewed as simply a matter of individual style.

## Rituals and Grief

Rituals are an important part of grieving. Archaeologists have found evidence of funeral ceremonies among prehistoric people. Human beings have a need to mark crises with ritual, whether it be infant baptism, bar mitzvah for the adolescent, the wedding ceremony, or the final ritual occurring after death.

Placing one's child with an adoptive family is another crisis which more and more is being marked with ritual. In open adoptions, the birthparents may formally present their baby to the adoptive parents. They may plan a service with a minister or family friend in charge. We have talked with several birthmothers whose adoption rituals involved taking their babies home for a few hours or several days before releasing them to their adoptive families.

> *Roseanne brought her daughter home from the hospital specifically to share her with her family and friends. Roseanne's mother fixed some snacks, and they had a small open house in celebration of little Shauna's birth.*
>
> *They called the adoptive parents who came over as planned. Roseanne and Doug then presented their child to her new parents. There were a lot of tears shed, but Roseanne and Doug feel this time with their daughter and their friends helped them deal with their grief.*

You may want to suggest to birthparents that they plan a dedication or presentation ceremony for their child. Such an event may help them face the reality of their loss, and at the same time, provide some precious memories.

## Grief Preparation

It is important to prepare the young woman, at least intellectually, for the grief she will feel from the loss of her child. Birthparents sometimes are angry and resentful because no one warned them of how they would feel. To minimize this grieving is *not* an appropriate approach. This actually amounts to a lie.

When you work with a group of young women, spend at least one session preparing them for grieving. Then when the first person in the group begins the grieving process, everyone will have been warned and will understand that this is normal. You'll find that the pain of one will probably be shared by all the others. This can offer a catharsis for everyone.

The first time this happened in one of my support groups, I (Catherine) was unprepared for it. I found myself frightened by the intensity of the grief one of my clients was expressing. I didn't know what to do, so I simply worked on listening to her with all of my senses and on staying caring and supportive. Soon, I found that everyone in the group, myself included, was in tears.

It is doubtful that I will ever forget that hour. It was the most painful of times. Yet, I also witnessed a profound sense of well-being come over that group after the grieving subsided. A healing happened for all of us. It was in that moment that I learned that the purpose and outcome of grief is healing.

I also learned that I often share in the birthmother's grief. It is no longer unusual for tears to fill my eyes as I see the baby of a beloved client. It is difficult for me to be completely detached when a birthmother picks up the pen to sign the relinquishment papers or holds the baby for the last time. If I have been closely involved with the young woman and with her family, I now expect to experience some of the loss with her.

At first, I was concerned about this, wondering if my role as a support person included such feelings. I have found, however, that if I am fully present for that young woman in her moment of pain, it would be dishonest for me to be other than genuine.

Over and over they have told me of their memories of me with them at those times, and that they treasure my participation with them.

To be in touch with your own feelings is one thing. To grieve with a client should never mean that you have lost control or become part of the problem. It merely means that you're in touch with the feelings going on in yourself and others. This is an important distinction that must be made. Your role continues to be that of support person and advocate throughout the process.

Cheri's counselor didn't help her through her grieving. Because of her experience, Cheri offers suggestions for other counselors who work with birthparents:

> *After my baby was placed, I talked with my counselor only once, and that was the day after I came home from the hospital. At the time I didn't think about asking for counseling. I had a real hard time that first year. I was crying every day for awhile, and I had almost no contact with anybody, teachers or counselors, during that time.*
>
> *If you can be supportive, help her go over her decision. You start evaluating again. Did I do the right thing? Encourage her to get out the list of reasons she had for deciding on adoption. I figure you have to put your emotions aside and do what's best for the baby. Encouragement and support that I did the right thing would have helped the most.*
>
> *I didn't know other birthmothers at that time, and I think a support group would have been helpful. Those who are still pregnant and those who have already released could get together and talk about it. I don't think adoption is right for everyone, but it was right for me.*

The birthparent who is not in touch with any emotions at all is in need of special help. Work with her, through questioning and conversation, to see if you can learn *why* she doesn't allow herself to feel.

This may be a lifelong pattern. It could be because of family or other outside pressure. It may be a means of self-punishment. Or it may be a sign of pathology. These women should be reminded frequently that they can seek out counseling at any time in the future. It is also fair to warn them that they may grieve this baby some day in association with another incident in their lives.

## Grieving Loss of Relationship

How can a person grieve someone she never knew? Wouldn't it be better for these young women never to see their babies? We often hear these questions.

Sharing one's body with another person is a *very* intimate relationship indeed! The maternal feelings which women experience generally begin during pregnancy. The nursing literature even has a name for it, "fetal embodiment." This is a task of normal development for the mother during the course of pregnancy.

Another equally important task for the woman carrying a child is the separation from that child at birth. They no longer share one body, but become individuals. This stage is also a normal part of the progression. Most birthmothers experience both of these phenomena. It is particularly important for them to progress as normally and as healthily through the process of childbearing as any other woman. This statement is as true for their psychological progress as for their physical. To inhibit the completion of their psychological tasks is as unhealthful for them emotionally as it would be to interfere with their biological functioning.

What they grieve is the loss of the continuation of that relationship. They are losing the opportunity to watch the child grow, to develop a relationship, to nurture that child. This is indeed a loss, regardless of whether or not they were "ready" for parenthood. Ready or not, they're still experiencing the loss of a child.

Most of the birthmothers we interviewed responded that they continue to experience emotional pain as a result of their experiences of having given birth to and relinquished a child for adoption. The amount and intensity of the grieving appears to vary considerably among individuals. For some, the grief is sporadic, while for others it is relatively constant.

---

*The most important issue was the feeling of control the birthmother had.*

---

Robin Winkler and Margaret van Keppel studied the long-term adjustment of 213 birthmothers in Australia. The most important issue, they found, was the feeling of control the birthmother had. Whether she wanted to see her baby or she didn't want to see him/her, those who healed fastest were those who knew what their choices were, knew the consequences, and got what they wanted.

"I have really come to understand that it's okay if a birthmother says, 'I don't want to see my child, I don't even want to know its sex,'" Sharon Kaplan, Parenting Resources, commented. "I'll reply, 'These are some things you need to be aware of but if, after you hear me out, you still don't want to see your baby, I'll support you.'"

Winkler and van Keppel also found that adjustment is greater in those women who were allowed to express their feelings openly and genuinely. In addition, their support persons were found to be crucial elements in the healthy adjustment of birthmothers.

The period of recovery varies from person to person. Most birthmothers report that grief is most intense immediately following the relinquishment, then gradually lessens over time. They also report periods when they feel quite peaceful, then suddenly notice a wave of sadness or depression coming over them. These periods appear less frequently with the passage of time. Birthmothers should be warned about these times and be assured that such feelings are normal.

Whenever possible, make yourself available to the grieving parent. Most often, all that is required is a listening empathetic ear. Don't try to talk them out of their pain. Many young women have expressed their frustration with individuals who try to offer platitudes about their having made the right decision or needing to get on with their lives. They usually know these things already. The grief will, however, take precedence at times over such positive assertions.

Sometimes a birthmother appears to hold onto her grief with tenacity and such behavior may seem confusing. However, to let go of one's grief is finally and completely to let go of the child. In some ways, the grief is perceived as the last link she has with the baby. Once she has begun truly to move on with her life, the loss is sealed emotionally.

Birthmothers report that they never forget the child, regardless of how good their subsequent adjustment. They will always continue to remember and to wonder about the child. Grieving appears to intensify at certain times such as birthdays and holidays. The first day of school the year the child turns six, or the child's eighteenth or twenty-first birthday are also commonly reported as meaningful occasions.

## Grieving Intensifies on Holidays

Holidays can be especially difficult for birthparents. It may not be *all* holidays, but there usually will be significant times that are harder than others.

Many women report that the baby's birthday is a particularly significant day for them. Perhaps she can plan ahead for this date. What she plans is not the issue. Rather, it is important that she prepare herself with a strategy for coping with a time that may be unusually stressful. The responses to this are as varied as the birthmothers we've known. One bakes a big birthday cake on her son's birthday every year and shares it with her close friends. Another sets that date aside to be completely alone. She takes out her album of baby pictures, puts on music, and allows herself the freedom to feel whatever comes up. It is important to trust our clients to know what kinds of activities will serve them best at crucial times.

Marty, a nursing student now, talked about her holidays:

*Holidays are real hard. Sometimes I'll be sitting with my boyfriend, and I'll picture my son at two running around the house. Sometimes that's all it takes and I end*

*up having one of my little crash spells. I sit down and
bawl my eyes out for an hour, and then I'm fine for the
next couple of months.*

*Then I start to feel blue again, a little more every
day. Something will set me off and I'll cry a few tears. It
gets worse the next day and the next, like in waves. I
think now it's because his birthday is coming up soon.
Actually it's kind of helpful because I've been trying so
hard to forget.*

*I haven't talked about it to my boyfriend for a long
time, but it's good for me to talk about it. I have to
realize that it's here, another year, and I have to deal
with it.*

*It's not something that ever goes away. You keep
waiting for it to magically disappear or something to
change, but it doesn't. You have to keep on fighting it,
working with it, dealing with it.*

Holidays that traditionally focus on children and families
may be especially difficult. It isn't hard to understand how a
birthmother may experience pain when she sees small children
the age of her child in line to see Santa Claus at Christmas.
Halloween and Easter may also intensify her grieving. More
common, however, is the impact of Mother's Day, when the
young woman who is a mother within herself is forgotten. It is at
these times that the birthmother needs her support persons. Just
as with the grieving process, she should be prepared that such
times are normal and transitory.

Cindy is a hard-working birthmother of nineteen who is now
employed full-time as a secretary in a large company. She
mentioned her Mother's Day feelings:

*The first Mother's Day nobody mentioned her birth
at all to me, and I was rotten to everyone. Half the day
went by before I realized why. I went, "Hey, I'm a mom
too. I may not be mothering, but I did give birth." Then
when the second Mother's Day came around, I got a
card from my mother.*

There are times when all of us feel sad or lonely. At times like this, we may think nostalgically of how things might have been. "If only. . ., then I would be happy." What we use to fill in the blank depends upon each of us. As for the birthmother, she may find that in these times she is tempted to believe that if she had her baby she would be happy.

Of course this could be true, and her feelings should not be discounted. At the same time, share with her that all of us occasionally feel this way, regardless of our circumstances. Help her to move back into a place of power by figuring out what she can do now to gain joy and peace within her life.

You may also want to remind birthparents that grief often comes up as part of normal developmental transition. A birth-mother may need to come back to talk with you because she's feeling grief over the loss of her child, grief which was triggered by such a normal event as her graduation, moving or marriage.

"Birthmothers expect only to be in pain again if something bad happens in their lives. I tell them, 'Sometimes very normal and happy events will be happening and you'll be grieving,'" Kaplan related.

## If It Hurts, Is the Decision Wrong?

It is not uncommon to hear a birthmother question why she feels so bad if she has made the right decision. Regardless of how sound the decision, the loss is still a reality. Birthparents and their families need reassurance that their grief is not an indication of faulty decision-making. Likewise, a state of intense grief is not a good condition to be in when making a decision. Encourage young women to forego the making or changing of decisions at this time.

It's important to prepare birthgrandparents for the grief their daughter will feel after placing her baby for adoption. They are likely to be frightened when they see their daughter in this stage. They feel supportive of the decision, but when they see her going through this grieving, they think, "Did we make the right decision? I can't stand seeing her go through this." They need to be aware that this will probably happen.

As professionals, we need to recognize grief and not be afraid of it as we work with birthparents. It's natural and normal, and it needs to be dealt with. If it isn't, it will almost certainly come up later.

There is little in the literature describing the grieving process of the relinquishing mother. Most of the literature likens it to other grieving processes, particularly those associated with the death of an infant.

However, adoption is distinctly different from loss through death. The child is still very much alive. The complete finality that accompanies death is not found in the relinquishment process.

Susan was in a support group for several months after her baby was born, and she may start attending the meetings again:

> I still feel secure about my choice, but I'm having a
> lot of pain with it. I think I didn't deal with the pain that
> first year, and it's beginning to surface.
>
> I know I'd probably be in a whole heap of hurt right
> now if I had kept him, but I miss him. I suppose that's
> funny to say after holding him for only two days, but I
> do miss him. I'd like to have him around and watch
> him grow.

"Society doesn't recognize adoption as a loss, yet it's worse than death because there is no body, no grave. There's a live child out there," Janet Cravens, Lutheran Social Service, Corpus Christi, Texas, explained. "The real loss of parenting that child is lost. You aren't going to get the homemade Valentines. You aren't going to get the hugs.

"We lose the extension of self that our children are. Birthparents deny the significance of this loss. I can counsel a person for six months before she tells me she placed a child for adoption. Resolution of adoption placement requires denial, fear, rage, depression, despair, and helplessness, disorganization, reorganization, and most importantly, finding a meaning in the loss. Good resolution of the grief requires resolution of all these feelings," Cravens concluded.

Almost four years ago Trisha placed her infant daughter with the family she selected. She talked about her early grieving and the resolution of that grief:

> *To tell you the truth, I feel like I had my baby for them, like it was theirs all along. I didn't at first, of course, right after I came from the hospital. For three months it was pretty hard. The first three weeks all I did was cry. I couldn't even look at a baby without crying. I thought I could never get over that pain.*
>
> *Now I'm like a new person. In some ways, it's like losing somebody in your family through death. You grieve but you finally accept it. The good thing is you get to keep seeing this person grow, and you know she's happy and living a full life. You have to put yourself in the right state of mind. You have to understand exactly what is going to happen, and you have to accept that from the beginning or else it will be a total shock to you.*
>
> *It's a shock anyway. No young girl can ever know what it feels like when she has her own child, she is holding that baby in her arms, and it's her own. I couldn't believe that was my baby. I really had to reinforce my adoption decision then.*
>
> *One thing that helped me was Ken and Jodi were there all the time at the hospital. It was like "We're taking our baby now. We love you and we thank you, but we need to go." I wanted to hold her and stay there, but there had to be a point of letting her go. I got over it. I'm happy with my life, and Ken and Jodi are happy.*

"Go for the Gold" by Fran Thoreen, adoption counselor, King County Adoption, Seattle, Washington, is reprinted in the Appendix, pages 257-267. Thoreen wrote the article in order to explain to birthparents the grieving process they face and the steps they will probably go through. She offers some excellent suggestions on coping with this grief. Permission is granted for reproduction of the article, and you may wish to offer copies to birthparents with whom you are working.

## Research Focuses on Birthmother Grief

The majority of the birthmothers in Monserrat's study (unpublished dissertation) are still grieving the loss of their children. All but two of them cried during the interviews. Their sadness was almost palpable.

Most have had ongoing contact with the adoptive parents and, therefore, know how their children are doing. Seeing the pictures and receiving letters from the adoptive parents greatly alleviated their fears and reassured them that they had made the right decision. This contact, however, did not provide resolution of their loss.

Some of these birthmothers engaged in fantasy as a response to their loss. The fantasizing seemed to occur when they were feeling sad or lonely, when things were not going well, or when another loss had occurred. They also mentioned fantasizing about having the child with them at special times, such as holidays and family get-togethers.

---

*It was as if that whole period of time
had been erased from her memory.*

---

Several of the birthmothers talked about having had periods of denial during which they felt no sadness about the loss. The timing and duration of these periods of denial seemed to vary considerably. However, in most cases, the onset was shortly after the relinquishment. One birthmother said that, although she does not remember being sad for the first six months after the placement, she couldn't remember much else that happened to her either. It was as if that whole period of time had been erased from her memory.

Two of the sixteen birthmothers said they had felt absolutely no grief since the placement. Both explained that because they were feeling so good about the adoption, they felt they had no reason to be sad. It is difficult to assess whether this is a continuation of the denial or whether these two birthmothers have brought the loss to this type of resolution. Both women had been counseled at the same agency, and both explained their lack of sadness in much the same way.

The grief experienced by birthmothers may be unique in at least two ways. First, there is the "head/heart" dilemma. Most of these birthmothers felt that they made a good decision and that adoption was the best plan for them at that time in their lives. They think they made the right decision, but they *feel* sad. Conflict results. As Paula put it, "It's real hard. In my mind, I knew adoption was the best. But physically and emotionally, I'm having a hard time."

The second unique factor in birthparent grief is that the loss is not entirely final. The child is, presumably, not dead. As a result, there are continuing thoughts about an individual who still exists, a child for whom they feel a tremendous amount of love. Perhaps it is one reason birthmothers appear to grieve for such long periods of time.

The teenage birthparent faces other losses in addition to the loss of her child. She has lost a part of her own childhood. She has lost the image of being the "perfect daughter." She has lost the support and identification with the peer group. Grief is an appropriate response to losses of all types. The grief of the adolescent birthmother is compounded by all these factors.

## Their Grieving Continues

Alena released her son for adoption nine years ago. It was a closed adoption and she hasn't even received a photo since he was a year old. Alena was married a few years later and now has a three-year-old daughter. She talked about the grief she still experiences:

> *For me, the grief process has been long. The first six months were especially difficult. I wasn't sure I'd made the right choice. The next year was a time of getting through the crisis. Then it gradually tapered down.*
>
> *I'm always surprised how hard it is. This morning I cried when I was making my daughter's birthday cake and thinking about all the birthdays I've missed with my son. Having my own baby that I can keep is special. What I've lost with my birthson hit me about two weeks before my daughter was born, and I cried and cried.*

Although Joanne had considered adoption throughout her pregnancy, she decided to bring her baby home. She and the baby lived for a week in the home of her aunt before the placement occurred. Joanne has been in contact with the adoptive family by letter. She has grieved intensely and still misses her baby, but time has eased her pain:

> *Sometimes I think I should have kept him, but I always know in the back of my mind that this was the best thing. I miss him and wonder what it would have been like. I don't talk to anyone about it, but I imagine him calling me mom.*
>
> *I'm glad I got to pick out the adoptive parents and that they send me pictures and write to me. It would have been even harder if I'd had to just give him away and never hear anything about him again. I feel better that I know how he's doing. It lets me know I did the right thing because he's happy and he has a good family.*
>
> *When he first left, there were times when I'd look at his pictures and I'd cry and cry. It's not as hard now as it was the first year. I look at his pictures now and I can smile.*

As helping persons, it is important that we assist birthparents in understanding, before their baby is born, that they will undoubtedly suffer intense grieving over the loss of their child. We need to be there for them as they grieve, understand them and support them as they work through their grief.

# CHAPTER 13

# Birthparents Forever — And Life Goes On

*When I have trouble with my boyfriend I keep think-*
*ing, "If I had the baby, if I had kept the baby, I wouldn't*
*have to deal with this." And at Christmas when all the*
*family is sitting around with my nieces and nephews,*
*I'm thinking, "They could be playing with my baby too."*

*Just this Sunday I was in church and my sister had*
*her daughter there. The baby was smiling and every-*
*body was saying, "Oh what a cute baby" and tweaking*
*her cheeks. I was thinking, "That could be my baby*
*they're looking at." I have a lot of thoughts like that.*
*(Brenda, 22)*

Ongoing support is crucial for birthparents. The kind of
bonds that occur during alternatives counseling are often endur-
ing. There may be times in the future when the need to remember, rethink, rework, or regrieve this decision will occur. It may
be that the birthmother will simply need you to recall these days

with her. Or she may be met with a new piece of grieving when she thought it was all gone. Often she may contact you about an issue that is seemingly unrelated to the adoption.

Regardless of the origin of her need, it is important that you be available when it surfaces. If you won't be there in the future, make sure someone can meet the needs of the birthparents who made this decision while working with you.

Because you were with her at a crisis time that was so intimate and when she was so vulnerable, she is likely to seek you out at crisis times in the future. This doesn't necessarily refer to "bad" crisis. She may also want to be in contact when she marries, has another child, or graduates from college. The issue is that you may always be a part of the lives of the young people with whom you work.

One of our dearest friends relinquished her child as a teenager. She later married and made the decision to begin her family. For many years, however, she was unable to conceive. This was a painful experience for her. It brought back memories of her lost child. She began to wonder if she was being punished, or if perhaps she made the wrong decision so long ago. This is not unusual, nor should it be viewed as unhealthy. There will be moments in everyone's life when the past resurfaces to be examined once more. Support during this time can help the individual view the situation from a realistic perspective.

Many people ask whether women who carry out an adoption plan get pregnant again in order to replace the lost baby. Although it is difficult to judge, it seems that this occurs most often when there has not been an adequate grieving process or when the child was released against the birthmother's will. It's as if she must go back and do it again if some aspect of it was not right for her. Actually, we have seen very few instances of repeat pregnancies following placement.

## Return to "Regular" Life

One of the things the birthmother must deal with is going back into her regular life. She returns to her job or her home school and resumes other activities. Birthmothers often report a feeling of estrangement from their peers. This can be readily

understood. A young woman who has faced a monumental
decision of this type, carried it out, and grown accordingly is no
longer like her peers in many ways.

A teenage birthmother may find that she enjoys being back in
the world of her peers. At the same time, she may find herself
dating a young man who is interested in cars and cruising the
main street. Her girlfriends care mostly about make-up, music
and boys. Although she interacts with them, she continues to
wonder about her child.

---

*The issue of who to tell and when
is a highly individual matter.*

---

She is also faced with the decision of whether or not she will
tell others about her experience of having given birth and placed
her child for adoption. Some birthmothers prefer to keep the
information to themselves and find this more comfortable.
Others elect to tell their friends the truth about the situation and
let them handle it in whatever way they wish. Most, however,
seem to be somewhere in the middle of these two extremes.
They don't want to advertise the fact that they had a baby and
released it for adoption. At the same time, they're interested in
having honest relationships with some of their peers. They feel
that this is an important part of themselves that should be
included in that relationship.

The issue of who to tell and when is a highly individual
matter. It is one that should be discussed with each young
woman, and the final decision depends upon what is most
peaceful for her. It is very important that she have someone in
her life with whom she can talk honestly about her baby and
about her feelings. Sometimes that person is a family member.
Other times, it's a close friend. Regardless of who the birthparent selects, encourage the establishment of a relationship
with *someone*.

Marty occasionally talks with her husband about her pain:

*I thought I was going to be all big and mature and
very strong about this whole thing, and that it wasn't*

*going to bother me. . .Now I usually try not to think
about the adoption at all. But when my husband and I
have a fight or something, it's like everything comes out.*

*Otherwise, I don't let it out. I just kind of push it back
down, don't deal with it right now. I've told my husband
the truth about it, and he's been honest about how
he feels.*

*I don't like the answers I get myself because I know
what they imply. I didn't want to know that I'd given my
baby up for adoption, plain and simple, but I had.*

Suzi didn't feel she was allowed to consider parenting her
child. For her, intense grieving continues:

*I can't say whether adoption was good for my baby
because I don't know how things would have been for
him with me. I feel like it's ruined my life. My life will
never be the same. It wasn't good for me.*

*I was the one that got hurt, not him. I'm the one
who's going to have to deal with it. I haven't found
peace or acceptance yet and haven't found forgiveness
in myself.*

*All I have experienced is pain. I have not experienced
any joy or happiness at all, not any aspect of it. Sure, I
know it was best for him, but that doesn't make me feel
any better.*

*If I had it to do over, I'd realize there is some way to
work it out. Everybody says how hard it would have
been to have kept him, with school and everything, but
that would be nothing in comparison to me giving him
up for adoption. That was a million, trillion times
harder than having to keep him. I'll live with that the
rest of my life, and I'd never do that again, never.*

Phyllis R. Silverman writes about the grief of birthmothers in
*Helping Women with Grief* (Sage Publications). However, her
discussion centers around the grief experienced by birthmothers
who released their babies for adoption in secrecy. The women

quoted speak primarily about hiding the pain they experienced when they released their children for adoption, and how difficult living with this pain was. The implication is that eliminating secrecy in adoption can eliminate some of the pain birthparents experience. At the very least, the lack of secrecy would appear to help birthparents deal with their pain.

## On-Going Counseling Is Vital

Birthmothers are often told to "put this behind" them and to "get on with life." These well-meaning comments come from those who believe that once the immediate pain over the loss has subsided, birthmothers will feel just fine. This is not the case with many birthmothers. Internally, many continue to experience the sadness associated with the loss. It doesn't appear to be as easy as it sounds to "go on" emotionally.

Paula's pregnancy resulted from a rape which she kept secret from everyone until her eighth month. She then moved back east and stayed with an aunt until her baby was born and placed for adoption. She returned to her private Christian high school for her senior year. Paula, too, is having a tough time:

> *Sometimes I lie there, and I feel so empty. I feel like, "Where is she at?" It's real hard. In my mind, I know that it's best, but physically and emotionally, it's very hard. At first I went back to school and kept real busy. So I was okay. I didn't have much time to myself.*
>
> *Then about three months later I had more time, and I really started thinking about her. I couldn't talk to anyone, but I'd think about it at home and in school. I started crying all the time.*
>
> *Then I started thinking, "Maybe I can get her back. I can still get her back." Then I thought, "No, it would hurt them too much." Then, "If I don't, I'll hurt myself." All of this kept going through my mind.*
>
> *Finally I asked my mom if I could call the teen parent program where I had gone to school and talk to everybody. She said I could, so I called long distance. They all got on the phone and listened to me. I got support.*

*They'd say, "Whatever you want to do, Paula, we'll*
*help you."*
    *They also said, "Think about it, think about what*
*you'd be doing to the adoptive parents and to the baby*
*and their bond." I knew they were right. It helped so*
*much to talk to them. It's still hard though.*

Linda Nunez, attorney in Tustin, California, has no official
follow-up plan for her clients although she strongly encourages
continuation of counseling during the first few months after
placement. In fact, she says, some birthmothers call two years
later and want counseling, and the adoptive parents generally
pay for it.

"I won't work with an adoptive family that isn't willing to
pay for counseling for the birthparents," Nunez said. "Two years
later the adoption would be finalized, but it's out of respect for
the birthmother of their child that the adoptive parents are still
willing to pay for counseling services."

In about one-third of Nunez' placements, there is on-going
contact between the birthparent(s) and the adoptive parents.
Almost all of them exchange letters and pictures. "We don't
have any cutting-off time on that, and they do this directly —
except for a few students who move around a lot. Their letters
and pictures are sent through me," she explained.

## She Needs a Listener

Birthmothers often report difficulty in finding someone to
talk to about the pain associated with the adoption. They report
not being able to find people with whom they can share their
sadness. Some share their grief with someone, but may be very
selective about this. Debbie, now twenty, is one of these. She
works part-time and attends college where she is studying
computer technology:

*I talk to my boyfriend. He's the **only** person I talk*
*with. I can't talk to my mom about it. I don't want to do*
*anything else, just let her know I'm fine, I'm okay with*
*everything that happened. So, for my mom, everything's*

*great. She has no idea what I'm going through now. She*
*doesn't need to. If I need her help, I guess I can go to*
*her. But I can find my own help. I don't see any reason*
*to hurt my mom anymore. My boyfriend helps a lot.*

A nurse in Portland, Oregon, discussed a patient who had not
had "closure" when she released her baby for adoption. When
the nurse first saw her, Janine was ambivalent about releasing.
She said she felt guilty thinking about adoption because she
should not have had her baby at this time. Therefore she should
keep it.

Janine did release her child. When she came back for her
postpartum checkup, she was a month late. She said she hadn't
wanted to come in because the hospital reminded her of her
baby. Then she burst into tears. "I asked Janine about the birth,"
the nurse related. "Did the baby look like you? What do you see
as the personality of your baby? How did you adopt?"

"Through a lawyer."

"What do you know about the family?"

"Nothing."

"Do you feel good about that?"

"No."

"Not knowing anything made her wonder if her baby was
okay. She had absolutely no information, just that it was a
'good' set of parents who wanted a child. She didn't name her
child because she didn't know she could name him. She didn't
write a letter.

"I think guilt may have been an important part of this situation," the nurse observed. "We talked about her negative
feelings and the hurting. I like to do a reversal of that. I say, 'I
see two things in a person like you — first, that adoption was
not easy, it wasn't an act of abandonment. It was an act of love,
a sacrifice you made. Second, what do people around you think
of this?' She said they think of it as abandonment.

"At this point I could see a glimmer in her eyes that yes, she
did give him up because she loved him. I really push the idea
that she is a good mother now, and she will be a good mother
later. Hopefully her self image will be boosted because of that.

"The woman I worry about," the nurse continued, "is the one who releases and says life can go on, it was no big thing. I stress most the options, the rights, and that the woman must be aware of the negative aspects of adoption. She must turn that hurt around into something positive."

## Birthparent Support Group Is Helpful

Birthparents so often feel isolated. They probably have matured more rapidly than have their peers. The challenges, responsibilities, and life changes associated with pregnancy cause most birthparents to feel more like adults than typical teenagers. This shift from feeling like a teenager to feeling like an adult may not be what they want. As Cindy put it, they often miss "that teenager feeling."

Because they see themselves as different from their peers, teenage birthmothers may have few if any people with whom they will share their feelings about the adoption. If the birthmother is older she, too, may feel no one is tuned in to her needs. A birthparent support group can provide an opportunity for this kind of sharing. In such a group, she may find peers with whom she can identify.

For awhile, Susan continued to talk with her counselor after her baby was born. Then she became part of a birthmother support group:

> *I talked to my counselor until she moved. And I talked to my friend, John, at school. Then we got this group together of birthmothers. All of us sat there and cried and talked. It helped because it's a bunch of people who know exactly what you're going through.*
>
> *It's not like my friends who didn't know what I'd been through, or even the girls at school who had gotten pregnant and kept their babies. It wasn't the same there either. In the group, we all knew what kind of pain we had, and we could relate to each other.*

Katheryn also felt the birthmother support group helped tremendously:

*After placement I had a lot of contact with my counselor. It's been four years and I don't talk to her quite as much now. I was going to most of the support group meetings afterward and was seeing Joan about once a month. Any time I wanted to talk, she was there.*

*Support meetings were basically a bunch of the girls who were either pregnant or had already placed their babies. We talked about how we were feeling. The counselor was there mostly for support, and we did most of the talking. Joan would bring in adoptive parents so we could hear their viewpoints.*

*Basically they were tear-jerking sessions. That was important, and it kept us all together. Everybody got to talk with other people who understood how they were feeling.*

*I'm working and going to school now so I don't get to all the meetings. The girls I was with still try to keep in contact with Joan. When something happens to one of us, Joan makes a point of sharing it with the others.*

*I feel very good about what I did. I feel the support group helped me a lot with my grieving. They knew how I was feeling.*

*I still have contact with the baby. Lately I see him about once a year. I get pictures and letters every couple of months, and that helps a lot.*

For the birthparent, as with the rest of us, life goes on. She will never forget the baby she placed for adoption. She may want to talk about her experience a lot or a little, or she may keep most of this part of her life to herself. As helping persons, our role is to be open to whatever sharing she wants to do, and to provide support for her as she works through her loss and goes on with her life.

# CHAPTER 14

# Whose Responsibility?

An individual who has made a conscious decision based on what she knows would be best for her and for her baby has matured. Regardless of which way she goes, she has matured.

The woman who decides, after looking at her choices, that she is ready and willing to be a mother has made a commitment to the parenting process. Likewise, a birthmother who feels strongly that adoption is best, that both she and her child will benefit from this choice, has made a quantum leap in her personal growth.

These are skills that will be useful throughout the lifetime of the individual. They do not apply only to this situation, nor will this individual face only one crisis in her life. To pass through this crisis successfully builds life skills that she will be able to use for the rest of her life. She will carry with her the confidence that she faced something extremely difficult and challenging, and that she was able to meet the challenge.

Most young women need a tremendous amount of help and support as they look at their alternatives and make the most difficult decision they may ever make. Who will provide that support and that help?

Whose responsibility is it anyway? The work we have talked about in this book is challenging. It requires extra time and extra energy. It demands courage and conviction. It demands that we control our biases. With so many teenagers electing to keep and rear their children, it seems far easier simply to "ride the horse in the direction it's going."

But whose responsibility is it to assure that pregnant teenagers and older women with crisis pregnancies are aware of their choices? Who is responsible if they don't get the assistance they need with the decision-making process? And what of the birthmothers who make the decision to release their children for adoption? Who will offer them support, advocacy, and assistance?

Clearly, no one is going to do the job for us. If it is to be done, it will have to be done by those of us who work with these young women. And though it requires much of us, it also offers tremendous rewards.

# Appendix

# Adoption Questionnaire

**Please answer the following questions as honestly and completely as possible. You do NOT need to sign your name.**

Your age___ Grade in school ___ Your due-date or baby's birth date: ___

Your relationship with your baby's father:

We are no longer together___
We are "together" but not living together___
We are living together (not married)___
We are married___
We were married, but are now separated___ divorced___

Do you live with your parents?___ Boyfriend___ Husband___
Other___ Alone___

Have you ever known anyone who was adopted? Yes___ No___
Have you ever known anyone who adopted a child? Yes___ No___
Anyone who released her child for adoption? Yes___ No___
Were you adopted? Yes___ No___

1. Did you ever consider or are you thinking about releasing your baby for adoption? Yes___ No___ Why or why not?

2. How does your baby's father feel about adoption?

3. How do your parents feel about adoption?

4. How have their opinions influenced your decision as to whether to keep your baby or to release him/her for adoption?

5. Please pretend that you are thinking of releasing your baby for adoption. Would you like to meet/interview/select his/her adoptive parents? Yes___ No___ Why or why not?

6. Would you like to stay in contact with your child's adoptive family? Exchange pictures occasionally? Yes___ No___ See your child occasionally? Yes___ No___ Please comment:

# Who Should Consider an Adoption Plan?

Please read the following examples. As you do so, pretend that you *are* that person. If you were, do you think you should or might consider an adoption plan for your baby? Number each paragraph as follows:

0 - absolutely should not/would not consider adoption.
1 - might consider adoption but would decide against it.
2 - would consider adoption and might carry out an adoption plan.
3 - probably would release baby for adoption.
4 - absolutely would plan adoption.

_____ 1. You are **Irene**, a seventeen-year-old eleventh grader. You and your baby's father had planned to get married but he split when you were six months pregnant. You don't especially like school and you have no particular career goal.

_____ 2. You are **Lisa,** and you came to the Teen Mother Program from a Christian high school. You would like to return to your high school next year. You have thought about adoption but your parents are opposed to the idea. Your mother works part-time, and you think you may be able to have your child cared for in your school's Infant Center. (If there is no room, you will have to drop out of school to care for your child.) You had planned to go on to college but know you must get a job as soon as you graduate if you keep your baby.

_____ 3. You are **Karen** and you are thirteen. Your boyfriend is fifteen. You live with your mother and four younger brothers. Your family receives AFDC (Aid to Families with Dependent Children). You have helped your mother care for your younger brothers and you have had baby-sitting jobs occasionally. You love babies. You mother says she will help you take care of your baby.

_____ 4. You are **Jeni,** and you and Raul were married when you were sixteen and he was seventeen. You didn't plan to have children right away but you got pregnant a month after your wedding. Both of you are determined to finish school and go on to college. You feel you must choose between abortion and adoption.

_____ 5. You are **Nicole** and you are seven months pregnant. You were a cheer-leader in your high school until two months ago, and you would like to go back to cheering as soon as possible. Next year after you graduate you had planned to enroll at the University of Hawaii. You and your baby's father are still close, and he is willing to accept whatever decision you make about the baby.

_____ 6. You are **Pauline,** and your parents kicked you out when they learned you were pregnant. You had already broken up with your boyfriend. You moved in with friends who said you could stay there until you have the baby. After that you must find a place of your own. You have not graduated from high school.

_____ 7. You are **Erin,** and your baby will be born in three weeks. You are fifteen and you live with your parents. Your baby's father will graduate from high school next spring. He is willing to marry you although this would mean he could not go on to college as he planned. He is also willing to go along with an adoption decision if that's what you want.

_____ 8. You are **Elaine,** and you are seventeen. Your boyfriend, twenty, wants to marry you. You think a baby should have two parents. However, your boyfriend is into drugs and you don't think he's ready to settle down yet.

_____ 9. You are **Christine,** and you are an eighth grader. Your mother, who is on welfare, tells you that you sinned by becoming pregnant. She says you must grow up quickly now and take responsibility for your soon-to-be-born child.

_____ 10. You are **Pati** and you are a senior. You live with your father and his wife. They say you must move out if you keep your baby. You don't want to live with them anyhow, and you've made plans to move in with a friend as soon as you have your baby. You plan to get a job, but you also hope to finish high school on schedule.

# Suggestions for Alternatives Group

## Clarify the purposes for holding such a group.
- Why are we holding the group? For support? For influence? For decision-making? For information sharing?
- The purpose may vary with the setting.
- The purpose should be made clear with the participants.
- Participation should be voluntary and based on the stated purpose.

## Establish Support and Cohesiveness.
- Early groups are facilitated by get-acquainted activities that will help teens move through feelings of estrangement and embarrassment.
- Discuss the confidentiality agreement.
- Discuss respect for differences in decisions.
- Make the group a safe environment for all types: verbal, nonverbal, various ethnic and religious backgrounds, etc.
- Integrate new members. Have older members take new ones around, meet for lunch, explain guidelines.
- Make group decisions as to speakers, topics for discussion, activities.
- Celebrate and play at times. Birthdays and holidays are significant for young people.

## Group Structure:
- For information sharing. Topics such as grief, father's rights, agency adoption, private adoption, legal information, etc., are important for anyone considering the adoption alternative.
- To paint a realistic picture.
- To meet and hear from various guest speakers, such as adoptees, adoptive parents, relinquishing mothers, teen mothers, agency workers, birthmothers who were involved in a search, etc.
- For personal exploration. Activities such as letter writing, goal setting, relaxation and fantasy can be safely structured.

## Nonstructured sessions provide the opportunity:

- For spontaneous sharing of feelings, thoughts, ideas, experiences, and attitudes.
- For support and feedback among group members.
- For grief work.
- For vacillations of one's decisions.
- For resolution of the head/heart dichotomy.

## Adoption Support Activities:

- Work with extended family. Grief work, anticipation of outcomes, etc. Assist them in making agreements prior to the birth.
- Contact with agencies, homes, etc.
- Hospital visits.
- Special advocacy issues:
  - Hospital personnel and policies (pictures of baby, time with baby, where they stay).
  - Fathers' rights (need to let young women know early on how that will affect decision).
  - Grieving (others may inhibit the process, attempt to talk her out of it).
  - Referrals to appropriate agencies, lawyers, etc. Know what's happening in your community along these lines.
  - Community relations on topic of adoption.

## Individual Counseling Sessions:

Early in your work you will find it helpful to evaluate each of your clients individually. The following are some guidelines for an informal assessment:

1. Informally assess the level of cognitive development of each client. Does this teenager appear to be able to think ahead? Hypothesize outcomes? Take a lot of risks? Seem capable of self-direction?

2. Look for signs of rebellion against adults and significant others.

3. Determine how much the client knows about her choices.

4. Who exerts the most pressure on her, is more significant to her right now?

5. Is the client in a state of denial at the present time?

6. Is the client aware of what she is feeling at the present moment? It is never true when they say they aren't feeling anything. It may be true that they are not aware of their feelings. There is a difference.

It will be of equal value to assess where you are with this client. We may, as professionals, strive to be nonjudgmental. However, we see the world through our own values, attitudes, beliefs, and experiences. Answering the following questions may be helpful:

1. What is my role in working with this young person?

2. Am I tempted to tell this client what to do?

3. Do I have strong feelings about her situation and the outcome?

4. Am I willing to explore all of her choices with her in an impartial manner?

5. Am I able to give her permission to be undecided and/or vacillate in her decision?

# Strengthening Support for Birthparents in a Teen Pregnancy Program: A Guideline for Helping Professionals

*By Bev Short, M.S.W., Director*
*Sierra Nueva, San Juan U.S.D., Carmichael, California*
Copyright © 1988 by Bev Short

1. Clarify your own feelings about adoption planning. Explore your values, your biases, your strengths, and your weaknesses. Decide if you should work in this area.

2. Create a program, group, or school atmosphere which is supportive and accepting of individual decisions, and which allows options to be explored and choices to be made. All staff members should be sensitized to be open, accepting, and nonjudgmental. Students should be expected to be sensitive to each other's needs and choices.

3. Help students take control of their lives and get out of the "victim" role.

<del>Victim</del>
Process of Choosing = Control
Control = Increased Self Confidence

4. Provide positive role models. Former students who have carried out an adoption plan and feel good about their decision should be invited to participate in groups, classes, or on panel presentations. Even better, if funding allows, hire them as peer counselors.

5. Have a special "Choices Day" once a year or once each semester in which an entire day or half day is devoted to exploring adoption. Since teens are more interested in hearing personal experiences rather than information from professionals, invite special guests to sit on a panel.

Include adoptive parents who have experienced various types of adoptions such as private and public agency, independent, open and closed. Include adoptees (present students or staff members could be utilized), and perhaps someone who searched for and found a birth parent. Have another panel of former students who have carried out adoption plans. Carefully select these guests as they must be able to **positively** present this choice.

Choose a few of the very special poems or letters written by teen birthparents and read to the group.

If possible, obtain permission from your panel participants to videotape the panels so that students who were absent or who enroll at a later date may view the tape and be exposed to this option. A video or film depicting this choice by a teen mother or teen couple could also be utilized.

Have handouts available with basic information about the types of adoptions possible, legal rights of fathers, possible referral resources, and a few of the special poems or letters.

6. Provide on-going support through intensive group and individual counseling:
- Allow students to explore feelings and alternatives.
- Support students in decision-making and grieving processes.
- Encourage students to build a support base by:
  - learning who among their friends, relatives and peers is supportive of their decision;
  - helping them learn to ask for support;
  - having them bring family, friends, husband, or boyfriend to group in order to increase understanding of the process and their needs;
  - helping them to identify and avoid those who are negative or discouraging.

7. Provide ongoing support through didactic and experiential activities:
- Have students list:
  - pros and cons of parenting versus adoption;
  - hopes and goals for the future both for themselves and for the baby;
- Have students plan, rehearse, discuss and share:
  - type of adoption desired;
  - type of adoptive parents desired;
  - what contact (if any) they want with the adoptive parents (meet, talk with, receive pictures from, etc.);

- when (if ever) and what (if any) contact they want with
  the child;
- their hopes for the life they want for the child;
- plans for the hospital stay;
- their future plans, hopes, goals and dreams.

- Support student's desire to make, create or purchase something to
  go with the baby. This often has symbolic meaning to her.
  Possible projects or items include blankets, wall hangings, rings
  or lockets, clothing.
- Encourage students to write any of the following:
  - a letter to the baby
  - a letter to the adoptive parents
  - poems
  - journals
- Assist the student in making a tape recording or a videotape of
  their experience and/or feelings.
- Provide opportunities where the student can listen to and
  talk with:
  - other students who carried out adoption plans;
  - adults who released for adoption many years ago;
  - students, children, staff, and others who are adopted;
  - adoptive parents.
- Encourage students to read books on adoption, letters from
  adoptive parents, letters from birthmothers to their children,
  poems and journals.
- Use guided imagery. Have students imagine what it would be
  like if they keep the baby — the day after birth — two years from
  now — and five years from now. Have them imagine what it
  would be like if they relinquish. Lead the students in a guided
  fantasy of a conversation they might have with the baby to
  explain why they chose adoption. Have them imagine a conversation they might have with someone from whom they need support
  or understanding.

- Don't be afraid of feelings. Encourage students to experience and to feel — to cry, laugh, grieve, hope, change their minds, accept, feel relieved, feel confused or happy or sad or angry or resigned or proud or unsure or sure — any feeling is okay. The sharing of the feelings creates understanding and acceptance.
- Provide opportunities where a student can affirm and reaffirm her decision such as on a panel or in a group.
- Provide as much information as possible about independent adoption and agency adoption. Provide names and numbers of referral resources if possible. Invite guest speakers.
- After the student has relinquished, encourage her to come back and be in a group or on panels to talk about her experience and to serve as a role model for other students. This can help her to reaffirm her decision while providing her a safe place in which to talk about her relinquishment and complete her grieving process.

Adoption is perhaps the most difficult, most unselfish decision anyone can ever make. Pain and joy, relief and grief are all a part of the very complex process. As helpers, we are all human. We wonder what will happen in the future — will there be regrets or will there be a belief and acceptance that the decision was the best one possible at that particular time?

We must keep in mind that we don't know what is best for anyone else. Ultimately, we must trust that each person — at some level — knows what is best for herself or himself. We must help each student or client reach that level.

Good luck!

# Single Parent Request Form

*Bergan Mercy Hospital, Omaha, Nebraska*
*Developed by Linda Howrey R.N.*
*with assistance from Laurie Cooley*

The staff at Bergan Mercy Hospital respect you and your decisions about your pregnancy. We ask that you answer the following questions so that we can be most helpful to you during your stay. This information is used to help us meet your needs. Please feel free to change your mind at any time.

1. Are you currently working with an agency or an attorney? _____

2. What is the name of your contact person? _____

Agency or Firm _____ Phone number _____

3. Would you like us to notify them of your delivery? _____

4. How much contact do you want with your baby after your delivery?
   (Please check those that apply)
   _____ a. No contact. I do not want any information about the baby.
   _____ b. I would like to see the baby in the delivery room.
   _____ c. I would like to hold the baby in the recovery room.
   _____ d. I would like the baby to visit me on the postpartum unit.
   _____ e. I want to see the baby and take care of him/her as much as possible.
   _____ f. I would like to have infant teaching while I'm in the hospital.
   _____ g. I would like a daily report from the pediatrician while I'm in the hospital.

5. Would you like to have:
   _____ a. Pictures
   _____ b. Boy/girl buttons
   _____ c. Footprints
   _____ d. Complimentary birth certificate
   _____ e. ID bands
   _____ f. Crib cards
   _____ g. Other. Please specify. _____

6. How much information do you want released about you while you
   are here?
   _____ No information
   _____ Presence here and room number only

7. Would you like to have your baby at the nursery window for
   viewing? _____
   (If you do not want to have your baby at the nursery window, we
   will require your presence any time the baby is shown.)

Thank you for your time in filling out this form. We offer you our
continued support and respect.

Additional comments:


                                        _____
                                                      Your signature


                                        _____
                                                      Date


Copies to:
          Postpartum
          Nursery
          Admitting Department
          Pastoral Care

# Swedish Hospital Medical Center, Seattle
# Open Adoption Consent

I am planning an open adoption for my infant at Swedish Hospital Medical Center. The following people named are the participants:

Birthmother _____

Agency worker/Attorney _____

I hereby give my permission for the following:

INITIALS
1. _____ Exchange of birth and adoptive parents' names (birthparents and adoptive parents have exchanged names).
2. _____ Adoptive parents may visit me in labor.
3. _____ Adoptive parents may be in attendance at delivery of infant.
4. _____ Information about infant's care and health may be given to my agency worker/attorney.
5. _____ Information about infant's care and health may be given to adoptive parents.
6. _____ Adoptive parents may visit me in hospital on the post-partum unit.
7. _____ Adoptive parents may visit infant in the hospital at the following times:

8. _____ Adoptive parents may take pictures of infant.
9. _____ Other:

I understand that the above will be in effect during my hospitalization and while I retain custody of my infant. The above may be changed, at my request, at any time during our hospitalization while I retain custody.

Signature of Birthmother: _____ Date: _____

Witness: _____

At this time I wish to make the following revisions to the above permission:

Signature of Birthmother _____ Date/Time: _____

Witness: _____

# Birth Plan for Baby

*Written by a birthmother at Swedish Hospital Medical Center, Seattle*
*Note: This was to be an independent adoption.*
*The plan can easily be adapted to an agency adoption plan.*

Attorney: _____

Social worker: _____

Hospital contact: _____

1. I know the names of the adopting couple, so confidentiality is no problem.

2. I do not want my name on the board (Initials are okay), and I want my chart kept out of sight.

3. Labor specifics:
     a. Coach's name _____
     b. Information can be given to the people with the listed last names without my consent:

          1. _____

          2. _____

          3. _____
     c. All others seeking information must be screened by me.
     d. The natural father is not involved.
     e. Medicated labor — epidural.
     f. Attended childbirth preparation classes with coach, but *please* help us if needed.

4. Delivery
     a. I want to know the baby's status immediately.
     b. I would like to see the baby in recovery.
     c. Amount of time I spend with the baby will vary depending on how I feel.

5. Postpartum — Depending on baby's status, I will have the baby in my room upon request. He can be shown to relatives when they are accompanied by me. I will *not* breastfeed the baby.

6. The baby must be circumcised before being discharged from the hospital.

7. Please send baby pictures (three sets) to:
>    Family Court Services
>    King County Superior Court
>    W-364 King County Courthouse
>    Seattle, WA 98104

>    Baby memorabilia are to be sent to:
>    (Birthmother's name and address)

 

 

    I request that I be allowed to change my mind about any of the aforementioned.
    Please ask if you have questions.
    Thank you.


_____                _____
Date                                              Signature

# Open Adoption Policy

*Swedish Hospital Medical Center, Seattle, Washington*

• Pre-hospitalization planning will assist greatly in providing a satisfactory hospital experience. We encourage birthparents and prospective adoptive parents to contact the Maternal-Newborn Patient Services R.N. for a private tour. At this time we will discuss their special requests and options and be prepared to provide for their needs at the time of birth. All arrangements for hospital visitation of the prospective adoptive parents with birthparents or the infant should also be made through the Maternal Newborn Patient Services R.N.

• Visitation by adoptive parents will take place only with prior approval of the birthmother. The birthmother will sign the consent form for visitation by the adoptive parents.

• To avoid possible breach of confidentiality, adoptive parents will be provided a private room away from the nursing unit for all visitation. They will not go to the nursing unit unless special arrangements have been made.

• A hospital staff member will accompany the infant during any visitation with adoptive parents until a court order is received placing the infant in their custody. Maternal-Newborn Patient Services R.N. will attempt to be present for all visits, but if one is not available, they will be responsible to designate another staff member to be present.

• During visitation with adoptive parents, the hospital identification bands of birthmother and infant will be covered with white tape. The nursing staff will be responsible for seeing that the identibands are covered prior to the visit.

• Mementos such as pictures and footprints should not be given to the adoptive parents until after we have received a court order placing the infant in their custody.

• Mementos may be given to the birthmother at any time with the exception of the infant identiband. Both identibands must remain on the infant until the baby is identified with court order at the time of discharge. After the discharge procedure one of the identibands may be given to the birthmother.

• **Note:** Ask birthmother if she knows the name of the adoptive parents and if they know her name. If so, we need not protect confidentiality of names.

• Information about the birth or the infant may not be given to the adoptive parents by hospital staff until they have legal custody. Direct questions by adoptive parents to their attorney or agency worker. The birthmother may give any information she wishes to adoptive parents.

# Your Reaction to Grief

*Adapted from "Grief History" prepared by*
*Lutheran Social Service, Texas*

1. Make a list of people, things, or situations that you have lost during your life. (List the hardest one first and the easiest one last.)

2. How did you feel about these losses? What did you do? (Cry? Go numb? Get mad? Nothing?)

3. Do you think you finally worked them through?

4. Did you get depressed with any of these losses? How did you act and feel when you were depressed?

5. What do the members of your family do when they have a loss? (Think about parents, brothers and sisters, etc.)

6. Does your family have any rituals for handling grief and loss? Please describe them.

# Go for the Gold

*By Fran Thoreen, M.S.W., Adoption Counselor*
*King County Adoption Service, Seattle, Washington*
Copyright © 1988 by Fran Thoreen

When you have a strong emotional reaction to a permanent loss, we call it grief. And, as you work at getting
through grief, we call it grief work. It is something you
will get through. Just as your pregnancy ended, so will
your grief.

Here's how it is with grief:   You can't jump over it.
                                You can't duck under it.
                                You can't get around it.
                                You gotta work through it.

These are some suggestions on understanding your grief
after completing an adoption plan for your baby. In spite of
your loss, life goes on. Your life can be full and it can be
happy. It is hoped these few pages of thoughts will support
you through your grief work, congratulate you along the
way, enable you to face your future with a smile and go for
the gold in your life.

**Facing Loss.** Choosing life for your baby, and passing
that precious life on to adoptive parents who are unable to
create life is a beautiful gift. . .unequaled and extraordinary.
Be proud and take credit for a difficult job well done. But
recognize it for what it is. . .a permanent loss. Your baby's
new parents have faced permanent loss, too. They had to
face the loss of their fertility, which means their genes,
family traits and resemblances will not be carried on. They
cannot get pregnant, give birth or breastfeed naturally.
And, until your gift, they couldn't be parents and share
their life with a child. They were fearful they might never
have a baby.

> *"Not everything that is faced can be changed,*
> *But, nothing can be changed until it's faced."*
>                          *George Baldwin*

So you have some feelings in common. You have all felt the grief of facing loss. You all probably felt some helplessness. They felt helpless trying to get a baby. You felt helpless facing an untimely pregnancy. Then you each took control of the crisis in your lives by deciding on adoption planning. Then you learned of each other and chose to join your lives by mutually planning an adoption for the baby you all love. You could have a baby, but at this time in your life, couldn't provide a home and stable upbringing. They could provide a home, stability and financial security, but they couldn't have a baby. So you took control, planned the adoption with the help of your counselor and lawyer, and believe this is the best plan for the well-being of your baby. And, it meets your needs and their needs.

Your baby will be raised to know about your love and your courage in choosing your baby's Mom and Dad. Your baby will know their family was built through adoption. Your baby will know about you and the birthfather through the background information you provided.

> *"Everybody has a history,*
> *Everybody has a name.*
> *Everybody has a story,*
> *No one's story is exactly the same."*
> *(from Mr. Roger's record, "Come On and Wake Up")*

**You Can Be in Control.** You have already taken control of one situation in your life, and that was continuing your pregnancy and making an adoption plan for your baby. You can now take control of this situation. . .your grief. . .and work it through. You can survive it, just like you survived the last nine month chapter of your life. And, you can begin planning the next chapter of your life. Grief is like a bridge in getting you from one chapter to the next. Grief is a transition period. It can be changed into personal growth. Make the most of this time of transition. Make the pain change you into a stronger, prouder, more confident you. Remember what Grandma used to say, "There's a silver lining to every cloud."

**What Is Grief?** Grief is a changing process. Your emotions may change hour by hour at first, then day by day, eventually month by month and longer. Grief is a variety of feelings underneath behaviors. . .sad, mad, lonely, relieved, anxious, confused, frustrated, guilty, hurt, apathetic, etc. The feelings are lumped together in what is called stages of grief because a person usually experiences these feelings in stages. Often you experience several feelings at once. Sometimes you may feel you've gone through several stages, and then slip backwards to an earlier stage. Sometimes the feelings are mild, sometimes raging, sometimes fleeting, sometimes ongoing, sometimes superficial, sometimes deep. Grief ebbs and flows. It washes over you in waves, then subsides. Be prepared for it. Go with the flow. It helps to recognize what is going on inside of you. This insight will help you feel more in control.

**Stages of Grief:**
   **1. Shock.** It's described like an unreal feeling; like being spacey or in a fog; like there is a drama going on and you are watching. You act temporarily anesthetized, managing to do what you must do but acting by rote or instinctively. You're not really "into" anything at first; you're emotionally flat or tearful. You may have no appetite, feel a knot in your stomach, feel numb and tired. This is the stage where people facing a loss are described as "It hasn't hit her yet." Worry if it doesn't *ever* hit you.

**2. Denial.** Intellectually you know what's happened but on a deeper level you don't want to believe it. It's hard to believe you had a baby and now you don't have a baby. You may wander around from place to place searching for your baby in a crowd. You may have requested lots of pictures and progress reports pretending on some level your loss isn't real. Or, the opposite. . .you may refuse all pictures, keepsakes and avoid baby departments in stores or being around other infants to avoid and deny the feelings of loss. For most birthmothers, keeping a few treasured photos and keepsakes is an affirmation of love, not denial. Dreams may reveal your conflict, and excessive daydreaming can indicate denial. A flurry of activity, overworking, or a merry-go-round of socializing may be an attempt to keep so busy you don't have time to think about your baby. Denial can trigger a desire for replacement. . .don't get pregnant again yet! Alcohol and drugs can seem to cover up the pain, and can become addictive if denial persists. Watch yourself.

**3. Anger.** When you're awfully angry, you usually focus on somebody. . .your boyfriend, your mom, your doctor, God, yourself, your baby's adoptive parents, your counselor. Recognize most of your anger is part of your grief, though some folks may deserve some of it! Minor, insensitive comments may cause an over-reactive emotional outburst. Anger needs to be expressed. . .talking, private yelling, exercising, punching pillows. Some women have trouble expressing anger, feeling it's unladylike. Baloney. Get it out. Prolonged or destructive anger needs professional attention, as in the beginnings of criminal, delinquent or physically abusive behavior stemming from bottled-up anger and frustration.

**4. Guilt and Bargaining.** You may torture yourself for a while with "if onlys." Feelings of guilt and regret over your decision are common. Whenever we make a major life decision of any kind (leaving home, quitting school or a job, deciding on major surgery, putting an elderly parent in a nursing home, buying a major purchase) we usually wonder "what if" and question our decision or feel some guilt. You might bargain with a higher power that if you win the lottery so you can keep your baby, you will donate money to a good cause, or never have sex again, or go to church every Sunday. Some birthmothers feel guilty because other people think they should feel worse than they do, when actually they feel mostly at peace with their decision. They feel guilty thinking there is something wrong with them. Sometimes there is bargaining to try to get your baby back when it's too late.

**5. Depression.** When the numbness wears off, and you can no longer deny your loss, your raging has quieted and you've anguished through all of your "if onlys" and "what ifs," depression hits quietly with a whimper. It is like thumping up against the wall of reality and experiencing the pain and tears. You may feel listless, tired, not hungry, have sleep disturbances, feel uninterested and hopeless. Depression isn't all bad. It gives you a second wind, after you've spent a lot of energy denying, bargaining, raging, feeling guilty about being angry. Now you're tired. You're at the bottom. There's nowhere to go except *up* to acceptance.

**6. Acceptance.** Now you will gain energy and interest. You will remember your baby but it will be less painful and there will eventually be warm memories that bring a smile. You can find ways for those memories to enrich your life. Sorrow doesn't last forever; love does.

**Time Heals, with Your Help.** It takes time to heal, but you can help time do its healing. Grieving deeply takes a year. . .or longer. Shakespeare even said something about sorrow taking four seasons. You've probably heard the advice about not making other major changes or decisions for a year. But that doesn't mean you sit around and do nothing but grieve for a year. Of course not! You do your grief work and get on with your life. Notice I didn't say you forget and get on with your life. You will never forget this baby, nor should you. This baby is a part of your family and has a place on your family tree. There is even a proper symbol for this. . .[name of baby] means adopted into your family and )name of baby( means placed outside your family with an adoptive family. If you don't know the name of your baby chosen by the adoptive parents, name your baby yourself for your own pleasure.

**Getting On With Your Life.** This involves *balancing* three areas: Private Time, Social Time and Busy Time. Balance solitude and reflective times with busy, distracting activities. Too much of each can be unhealthy. Some of each is your best bet.

**1. Private Time.** Plan quiet time to be alone with your-self. Think and reflect on all that's happened and who has been involved. . .your boyfriend, your parents, your friends, doctor, counselor, hospital staff, baby's new parents. Think of yourself, who you were and who you are now. You're between roles. . .a mother, yet not exactly a mother. So you begin to call yourself a birthmother and refer to your baby's adoptive mother as "her Mom." You don't exactly know how to act. . .just like before? Only you're not exactly just like before. It's kind of scary, trying to figure out who you are now. As you feel mixed up, *CRY*. Crying helps get out the sad and the mad.

**2. Social Time.** Plan for shared time with trusted others. You might really need your own mom now, like a little kid. Choose your friends selectively to be your sounding board, to listen to you ramble and work out your feelings. Forget about people who say, "How *could* you!" You can deal with them later when you're stronger. Talk with other trusted, supportive people. . .the baby's father (maybe), clergy, your obstetrician, your favorite nurse or hospital social worker. Join a birthparent support group for that special understanding you get only from another birthparent. And, be sure to make appointments with your counselor because she really understands the process you're going through. She has the professional skills to help you work through your grief. If you have concealed your pregnancy, your counselor will be very important, as are the hospital staff where you gave birth because others in your life will be unknowledgeable about what you are going through. In other words, *TALK*. Talking it out is a key factor in grief work.

**3. Busy Time.** Take action. Do something. Be productive.

**A. Ritualize your goodbye.** Decide how much you want to see your baby in the hospital, if at all, and whether or not you want to provide care, such as bathing and feeding. You may want to talk to your baby, explain why you are making this adoption plan, express your love and say goodbye. You may want to do this in a letter and include a picture of yourself, birthfather or your family or his. You may want keepsakes: pictures, hair lock, blanket, cap, ribbon, wristband, feet/hand prints, birth record. Make a photo album or memorabilia box for yourself. . .something to do as a tribute to your baby. You may want to send birth announcements to close friends and family including a statement like, "Melissa joined her adoptive parents, Bill and Sue, on August first." You may want to send a family heirloom to your baby, or make a gift, or purchase something special. One birthfamily had a shower and sent the gifts to the adoptive family with many personal notes of best wishes for a happy life. You may want to hand your baby over to his new parents. You may not want to do any of the above, or only one or two. Some birthmothers want their counselor to phone them after the court hearing to say, "It's done."

**B. Take care of yourself.** Eat a balanced diet, sleep enough, begin exercising, maybe continue your prenatal vitamins and iron until your postpartum checkup but call the doctor with any worrisome physical complaints. You need to heal physically to heal emotionally. Realize your hormones are swinging back to their pre-pregnant state and baby-blues tears are a normal part of postpartum recovery. Think about your body; nourish it and shape it to the way you fantasize yourself. Put a skinny lady picture on your refrigerator door to help you eat prudently and healthfully, with no crash diets.

**C. Write.** If you are inclined to write, keep a *diary* and record your thoughts and feelings. It will serve as a release now. Later, when you read it, you'll feel a sense of accomplishment, seeing how far you've come.

Write up *one-liners* or responses to questions or comments from outsiders. Use positive adoption language, like "I made an adoption plan for my baby," not "I gave up my baby." Say things like, "I'm lucky I found my baby such great parents." One birthmother said, "Anyone can get pregnant by mistake and have a baby. But I'm special. I made an adoption plan for my baby and *I did it!*" Don't be defensive; be proud. Educate others on the positive aspects of adoption planning. You'll feel self-respect. Others will learn from you. If someone asks a really rude question, try "Now why would you ask a question like that?" You don't *owe* anyone answers. By writing up responses to questions you've been asked, or expect to be asked, you'll be better prepared.

Write up lists for goal planning. This is an excellent way to move ahead in your life. Successful homemakers, students and career women use lists to discipline themselves in accomplishing goals. Make realistic goals, with some easily within reach and others more challenging. When you use this method, you will be pleased with yourself and what you have accomplished. Also, some of your reasons for making the adoption plan for your baby were because you felt you needed to accomplish more in your life before you begin parenting. So start working toward those goals now, giving credit to your adoption plan. Your child will be proud of you, as will his parents, in addition to your own self-pride.

Make three kinds of lists. One for your general life goals, what you hope to accomplish in your lifetime, with a list of your strengths in meeting these goals and a list of shortcomings you need to build on. A second list will be for the next twelve months, beginning with the month after your baby's birth. Set goals for the year and each month list what you expect to accomplish toward those goals. Lastly make a list for tomorrow. Let's take this day by day and get started now! For your goals think in terms of personal appearance, education, earning power, rewarding work, family life, health, home, environment, etc. Good luck!

**4. Help Others.** As you heal and become less sensitive, you will be able to talk more about your experience. As you share your experience and decision making with others, they learn from you and get comfort from you. You may share in a birthparent support group. You may be a guest speaker for a community conference or meeting. You may be interviewed for your views for a newspaper or magazine article, or a T.V. special. Or, you may help others privately one to one. . .just one friend helping another.

**5. Ask for Help.** Tell others what you need and when you need it. They can't read your mind and it's not fair to expect them to understand your feelings if you don't try to explain.

If you feel stuck in any one of the stages of grief, with prolonged, immobilizing or hurtful behaviors to yourself or others, ask your counselor for help. She may be able to help you help yourself over that hump. She can also give referrals to therapists who have expertise in helping grieving birthmothers.

**Be Patient with Yourself.** It's okay to be inconsistent in going through the stages and to have normal setbacks. It's okay to be human! Be prepared for your emotions to get stronger around Christmas, Mother's Day, your baby's first birthday, and even monthly on significant days. Plan an activity or a special treat for yourself to short-circuit depression. Don't feel disappointed in yourself if you're not getting over "it" as fast as you want. It's usually slow going.

In closing, again I remind you that choosing life for your baby, and choosing wonderful parents with a bright future for your baby is a most beautiful, loving gift. . .unequaled and extraordinary. Your gift has made them enormously happy and forever grateful to you.

These two poems reflect feelings as expressed by birthfamilies and adoptive families:

*Now you must leave, Love,*
*To walk where you must,*
*To fly like an eagle,*
*To touch whom you trust.*

*But remember we love you*
*Remember we're here,*
*Remember we'll think of you,*
*Remember we care.*
*(Author unknown)*

*And, oh, thank God, this child is here,*
*That another mother loved him so,*
*She had the strength to let him go.*
*And, may our lives be worthy of*
*That final, total gift of Love.*
*(Author unknown)*

Bless you. You are special. Your baby is special. Your baby's Mom and Dad are special. May your dreams come true, as you have made theirs come true.

So smile. . .and go for the gold!

# Annotated
# Bibliography

About 120 titles in the 1988-1989 edition of *Books in Print* are listed under the subject of adoption. Most of these books are written for professionals dealing with adoption, for adoptive parents, their adopted children, and for adult adoptees. A few books are listed for birthmothers who relinquished for adoption in the past. Even fewer are designed for pregnant women considering an adoption plan, and none appear to be written for the families of birthparents. Titles for professionals appear also to concentrate on the adoptive family rather than the birthfamily. Yet it is with the birthfamily that adoption begins.

Some of the following books deal with crisis pregnancy and/or adoption from the professional's viewpoint. Others are written specifically for teenagers facing early pregnancy. A few of these books are also appropriate for older women facing a crisis pregnancy. Not included are the many books available which focus on adoptive parents and/or adoptees.

These books for birthparents deal primarily with the dilemma of unplanned pregnancy. Some focus on decision-making generally, others on adoption specifically. Others provide guidance during pregnancy, while some stress the realities of parenting a child and/or premature marriage.

Prices, when given, are from the 1988-1989 edition of *Books in Print*. If you order a book directly from the publisher, check first with your public library or a bookstore to learn current prices. Then add $2.00 for shipping.

---

Aigner, Hal. *Adoption in America: Coming of Age.* 1986. Paradigm Press, 127 Greenbrae Boardwalk, Greenbrae, CA 94904. Paper, 216 p. $8.95.
*Aigner is concerned with the interests of adoptees, their birth-parents, and their adoptive parents as he documents and analyzes the major challenges faced in adoption reform efforts. He also provides a fascinating and detailed look at the history of adoption in the United States.*

Anderson, Carole, Lee Campbell, and Mary Anne Manning Cohen. *Choices, Chances, Changes: A Guide to Making an Informed Choice About Your Untimely Pregnancy.* 1981. CUB, Inc., P.O. Box 573, Milford, MA 01757. 63 p. $5.
*Book offers constructive suggestions for questions a young person should ask if she approaches an adoption agency for help. Mainly it is a reassuring booklet for young mothers who want to keep their babies to rear themselves.*

Arms, Suzanne. *To Love and Let Go.* 1983. Alfred A. Knopf, 201 East 50th Street, New York, NY 10022. Hardcover, 240 p. $17.95.
*Presents the stories of several young women who release their babies for adoption and of the parents these birthmothers choose. Arms' emphasis is on the needs of the birthmothers and of the positive effects of adoptive parents and birthparents meeting and developing a relationship.*

Barr, Linda, and Catherine Monserrat. *Teenage Pregnancy: A New Beginning.* Revised 1987. New Futures, Inc. Also available from Morning Glory Press, 6595 San Haroldo Way, Buena Park, CA 90620. 98 p. Illustrated. $10. Quantity discount. Student Study Guide, $2.

*This book was written specifically for pregnant adolescents.*
*Topics include prenatal health care, nutrition during pregnancy,*
*fetal development, preparation for labor and delivery, decision-*
*making, emotional effects of adolescent pregnancy, and others.*
*The authors have obviously known, worked with, and loved many*
*school-age parents.*

_____. **Working with Childbearing Adolescents: A Guide for Use**
**with Teenage Pregnancy, A New Beginning.** New Futures Inc.
Also available from Morning Glory Press. Revised 1986. 159 p.
Spiral, $12.95.
*Introductory chapter presents overview of teen pregnancy and*
*parenthood in the United States. In addition, adolescent develop-*
*ment and sexuality are explored. Authors include their experiences,*
*ideas, and insights gained through working with pregnant*
*adolescents.*

Becker, Kayla, with Connie K. Heckert. **To Keera with Love: The**
**Story of One Teen's Choice.** 1987. 170 p. Sheed and Ward. Also
available from Morning Glory Press, 6595 San Haroldo Way, Buena
Park, CA 90620. Paper, $7.95
*Dramatic first-person story of Kayla's journey from early childhood*
*in a happy and protected home environment in Iowa to the harsh*
*reality of becoming a mother too soon. . .and through her grieving*
*as she places her beloved Keera for adoption. Absorbing story of*
*one pregnant teen's decision.*

Brandsen, Cheryl Kreykes, M.S.W. A **Case for Adoption: A Guide to**
**Presenting the Option of Adoption.** 1985. Bethany Christian
Services, 901 Eastern N.E., Grand Rapids, MI 49503. 48 p. $2.
*Well-written booklet designed for counselors who work with*
*pregnant teenagers and older women facing a crisis pregnancy. It*
*stresses respect and caring concern for birthparents, and does not*
*suggest that adoption is the only option a young person could or*
*should choose. Rather, it addresses the concerns and frustrations*
*counselors have expressed about representing adoption as a loving,*
*responsible, and mature choice that must be considered as seriously*
*as parenting or marriage.*

Children's Home Society of California. *The Changing Picture of Adoption*. 1984. 138 p. Children's Home Society of California, 2727 West Fifth Street, Los Angeles, CA 90057. $14.95.
*An objectively presented overview of adoption in the United States. Information was compiled through interviews with people from throughout the country.*

Colgrove, Melba, Harold Bloomfield, and Peter McWilliams. *How to Survive the Loss of a Love*. 1982. Bantam, 666 Fifth Avenue, New York, NY 10103. $3.95.
*A wonderful book for facing losses of all types. It explains the normal reactions to loss and provides suggestions for moving through the process. Includes poems and scenarios to support the feelings of the reader. Doesn't deal specifically with loss through adoption, but is nevertheless appropriate.*

Ewy, Donna and Rodger. *Teen Pregnancy: The Challenges We Faced, The Choices We Made*. 1985. New American Library, 120 Woodbine Street, Bergenfield, NJ 07621. Paper, $3.95.
*A refreshingly practical guide for teenagers facing the hard choices and special challenges of pregnancy in the teen years. Good advice is coupled with quotes from pregnant and parenting teenagers.*

Hansen, Caryl. *Your Choice: A Young Woman's Guide to Making Decisions About Unmarried Pregnancy*. 1980. 176 p. Avon, 105 Madison Avenue, New York, NY 10016. $2.25.
*A comprehensive guide to the options open to pregnant teenagers. The author emphasizes the need for choosing an option rather than going into motherhood without making a decision. Suggested is a "Pregnancy Timeline" to be used in decision-making.*

Johnston, Patricia Irwin, Ed. *Perspectives on a Grafted Tree*. 1983. 144 p. Perspectives Press, P.O. Box 90318, Indianapolis, IN 46290-0318. Hardcover. $12.95.
*A beautiful collection of poems written by birthparents, adoptees, adoptive parents, and extended family members. They express a variety of positive and negative feelings which are part of the gains and losses, happiness and pain felt by all those touched by adoption.*

Lewis, Gay. *Bittersweet*. 1984, 206 p. Bridge Publishing, Inc., South Plainfield, NJ 07080. $3.95.
*Laurie Lewis' mother tells the story of Laurie's pregnancy and the adoption of her child. Strong religious perspective.*

Lifton, Betty Jean. *I'm Still Me*. 1981. 224 p. Knopf, 201 East 50th Street, New York, NY 10022. $9.95; Bantam, 1986. $2.50.
*Fiction. Story of a teenaged adoptee's search for and reunion with her birthmother. The author of this novel is an adoptee who searched for and found her birthmother.*

Lindsay, Jeanne Warren. *Do I Have a Daddy? A Story About a Single-Parent Child*. Illustrated by DeeDee Upton Warr. 1982. 46 p. Color. Morning Glory Press, 6595 San Haroldo Way, Buena Park, CA 90620. Hardcover, $7.95. Paper, $3.95.
*This is a picture book/story in which a single mother explains to her son that his daddy left soon after he was born. It contains a twelve-page section of suggestions for single parents, based on comments from teenage mothers facing this question.*

_____. *Open Adoption: A Caring Option*. 1987. 256 p. Photos. Morning Glory Press. Hardcover, $15.95; paper, $9.95.
*A fascinating and sensitive account of the new world of adoption where birthparents choose their child's adoptive parents and may remain in contact with their child's new family. Written for birthparents, adoptive parents, and professionals. Includes personal experiences of many birthparent(s) and the adoptive parents she/ they chose for their baby.*

_____. *Parents, Pregnant Teens and the Adoption Option: Help for Families*. 1989. 208 p. Morning Glory Press. Hardcover, $13.95; Paper, $8.95.
*Guidance for parents of pregnant teenagers, especially those considering the adoption alternative. Offers practical suggestions for providing support while encouraging the young person to take responsibility for her decisions. Includes experiences of and suggestions from parents and counselors. Much of book is in words of birthgrandparents.*

_____. *Pregnant Too Soon: Adoption Is an Option.* Revised 1988.
224 p. Morning Glory Press. Hardcover, $15.95; Paper, $9.95.
Teacher's Guide and Study Guide, 16 p. ea., $2.00.
*Young women who were, by their own admission, "pregnant too
soon," tell their stories. Most made the unpopular decision to
release for adoption. They share their reasons for doing so. Included with the personal stories is information on agency and
independent adoption, fathers' rights, dealing with grief, and other
aspects of adoption. Especially written for young birthmothers.*

_____. *Teenage Marriage: Coping with Reality.* Revised 1988.
208 p. Photos. Morning Glory Press. Hardcover, $15.95. Paper,
$9.95. Teacher's guide, $5.95. Student study guide, $2.50.
*Marriage book written especially for teenagers. Based on in-depth
interviews with married teens and on nationwide survey of teenagers' attitudes toward marriage. Extremely realistic.*

_____. *Teens Look at Marriage: Rainbows, Roles and Reality.*
1985. 256 p. Photos. Morning Glory Press. Hardcover, $15.95.
Paper, $9.95. Study Guide, $2.50.
*An in-depth coverage of the research behind Teenage Marriage:
Coping with Reality. Attitudes of teenagers not yet married are
compared with those who are. Provides insight into world of
teenage couples. Thirty-four bar graphs, 130 tables, eight photos.*

_____. *Teens Parenting: The Challenge of Babies and Toddlers.*
1981. 308 p. Illustrated by Pam Patterson Morford. Morning Glory
Press. Hardcover, $14.95; paper, $9.95. TG, $5.95. SG, $2.50.
*Basic how-to-parent book based on interviews with sixty-one
teenage mothers. Their comments are incorporated throughout the
book. Sixth grade reading level.*

Lowry, Lois. *Find a Stranger, Say Goodbye.* 1978. 192 p. Houghton
Mifflin Co., Wayside Road, Burlington, MA 01803. $10.95.
*Fiction. Teenage adoptee's search for and reunion with her
birthmother, and her relationship with her adoptive family during
these experiences.*

McGuire, Paula. *It Won't Happen to Me: Teenagers Talk About Pregnancy.* 1983. Delacourte, 234 p. $14.95. Dell, 1986, $7.95.
*Fifteen teenagers talk about their unplanned pregnancies, the decisions they made, and the changes in their lives.*

Mueller, Candace P. *The Adoption Option: A Guidebook for Pregnancy Counselors.* 1986. 72 p. Project SHARE, P.O. Box 2309, Rockville, MD 20852.
*This guidebook was developed and written under the auspices of the Office of Population Affairs of the Department of Health and Human Services. It provides a general explanation of the adoption process and highlights important points that counselors should be aware of in counseling young women about adoption.*

Musser, Sandra Kay. *I Would Have Searched Forever.* 1985. Jan Publications, Inc., P.O. Box 1860, Cape Coral, FL 33910. $6.95.
*A moving story of Musser's teenage pregnancy, the surrender of her daughter, the ensuing grief, and the subsequent, successful search to locate her daughter. Book lends insight into ongoing feelings that may occur after releasing a child for adoption.*

_____. *What Kind of Love Is This? A Story of Adoption Reconciliation.* 1982. Jan Publications Inc. $7.95.
*Musser's continuing story of building a relationship with her birthdaughter, plus similar stories from other people. The need for open records and openness in adoption is discussed.*

Myers, Walter Dean. *Sweet Illusions.* 1986. 146 p. Teachers & Writers Collaborative. Available from Morning Glory Press, 6595 San Haroldo Way, Buena Park, CA 90620. Paper, $5.95. Cloth, $9.95.
*Absorbing fictional accounts of the lives of very young mothers and fathers. Eleven young people tell their stories, the whole threaded together by their involvement in the Piedmont Counseling Center. One story concerns a young woman who placed her child for adoption, considered getting him back two months later, then decided to leave him with his adoptive parents.*

O'Brien, Bev. *Mom, I'm Pregnant.* 1982. Tyndale House Publishers,
   P.O. Box 80, Wheaton, IL 60189. 125 p. $4.95.
   *Written by the mother of a pregnant teenager, this book has a strong
   religious slant. Emphasis is on the adoption decision.*

Pannor, Reuben, Fred Massarik, and Byron Evans. *The Unmarried
   Father: New Helping Approaches for Unmarried Young Parents.*
   1971.196 p.  Springer Publishing Company, Inc., 200 Park Avenue
   South, New York, NY 10012.
   *Perhaps the earliest book focusing on the dilemma of unmarried
   fathers. It is a report of a comprehensive study of the unmarried
   father and his impact upon the unmarried mother and the decision-
   making about the baby. Theme is to provide services to help
   young fathers.*

Pierson, Anne. *Mending Hearts, Mending Lives: A Guide to Extended
   Family Living.* 1987. Loving and Caring, Inc., 100 Foxshire Drive,
   Lancaster, PA 17601. 156 p. Paper, $4.95.
   *Book written for families providing shelter in their homes for single
   pregnant women. Offers excellent guidance and shows real respect
   and caring for the young women involved.*

Pierson, Anne. **"My Baby and Me: Basic Decision-Making."** 1984.
   Loving and Caring, Inc. 34 p. workbook. $3.00.
   *Packed with "thinking" questions concerning goals in life, plans for
   the baby, and other areas of concern for pregnant teenagers.*

Richards, Arlene Kramer, and Irene Willis. *What to Do If You or
   Someone You Know Is Under 18 and Pregnant.* 1983. 254 p.
   Lothrop, Lee & Shepherd Books, 105 Madison Ave., New York,
   NY 10016. $10.88. Paper, $7.00.
   *A very readable discussion of possible alternatives for pregnant
   teenagers.*

Rillera, Mary Jo, and Sharon Kaplan. *Cooperative Adoption:
   A Handbook.* 1985: Triadoption Publications, P.O. Box 638,
   Westminster, CA 92684. 158 p. Paper. $14.95.

*Offers excellent guidelines for birthparents and adoptive parents
planning an open adoption. Authors do not recommend co-parenting
except in the sense of both sets of parents being actively involved
with the child. The adoptive parents are the legal and psychological
day-to-day parents, but the birthparents may be as close to the
adoptive family as desired by everyone involved. Suggested
cooperative adoption documents are included.*

Roggow, Linda, and Carolyn Owens. ***A Handbook for Pregnant
Teenagers.*** Zondervan Publishing House, 1415 Lake Drive, SE,
Grand Rapids, MI 49506. Paper, $5.95.
*Appropriate for young women whose religious convictions make
abortion an impossible choice. Alternatives of marriage, adoption,
and raising the baby alone are presented.*

Roles, Patricia. ***Facing Teenage Pregnancy: A Handbook for the
Pregnant Teen***. 1984. Eterna Press, P.O. Box 1344, Oak Brook, IL
60521. 123 p. Paper, $5.95.
*This is a personal guidebook with a non-directive and supportive
approach. Included are several first-person accounts of early
pregnancy, adoption, abortion, and parenthood.*

_____. ***Saying Goodbye to a Baby: A Book About Loss and Grief in
Adoption.*** 1989. Child Welfare League of America, Inc., 440 First
St., NW, Suite 310, Washington, D.C. 20001. Paper, $10.95.
*Deals with birthparent grief after adoption and throughout life.
Contents include the original adoption decision, living with the
decision in later life, the adoption triangle, searching and reunions,
guilt and anger when looking back on the decision, and when to get
counseling. Also includes worksheets to be used during pregnancy
and after the birth to help deal with grief and loss.*

Silber, Kathleen, and Phylis Speedlin. ***Dear Birthmother: Thank You
for Our Baby.*** 1983. 193 p. Corona Publishing Company, 1037
South Alamo, San Antonio, TX 78210. Trade, $7.95.

*An excellent book. Refutes such myths of adoption as the idea that
birthparents don't care about their babies. Includes many beautiful
letters from adoptive parents to birthparents and from birthparents
to adoptive parents.*

Silverman, Phyllis R. *Helping Women Cope with Grief.* 1981. 110 p.
Sage Publications, Inc., 2111 West Hillcrest Drive, Newbury Park,
CA 91320. $9.95.
*Discussion of the grief felt by widows, birthmothers, and abused
women. Birthmother section centers on birthmothers who released
their babies for adoption in secrecy.*

Sorosky, Arthur D., M.D., Annette Baran, and Reuben Pannor. *The
Adoption Triangle: The Effects of the Sealed Record on Adoptees,
Birthparents, and Adoptive Parents.* 1984. Doubleday, 666 Fifth
Avenue, New York, NY 10103. Paper, $9.95.
*Probably the first book to promote more openness in adoption. The
authors see adoption as a life-long process, and they suggest that we
need to reform our attitudes and policies regarding adoption. They
discuss the effects of reunion experiences between adoptees and
their birthparents.*

Witt, Reni L., and Jeannine Masterson Michael. *Mom, I'm Pregnant!
A Personal Guide for Teenagers.* 1982.  Stein & Day.  239  p.
$6.95.
*Excellent book for young people facing decisions about unplanned
pregnancy.*

Zimmerman, Martha. *Should I Keep My Baby?* 112 p. 1983. Bethany
House, 6820 Auto Club Road, Minneapolis, MN 55438. $3.95.
*Offers help and direction for facing pregnancy outside of marriage.
Argues against abortion, helps evaluate marriage, single
motherhood, and adoption.*

# Research Focusing on Adoption

Barth, Richard P. 1987. **"Adolescent Mothers' Beliefs About Open Adoption."** *Social Casework, 68*, pp. 323-331.

McLaughlin, S. D., Manninen, D. L., and Winge, L. D. 1987. *The Consequences of the Adoption Decision.* Seattle: Battelle Human Resources Institute.

Mech, Edmund. 1984. *Orientations of Pregnancy Counselors Toward Adoption* (Final report). Washington, D.C.: Office of Adolescent Pregnancy Programs, Department of Health and Human Services.

Monserrat, Catherine. 1988. *The Adoption/Relinquishment Process in Adolescent Pregnancy.* Unpublished doctoral dissertation, The Fielding Institute, Santa Barbara, California. 238 p.

Musick, J. S., Handler, A. and Waddill, K. D. 1984. **"Teens and Adoption: A Pregnancy Resolution Alternative?"** *Children Today*, November-December. pp. 24-29.

Pannor, Reuben, Baran, A. and Sorosky, A. D. 1978. **"Birthparents Who Relinquished Babies for Adoption Revisited."** *Family Process, 17*, pp. 329-337.

Winkler, Robin, and Margaret van Keppel. *Relinquishing Mothers in Adoption: Their Long-Term Adjustment.* 1984. 100 p. Institute of Family Studies, 766 Elizabeth Street, Melbourne 3000, Australia.

# Adoption Films and Videos

The media tends to print and exploit the sensational because this makes news and raises ratings. Unfortunately, this often gives the public a narrow or distorted view of a topic. Adoption, in its various forms, is no exception. When asked what they know about adoption, many teenagers will recount a scenario from a soap opera or situation comedy in which the members of the adoption triangle are portrayed as less than healthy human beings.

It is important to expose teenagers to birthparents, adoptive parents, and adoptees who can present adoption in a more balanced, realistic fashion. When this is not possible, the use of audiovisuals can be helpful. The following videotapes and audiotapes are concerned with adoption. Viewers may welcome the opportunity to discuss their attitudes and feelings with the help of a skilled facilitator.

It is always best to preview any visual before using it to make sure you're comfortable with the content and feel the film will be interesting and appropriate for the group with whom you're working.

**"Adoption: An Option."** The Wisconsin Human Services Information Center, 317 Knutson Drive, Madison, WI 53704. 15 minutes. May be borrowed without charge. $30.
*Two young women and a young couple who make adoption plans share their stories. One talks about the open adoption she planned and stresses that was the only way she could cope with adoption. Each birthparent stresses the choices offered to her/them, and that she/they were not pushed into this decision.*

**"Bittersweet."** Produced by Watts Media Productions. Order from New Hope of Washington, 2611 NE 125th, Seattle, WA 98125. 1988. 17.5 minutes. $49.95 + $3 shipping.
*Slick and professional, but quite real and very sensitive treatment of adoption, mostly from the birthparents' standpoint. Letters, from the birthmother to her baby, from the birthgrandmother to her daughter, and from the adoptive parents to the birthmother, provide a dramatic approach to sharing feelings.*

**"Decisions – Teens, Sex and Pregnancy."** 1986. 26 min. Leader's guide plus blackline masters. $89.95. United Learning, 6633 West Howard Street, Niles, IL 60648.

*Three teenage women describe the changes in their lives which occurred during their pregnancies and afterward. One placed her baby for adoption and life goes on, but "I still hurt," she says.*

**"The Adoption Experience – Perceptive Health Care for the Relinquishing Mother."** 33 min. $250. Adoptive Parents' Education Program, P.O. Box 32114, Phoenix, AZ 85064.

*Excellent film for hospital in-service. Three birthmothers share their experiences, positive and negative, of placing their children for adoption. Each offers helpful suggestions to health care professionals. An obstetrician, nurse, and adoption counselor present valid and much-needed suggestions.*

**"If You Want to Dance."** New Dimensions Films, 85895 Lorane Highway, Eugene, OR 97405.

*Pregnancy-prevention film about an unmarried teenage boy and girl faced wtih pregnancy. A main objectives is to impress upon boys that pregnancy is not just a girl's problem. Despite peer pressure, it is not "cool" to get a girl pregnant. The adoption option is covered.*

**"A Matter of Love."** 43 min. $295. Produced by Catholic Charities/ Catholic Family Services. Perennial Education, Inc., 930 Pitner Avenue, Evanston, IL 60202.

*Portrays Karen and Peter's reaction to their pregnancy, their adoption planning, reaction of adoptive couple (very nervous), and ends with adoptee eighteen years later reading the letter Karen had written to him before he was born.*

**"A Special Kind of Love."** 15 min. $69.95. Bethany Christian Services, Video Sales, 901 Eastern Avenue, Grand Rapids, MI 49503-1295.

*Video can help counselors present adoption as a loving alternative
to young women facing unplanned pregnancies. Can be used to
educate young people and adults about adoption and the role it
plays in society.*

**"Teenage Father."** Children's Home Society of California, 2727 West
Sixth Street, Los Angeles, CA 90057. Phone 213/389-6750.
*Classic film shows young couple deciding on adoption during
pregnancy — but at birth, to the young man's consternation, the
young mother and her mother decide she will keep the baby.*

**"To Love and Let Go."** Department of Communications Media, SS
107, The University of Calgary, 2500 University Drive N.W.,
Calgary, Alberta, Canada T2N 1N4. Video, $140.
*Focus of film is on the grieving process involved in releasing a
newborn baby for adoption. Reinforces the need for support services
for birthmothers. May be too long for use in classroom, but can help
professionals gain added insight into world of adoption.*

## Adoption Tapes

**"Adoption Adventure: A Unique Collection of Songs About
Adoption."** 1986. Beth Lockhart, Adoptive Parents' Education
Program, P.O. Box 32114, Phoenix, AZ 85064. 602/957-2896.
*Wonderful collection of songs beautifully performed. My favorites
are "Always Remember" (for birthparent) and "I Will Tell Her You
Love Her."*

**"Adoption/Abortion."** Rev. Jeff Johnson, Calvary Chapel, 12808
Woodruff Avenue, Downey, CA 90242. $6.95.
*The two tapes are Rev. Johnson's sermons on the abortion (nega-
tive) and adoption (positive) alternatives. Calvary Chapel is
extremely involved in adoption counseling through the church's
House of Ruth ministry.*

**"Problem Pregnancy."** The Church of Jesus Christ of Latter-Day
Saints, 50 East North Temple Street, Salt Lake City, UT 84150.
Filmstrip and tape.
*Filmstrip and tape prepared for use with unmarried parents.*

**"To Grieve, To Grow."** By Judy Tatelbaum. 1984. The Soundworks,
Inc., 1912 North Lincoln Street, Arlington, VA 22207.
*Suggestions for transforming grief into an opportunity for personal
growth.*

# Adoption Posters

Contact the following groups for information about adoption posters:

Adoption Information Center
1212 S. 70th Street
West Allis, WI 53214.

Adoption Education Project
Independent Adoption Center
3333 Vincent Road, Suite 222
Pleasant Hill, CA 94523.

Children's Home Society
2727 West Sixth Street
Los Angeles, CA 90057

# About the Authors

Jeanne Warren Lindsay, M.A., C.H.E., and Catherine Monserrat, Ph. D., have worked with hundreds of teenage and older women facing crisis pregnancy. They frequently present workshops and seminars on adoption across the country, and each has written extensively on the subject.

Catherine is a clinical psychologist practicing in Seattle, Washington. She worked as a counselor and a teacher for fifteen years at New Futures School, Albuquerque, New Mexico, a model comprehensive school for pregnant and parenting teenagers. For several years Catherine led the Alternatives Group at New Futures, a group composed of young women considering the adoption alternative. She is the co-author of the widely-used *Teenage Pregnancy: A New Beginning* and its companion volume, *Working with Childbearing Adolescents*.

Catherine and Bernardo have been married fourteen years and they have two children.

Jeanne founded the Teen Mother Program in the ABC Unified School District, Cerritos, California. This program, which she directed for sixteen years and where she continues as a consultant, is offered as a choice to pregnant and parenting teenagers.

Jeanne is the author of *Pregnant Too Soon: Adoption Is an Option, Parents, Pregnant Teens and the Adoption Option: Help for Families, Open Adoption: A Caring Option, Teens Parenting: The Challenge of Babies and Toddlers,* and three other books dealing with teenage marriage and single parenting. She edits the *NOAPP Network,* newsletter of the National Organization on Adolescent Pregnancy and Parenting. She has been married to Bob for 38 years and they have five children.

# Index

# OTHER BOOKS BY JEANNE WARREN LINDSAY

*PREGNANT TOO SOON: Adoption Is an Option*
Advocates choice. Young women who were, by their own admission, "pregnant too soon," tell their stories. Most made the unpopular decision to release for adoption. They share their reasons for doing so.

*OPEN ADOPTION: A Caring Option*
A fascinating and sensitive account of the new world of adoption. Read about birthparents choosing adoptive parents for their baby and adoptive parents maintaining contact with their baby's birthparents.

*ADOPTION AWARENESS: A Guide for Teachers, Nurses, Counselors and Caring Others* (with Catherine Monserrat)
Offers a philosophical framework and practical suggestions for presenting adoption as a choice. Guidelines for assisting birthparents in the classroom, in the counseling setting, and in the hospital.

*PARENTS, PREGNANT TEENS AND THE ADOPTION OPTION: Help for Families*
For all parents who feel alone and without support for themselves as their daughter faces too-early pregnancy and the difficult adoption/keeping decision.

*TEENAGE MARRIAGE: Coping with Reality*
Gives teenagers a picture of the realities of marriage – a look at the difficulties they may encounter if they say "I do"...or simply move in together ...too soon.

*TEENS LOOK AT MARRIAGE: Rainbows, Roles and Reality*
Helps you understand the culture of teenage couples. Includes statistical information about teenagers' attitudes toward marriage and living together. Attitudes of teenagers not yet married are compared with those who are.

*DO I HAVE A DADDY? A Story About a Single-Parent Child*
Picture/story book especially for children with only one parent. Includes special ten-page section for single parent.

---

## Books by Linda Barr and Catherine Monserrat:
*TEENAGE PREGNANCY: A New Beginning*
Prenatal health book written especially for pregnant teenagers. Covers not only the medical, but also the social and practical aspects of being a pregnant or parenting teen.

*WORKING WITH CHILDBEARING ADOLESCENTS*
Designed for use by professionals from various disciplines. Will help improve effectiveness in working with pregnant teenagers and teenage parents.

Please see other side for ordering information.

# MORNING GLORY PRESS
## 6595 San Haroldo Way, Buena Park, CA 90620
## 714/828-1998

Please send me the following:

| Quantity | Title | Price | Total |
|---|---|---|---|

**Parents, Pregnant Teens and the Adoption Option**

_____ Paper, ISBN 0-930934-28-8     8.95 _____
_____ Cloth, ISBN 0-930934-29-6     13.95 _____

**Adoption Awareness**

_____ Paper, ISBN 0-930934-32-6     $12.95 _____
_____ Cloth, ISBN 0-930934-33-4     17.95 _____

**Pregnant Too Soon: Adoption Is an Option**

_____ Paper, ISBN 0-930934-25-3     $9.95 _____
_____ Cloth, ISBN 0-930934-26-1     15.95 _____

**Open Adoption: A Caring Option**

_____ Paper, ISBN 0-930934-23-7     9.95 _____
_____ Cloth, ISBN 0-930934-22-9     15.95 _____

**Teenage Pregnancy: A New Beginning**

_____ Spiral     10.00 _____

**Working with Childbearing Adolescents**

_____ Spiral     12.95 _____

**Teens Parenting: The Challenge of Babies and Toddlers**

_____ Paper, ISBN 0-930934-06-7     9.95 _____
_____ Cloth, ISBN 0-930934-07-5     14.95 _____

**Teenage Marriage: Coping with Reality**

_____ Paper, ISBN 0-930934-30-x     9.95 _____
_____ Cloth, ISBN 0-930934-31-8     15.95 _____

**Teens Look at Marriage: Rainbows, Roles and Reality**

_____ Paper, ISBN 0-930934-15-6     9.95 _____
_____ Cloth, ISBN 0-930934-16-4     15.95 _____

**Do I Have a Daddy? A Story About a Single-Parent Child**

_____ Paper, ISBN 0-930934-17-2     3.95 _____
_____ Cloth, ISBN 0-930934-10-5     7.95 _____

**TOTAL** _____

Please add postage: 1-3 books, $2.00; 4+, 60¢ per book. _____
California residents - add 6% sales tax _____

**TOTAL ENCLOSED** _____

Ask about quantity discounts, Teacher's Guides, Study Guides.

Prepayment requested. School/library purchase orders accepted.
If not satisfied, return in 15 days for refund.

NAME _____

ADDRESS_____

7327  31  89